NEW
HANDBOOK OF COMPOSITION

RULES AND EXERCISES

REGARDING

GOOD ENGLISH, GRAMMAR, SENTENCE STRUCTURE,
PARAGRAPHING, MANUSCRIPT ARRANGEMENT,
PUNCTUATION, SPELLING, ESSAY WRITING, OUT-
LINING, LETTER WRITING, AND THE MAKING
OF BIBLIOGRAPHIES

BY

EDWIN C. WOOLLEY, Ph.D.

ASSISTANT PROFESSOR OF ENGLISH IN THE
UNIVERSITY OF WISCONSIN

REVISED AND ENLARGED
BY

FRANKLIN W. SCOTT

FORMERLY HEAD OF THE DEPARTMENT OF ENGLISH
UNIVERSITY OF ILLINOIS

D. C. HEATH AND COMPANY

BOSTON   NEW YORK   CHICAGO   LONDON
ATLANTA   SAN FRANCISCO   DALLAS

PE1408
.W7
1926

PREFACE TO THE FIRST EDITION

THIS manual is designed for two uses. It may be used, first, by students of composition for reference, at the direction of the instructor, in case of errors in themes. Second, it may be used for independent reference by persons who have writing of any kind to do and who want occasional information on matters of good usage, grammar, spelling, punctuation, paragraphing, manuscript-arrangement, or letter-writing.

The aim of the book is not scientific, but practical. The purpose is to make clear the rules in regard to which many people make mistakes. No material has been put into the book for the sake of formal completeness. Many statements that would be essential to a treatise designed to exhaust the subjects here discussed (a treatise, for instance, on grammar, or composition-structure, or punctuation) have been omitted because they concern matters about which the persons who may use the book do not need to be told. In the knowledge and the observance of the rules fixed by good usage and suggested by common sense for the expression of thoughts in English and the representation of them on paper, there are many widely prevalent deficiencies, some natural enough, some very odd, but all shared by many people. The purpose of this manual is simply to help correct some of these deficiencies.

Some of the rules in this book, making no mention of exceptions, modifications, or allowable alternatives, may perhaps be charged with being dogmatic. They *are* dogmatic — purposely so. Suppose a youth, astray and confused in a maze of city streets, asks the way to a certain place. If one enumerates to him the several possible routes, with comments and admonitions and cautions about each, he will probably continue astray and confused. If one sends him peremptorily on one route, not mentioning permissible deviations or equally good alternative ways, the chance is much greater that he will reach his destination. Likewise, the erring composer of anarchic discourse can best be set right by concise and simple directions. This is one reason for the stringency of some of the rules. There is another reason; let me use another parable in explaining it. A student of piano-playing is held rigidly, during the early period of his study, to certain rules of finger movement. Those rules are sometimes varied or ignored by musicians. But the student, in order to progress in the art, must for a certain time treat the rules as stringent and invariable; the variations and exceptions are studied only at a later stage of his progress. So, in acquiring skill in the art of composition, it is necessary for most students to observe rigidly and invariably rules to which masters of the art make exceptions. I believe that Rules 63, 69, 78, 98, 99, 112, and 115, for example, should be so treated by most apprentices in composition.

A word about the literary obligations I have incurred. So far as concerns my indebtedness to that great common fund of grammatical and rhetorical doctrine on which he who will may draw, it may truly be said of me, as it has been said of Homer,

> "What he thought he might require
> He went and took."

To individual authors I may owe debts of which I am not aware; for when a man has accumulated a store of thoughts, some from individual writers, some from many writers in common, and some, perhaps, from his own psychic processes, he inevitably forgets the source of many elements of the mass. I know, however, that my thanks are due to Professors Adams Sherman Hill, William Dwight Whitney, Alphonso G. Newcomer,

John Duncan Quackenbos, Fred Newton Scott, and
Joseph Villiers Denney, for a number of ideas suggested
by my acquaintance with their works.

I gratefully acknowledge here my obligation to Professor Frank Gaylord Hubbard, of the University of
Wisconsin, and to Miss Rose M. Kavana, of the Medill
High School, in Chicago, who gave me much acute and
valuable criticism during the preparation of the manuscript; and to several gentlemen (unknown to me) who,
at the instance of the publishers, suggested some much-
needed emendations before the book went to press, and
also during its passage through the press. Though the
book is probably not what Captain Costigan would call
a "meritorious performance," it is in many respects
nearer that character than it would be but for the
generous aid of these known and unknown counselors.

E. C. W.

Madison, Wisconsin

PREFACE TO EDITION OF 1926

THIS revision aims to adapt the rules to such modifications in the use of English as have been established beyond question in the time since the first edition was published. The changes made in that respect are comparatively few, for the aim of the author has been kept in mind to require the student to observe rigidly and invariably rules to which masters of the art make exceptions. When many masters of the art have consistently made the same exceptions for some time, the student may properly be allowed to follow the plain and well-established example. The wording of a number of the rules has been simplified; some have been clarified, others made more explicit. In no case has a rule been modified in meaning except in conformity to change in usage about which there can be little or no question. As Professor Gardner wrote, a hard matter is not made easier by shortening the rule.

The change most readily apparent places the exercises as near as possible to the rules they aim to apply. Many exercises have been added, affording a greater variety of drill material than has hitherto been offered. Most of the additions have been drawn from other books by the author, but a considerable number are new. The section on letter writing has been revised to take into account the two prevalent styles of punctuation and the many changes made by the common use of the typewriter. One entirely new section, on bibliography and footnotes, has been introduced.

Although a score of new rules have been included and a few old ones omitted, the old numbering has been preserved without change down to Rule 245, in the section on Punctuation. From that point on to Rule

261, and from 307 to 337, the numbers of several rules have of necessity been altered.

I wish to make grateful acknowledgement of the assistance of Miss Evelyn A. Tripp of the English Department of the University of Illinois, and of many others in high schools and colleges who out of their long experience in the use of the Handbook have helped to make this revision.

F. W. S.

NEW YORK,
  March, 1926

TABLE OF CONTENTS[1]

TABLE OF EXERCISES

DETAILED SYNOPSIS OF THE NUMBERED RULES

Numbers enclosed in parenthesis refer to rules

I. THE COMPOSITION OF DISCOURSE

II. PUTTING DISCOURSE ON PAPER

NEW

HANDBOOK OF COMPOSITION

I. THE COMPOSITION OF DISCOURSE

THE STANDARD OF GOOD USAGE

1. Good English follows the standard of good usage.
By good usage is meant the usage generally observed
in the writings of the best English authors and in the
speech of well-educated people. Dictionaries, gram-
mars, and books on rhetoric and composition record
this usage, on the basis of wide observation and study.

Good usage defined

(*a*) **A single standard of usage is thus set up for the
entire nation.** Sectionalism is reduced and national
unity is fostered by this means, for there is nothing so
national as language. A pride in our common Americanism is today the most powerful incentive for sup-
porting a single standard of good English.

A single standard of good English

(*b*) **Different levels of usage exist, and what is
proper to one level may not be proper to another.**
Common usage represents the center of the language.
Literary usage is somewhat above common usage;
colloquial usage is below it; *slang* is below them all.
In general, written discourse is more precise and more
condensed than spoken discourse, which often tends
toward the more free-and-easy colloquial usage. Col-
loquialisms may be allowable in informal writing that
are not allowable in formal writing. The lower levels

Common literary and colloquial usage

of usage, including slang, have no place in written discourse, except in narrative that reproduces the conversation of people who employ them.

Changing usage

(*c*) **Usage changes from time to time.** This is because language is a living thing, and grows by the addition of words, or by employing words in new senses and combinations. But these changes are so few, relatively speaking, that they need not occupy the attention of the student who is learning to speak and write good English.

Mistaken standards

2. There are several mistaken standards of good English.

Colloquial usage

(*a*) **An expression current in common conversation is not thereby proved to be good English.** If currency in common conversation were a valid test, such expressions as " ain't," " I says," " them fellows," " he laid down," " you hadn't ought," and " has went " would be good English.

Limited usage

(*b*) **The usage of a limited number of persons does not establish an expression as good English.** Otherwise a national standard would be impossible, and each section, even each town, would be a law unto itself. Even well-educated people, moreover, may make some mistakes, such as saying " he don't " for " he doesn't " and " affect " for " effect."

Newspaper usage

(*c*) **Newspaper usage does not establish an expression as good English.** The best newspapers set high standards, and oblige their writers to study " style books " similar to this Handbook, in order to avoid offenses against good English. But many newspapers have no such standards, and employ provincial and vulgar language. (Cf. Rule 16 and the note to Rule 129.)

(*d*) **The usage of recent writers of popular fiction does not prove that an expression is good English.** The right of an author to rank among the best English authors can be determined only by the general judgment of scholars and critics, as well as of the reading public, and only after that judgment has endured a sufficient length of time to become established.

(*e*) **A single instance of the use of a word even by one of the best English authors does not prove the word to be good English.** The word must be shown to be in general use among such authors, in order to give it the sanction of good usage.

3. **In order to learn what is good English, accordingly, the student should cultivate the habit of prompt reference to books on grammar, rhetoric, and composition, and to good dictionaries.** The best dictionaries are Webster's New International Dictionary, the Standard Dictionary, and Murray's New English Dictionary. There are numerous short dictionaries — such as Webster's Collegiate Dictionary, Webster's High School Dictionary, the Desk Standard Dictionary, the Student's Standard Dictionary — produced by omitting much material given in the unabridged dictionaries. Any of these short dictionaries is far inferior, for the purposes of a student of English, to an unabridged dictionary. The larger volume gives fuller explanations and examples showing how words are actually used. These explanations and examples, dispensed with in the shorter works, the student cannot well do without.

EXERCISE 1

Look up each of the following words both in an unabridged dictionary and in an abridged one, and write a

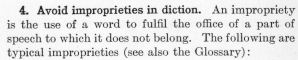

report showing how much more fully and clearly the larger volume explains the use of each word than the smaller one does: *avail, aversion, comment, decoction, ingratiate, ludicrous, neutral, sardonic, satiate, sequester.* State the exact title and the publisher of each of the dictionaries consulted.

Diction
Improprieties and Barbarisms

Error regarding parts of speech

4. Avoid improprieties in diction. An impropriety is the use of a word to fulfil the office of a part of speech to which it does not belong. The following are typical improprieties (see also the Glossary):

(*a*) Nouns used as verbs: *to suicide, to suspicion, to film.*

(*b*) Verbs used as nouns: *a combine, an invite, a steal, eats.*

(*c*) Adjectives used as nouns: *a canine, a feline, a drunk.*

(*d*) Adjectives used as adverbs: *real, some, this* (see the Glossary for these three words), *good, considerable, friendly, tolerable, powerful.*

NOTE. — As examples of the value of the use of a dictionary to determine whether a word is established in good usage, observe that *to motor* and *to finance*, both formerly used only as nouns, are found in Webster's and the New Standard, while *to film* (*to take a picture*) is found in neither.

EXERCISE 2

Adjectives misused for adverbs

Write the following sentences, filling the blanks with adverbs: 1. Do it as —— as you can. 2. He managed it very ——. 3. She stitched much —— than I. 4. You'd better treat me —— than you treated him. 5. The house was furnished as —— as one could wish.

Unauthorized formations

5. Avoid barbarisms in diction. Barbarisms are current words coined without authority from words in good standing.

Typical barbarisms are the following (see also the Glossary): *to enthuse* (see Glossary), *to burglarize, to jell* (for *to jelly*), *tasty* (for *tasteful*), *homey* (for *homelike*), *newsy*, *musicianly*, *complected* (see Glossary), *preventative* (for *preventive*), *illy* (for *ill*), *overly* (see Glossary), and the contractions *'gent*, *most* (for *almost*), and *way* (for *away*).

NOTE. — The standing of a word depends, not on the nature of its formation, but solely on its acceptance or non-acceptance by good usage (see Rules 1 and 2). "Baseballist" and "cheesery" are bad English, though they are formed after the analogy of *pianist* and *creamery*, which are good English. *(margin: Analogy not decisive)*

5a. Avoid confusing words of somewhat similar pronunciation. For example, distinguish between *allusion* and *illusion*, *conscience* and *conscious*, *deceased* and *diseased*, *formerly* and *formally*, *respectfully* and *respectively*. For definitions of these and other words often confused, see the list of words often misspelled under 162, and the Glossary. *(margin: "Malaprops")*

EXERCISE 3

Fill the blanks with appropriate words: 1. Please make no ——— to what has happened. 2. The appearance of land is an ———. 3. He is suffering from the ——— that he is a king, and often makes some ——— to his ungrateful subjects. 4. He is not ——— of having done wrong. 5. A tender ——— makes one ——— of some mistakes. 6. The ——— limb was cut off. 7. He was appointed administrator of the estate of the ——— doctor. 8. The family that ——— lived here has gone to Chicago. 9. The meetings were ——— opened informally, but are now opened ———. 10. If he had spoken ——— he would have been more cordially received. 11. John, James, and William spoke ——— at the first three meetings. 12. In closing a letter to a superior you may subscribe yourself "Yours ———." *(margin: "Malaprops")*

6. Except as a humorous device, do not use words of your own coining, without ascertaining from a dictionary whether they are authorized. *(margin: Extemporized formations)*

General Exercises in the Use of the Dictionary

Exercise 4

Words
designated
as bad
English

A word is not proved to be correct English by the mere fact that it is found in a dictionary, for the modern dictionary explains numerous slang words and other incorrect words. But incorrect words defined in a dictionary are clearly marked as incorrect by such expressions as *obsolete, slang, cant, dialectal, low, vulgar,* printed after the definition. In consulting a dictionary for the standing of a word, observe whether it is marked with one of the above-mentioned expressions. Look up the following words in an unabridged dictionary; read all that the dictionary says about each word; and write a report discussing each word and stating what sort of English it is: *deal* in the sense of *bargain, enthuse, resurrect, to down, complected, preventative, jell, sleeper* meaning *sleeping car, to wire, illy, to vamose, brace up, humbug, boodle, pal, rampage, parson, to duck, rough it, cavort, scrumptious, in cahoots, right off, right along, grouch, swipe, swell* (adj.). State the exact title and the publisher of the dictionary consulted.

Exercise 5

Collo-
quialisms

Opposite many words in a dictionary is printed *Colloquial.* This means that the word is used only in familiar conversation and informal writing, and not found — or very seldom found — in the written English of good authors. A word marked *Colloquial,* then, is unfit for use in formal composition. Look up the following words in an unabridged dictionary; write a report stating whether each word is fit for use in formal composition, and if not, what word is preferable: *cute, tantrum, gumption, proxy, whoop, to butt, duds, skinflint, boss, rum* (adj.), *to peek, to fix, a fix, hired help, ninney, hustle, gullet, rooster, ruction, dude, graft* (political), *to collar, to wallop, stunt, twaddle, scrappy, materialize, crank* (a person), *flabbergast, cantankerous.* State the exact title and the publisher of the dictionary consulted.

EXERCISE 6

In consulting a dictionary about a word, always notice the part of speech. This is indicated by an abbreviation following the word. The abbreviations (*a.* for *adjective*, *n.* for *noun*, etc.) are explained in the front part of the dictionary. Look up the following words in a dictionary; write a report stating what part of speech each word belongs to, and illustrating the correct use of the word: *illicit, impugn, vacillate, surgeon, brawn, riparian, tact, writhe, cowardly, dual, gyrate, rift, vagary, adept, invective, vitiate, suspicion.*

Part of speech of word sought

EXERCISE 7

In consulting a dictionary about a verb, always notice whether the verb is transitive or intransitive. If transitive, a verb is followed by *v. t.;* if intransitive, by *v. i.* Look up the following verbs in a dictionary; write a report stating whether each verb is transitive or intransitive, and illustrating the correct use of each verb: *dismay, deviate, recant, procrastinate, banter, retract, vibrate, harass, acclimate, ingratiate, stipulate, capitulate, locate, disaffect, metamorphose, concur, demur, debilitate, debouch, vitiate, lay, raise, accede, desist, acquiesce, coalesce.*

Verb transitive or intransitive?

EXERCISE 8

In consulting a dictionary about the use of a word, try not merely to get a general idea of the meaning of the word, but to discover within what *limits of meaning* the word is confined. To this end read the definition *as a whole;* do not pick out a single synonym and suppose that this and the word defined are interchangeable. *Cut* is defined thus: "To separate the parts of with, or as with, a sharp instrument; to make an incision in; to gash; to sever; to divide." To pick out the last synonym ("to divide") and reason that since *cut* means *divide*, one may say "I will cut the money among them" would be absurd. What *cut* means is ascertained not from one synonym taken separately but from the definition read *as a whole.* Look up the following words in an unabridged dictionary; read each definition as a whole, and read the examples; write sentences illustrating the correct use of each word: *broach, manifest, divert, descry, descant, indeterminate, in-*

Definition to be read as a whole

flux, forage, equanimity, compromise, vicissitude, intermit, analogy, transmute, diversify, poignant, exigency, derogatory, eradicate, incompatible, effete, extirpate, cavil, propitiate, deprecate, amenable, precedence, apropos, obligatory, alias, incognito, sinecure, stupor, ebullition, potent, divulge, deprave, pervert, acumen, insidious, peremptory, contiguous, submerge, emerge, immerse, circumvent, brusque, drastic, dulcet. State the exact title and the publisher of the dictionary consulted.

EXERCISE 9

Idiomatic construction to be sought

In consulting a dictionary about the correct use of a word, try to discover what idiomatic construction the word requires. In some cases this is specifically explained; in others it is suggested by the examples. For instance, under *ingratiate* we find this statement: "used reflexively, and followed by *with*" (*e.g.,* George *ingratiates himself with* Henry); under *accuse* we find "used with *of*" (*e.g.,* He was *accused of* treachery); under *charge* (meaning *accuse*) we find the example "I charge you *with* robbery," which shows that *charge* in this sense requires *with*. Look up the following words in an unabridged dictionary; find out, either from explicit statements in the definitions or from the examples, what idiomatic construction — especially what preposition — is required with each word; and write sentences illustrating the correct use of each word: *avail* (v. t.), *prevail* (v. t.), *substitute* (v.), *averse, compensate, confide* (v. t.), *confide* (v. i.), *demand, atone, treat* (v. i.), *deprive, different, demur* (v. i.), *accordance, attend* (v. i.), *tend* (v. t.), *rid* (v. t.), *free* (v. t.), *enamor, accustom, absolve, acquit, bestow, conform* (v. t.), *conversant, proficient, dependent, independent, derogatory, versed* (adj.), *inasmuch.* State the exact title and the publisher of the dictionary consulted.

EXERCISE 10

Limitation of words to special uses

Do not overlook the notes which indicate that words are confined to certain special uses — such notes as *Typ., Med., Naut., Mech., Machin., Mus., Her., Arch.* The meanings of such notes are stated in the list of abbreviations in the front part of the dictionary. Look up the following words in a dictionary; write a report stating to what occupation, art, or science each appertains: *necronite, spandrel, quindecemvir, bimanous, solenoid, cresselle, cuddy, sister block, barbara, mullion, fascine, semibull, meniscus, corona, stalagmite, tenaculum, anamorphosis, brontotherium, pediment, semibreve, tenon.*

See that you understand every statement, every abbreviation, every mark which you find under the word you are investigating. Use the list of abbreviations and the explanatory notes in the front part of the dictionary. Study the following definitions:

Thorough understanding of abbreviations, etc.

pet′ty (pĕt′Ĭ), *a.*; PET′TI-ER (-Ĭ-ẽr); PET′TI-EST. [ME. *petit,* F. *petit;* probably of Celtic origin and akin to E. *piece.* Cf. PETIT.] **1.** Of small size. *Obs.*

2. Of small importance; little; trifling; inconsiderable; also, inferior; subordinate; as, a *petty* fault; a *petty* prince.

im′pro-vise′, (ĭm′prŏ-vīz′). *v. t.*; IM′PRO-VISED′ (-vīzd′); IM′PRO-VIS′ING (-vīz-ĭng). [F. *improviser,* It. *improvvisare,* fr. *improvviso* unprovided, sudden, extempore, L. *improvisus; im-* not + *provisus* foreseen, provided. See PROVISO.]

1. To compose, recite, or sing extemporaneously, esp. in verse; to extemporize; also, to play upon an instrument, or to act, extemporaneously.

2. To bring about, arrange, or make, on a sudden, or without previous preparation; to invent, or provide, off hand; as, he *improvised* a hammer out of a stone.

Charles attempted to *improvise* a peace. *Motley.*

run (rŭn), *v. i.*; *pret.* RAN (răn) or RUN; *p.p.* RUN; *p.pr. & vb. n.* RUN′NING. [ME. *rinnen, rennen* (pret. *ran,* p.p. *runnen, ronnen*), AS. *rinnen* to flow. . . .]

run (rŭn), *v. t.* . . . **14.** To conduct; manage; carry on; as, to *run* a factory, a hotel, or a business. [*Colloq., U. S.*]

NOTE. — See in Webster's New International Dictionary, almost a whole page devoted to this word.

runt . . . 4. The dead stump of a tree. [*Obs. or Prov. Eng.*]

Pope, *n.* [AS. *papa*, L. *papa*, father, bishop. Cf. PAPA, PAPAL.]

1. Any ecclesiastic, esp. a bishop. [*Obs.*]

gules, *n.* (Her.) The tincture red.

article, *v. i.* To agree; to stipulate. [*R.*]

the, *adv.* By how much; by so much; used before comparatives; as, the colder it is, the happier I am.

incident, *a.* [L. *incidens, -entis*, p. pr. of *incidere* to fall into or upon; pref. *in-* in, on + *cadere* to fall; cf. F. *incident*. See CADENCE.] Falling or striking upon, as a ray of light upon a reflecting surface.

EXERCISE 11

Write a report answering the following questions: 1. The information given concerning *improvise* consists of five parts: first, the expression in parentheses following *improvise;* second, the expression "v. t."; third, the forms before the bracketed part; fourth, the bracketed part; fifth, the remainder. What five subjects are treated in these five parts (answer very briefly)? 2. What information is conveyed by the bracketed part under *incident* (answer fully and clearly)? 3. Under *incident* what does "see CADENCE" mean? for what purpose is the reader told to look up the word *cadence?* 4. What does "(-ty)" after *petty* mean? 5. What is meant by the numbers 14 and 4 under *run* and *runt?* 6. What information is conveyed by the bracketed expression under *run* (explain fully and clearly)? 7. Tabulate the following abbreviations and write opposite each its meaning:

a., compar., superl., OE., F., cf. (under *petty*)

v. t., imp., p. p., p. pr., vb. n., It., fr., L., pref. (under *improvise*)

obs., prov. Eng. (under *runt*)

n., AS. (under *pope*)

Her. (under *gules*)

v. i., R. (under *article*)

adv. (under *the*)

EXERCISE 12

(a) Usually only the chief inflectional form of a regularly inflected word is entered alphabetically in a dictionary; for other forms look under the chief form. Look up the following words in a dictionary; write a report stating where each word is found; if you find any entered alphabetically, state why it is entered: *birds, boxes, oxen, leaves, picnicking, dazzled, woods, happier, maddest, sourer, stole, killed, went, stood, cliffs, saddling, studying, chid.* (b) Answer the following questions by means of a dictionary, and state where in the dictionary the information on each point can be found: 1. Which is correct — *he sang,* or *he sung?* 2. *I dreamed,* or *I dreamt?* 3. *It is froze,* or *it is frozen?* 4. *A dollar was bet,* or *was betted?* 5. *I have drank,* or *I have drunk?* 6. *I have swam,* or *I have swum?* 7. *He has long lain unconscious,* or *long laid unconscious?* 8. *He spit* (past tense), or *he spat?*

Inflectional forms, how found

EXERCISE 13

Usually plurals regularly formed are not given in a dictionary. If no plural is given, the inference is that the plural consists of the singular plus *s* or *es.* Whether *s* or *es* is to be added is explained in the front part of the dictionary. Look up the following words in a dictionary; write a report stating what is the plural of each word, what plurals are given in the dictionary and what not: *road, wheel, glass, bunch, sheep, cannon, datum, phenomenon, stratum, species, index, penny, die, freak, flash, wolf, leaf, lady, attorney, tract.*

Plurals, how found

EXERCISE 14

Hyphens printed short and light in a dictionary are used only to show the division of a word into syllables; they should not be used in writing the word. A hyphen that should be used when the word is written is printed large and heavy. (One dictionary uses two short parallel lines.) Look up the following words in a dictionary; then copy the list writing the words correctly — with or without hyphens:

Use of hyphen in dictionaries

passerby	somebody
halfbreed	whoever
halfmoon	without
childlike	withstand
childhood	overcome
eagleeyed	together
whatever	whenever
yourself	outside
somewhat	moreover
notwithstanding	nowadays
instead	overcoat
nevertheless	outburst
inasmuch	offspring
selfpossessed	afternoon

Contractions

Inappro-
priate in
formal
composition

7. The contractions *don't, isn't, haven't,* etc., are not appropriate in formal composition. They are proper in conversation and in composition of a colloquial style.

Misuses of Pronouns

Indefinite
you

8. Avoid the indefinite use of *you* in formal composition. The fault may be corrected by using either the passive voice or the pronoun *one,* or by substituting the noun or pronoun which is really intended. (For the fault of shifting from *you* to *one* and to *we,* see Rule 139.)

> Vague: You should not use *they* indefinitely.
> Definite: *They* should not be used indefinitely; [or] One should not use *they* indefinitely.

Indefinite
they

9. Avoid using *they* indefinitely; use the passive voice, or recast the sentence otherwise.

> Wrong: They make bricks in Fostoria.
> Right: Bricks are made in Fostoria.
> Wrong: They had a collision on the electric road.
> Right: There was a collision; [or] A collision occurred (more formal).

Wrong: They don't have redbirds in Wisconsin.
Right: There are no redbirds in Wisconsin; [or]
Redbirds are not found in Wisconsin (more formal).

10. Except in impersonal expressions, such as *it* **Indefinite**
rains, it seems, it is cold, **do not use** *it* **without ante-** *it*
cedent; recast the sentence.

Wrong: In the notice on the bulletin board it says
the drill is held at four.
Right: The notice on the bulletin board says the
drill is held at four.
Wrong: In Garland's *Life Among the Corn Rows* it
gives a description of life among the farmers.
Right: Garland's *Life Among the Corn Rows* gives a
description; [or] In Garland's *Life Among the Corn
Rows* there is a description.
Wrong: Does it say "Fair Oaks" on that car?
Right: Is that car marked "Fair Oaks"?

NOTE. — The habit of beginning sentences with *it is* or
it seems, even when these expressions are grammatically
correct, makes a weak style and often leads to confusion
of pronouns (see Rule 55).

11. The use of a demonstrative adjective (espe- **Indefinite**
cially *that* **or** *those***) without the relative clause needed** *that* and
to make clear what is meant is a colloquialism. (For *those*
the misuse of the pronoun involving weak reference,
see Rule 59.)

Wrong: I observed that the building was one of
those rambling old mansions.
Right: I observed that the building was a rambling
old mansion; [or] . . . one of those rambling old
mansions that one often sees in New England towns.

12. The compound personal pronoun is used to **Misuse of**
refer back to the subject or to emphasize the noun or intensives
pronoun to which it is attached. *Myself* **should not be**

used for *I,* and not, as a rule, for *me. Himself, herself,* and *themselves* are used like *myself.*

> Right: I myself will attend to it.
> Wrong: My wife and myself will go.
> Right: My wife and I will go.
> Wrong: This is for yourself.
> Right: This is for you.

Especially avoid expressions like " yourself and guests," " myself and brother." Say " you and your guests," " my brother and I."

Misuse of *either* and *neither*

13. The best standard of usage restricts *either* and *neither* to two objects; it is rare to find a good author using it with three objects.

> Right: Either the conductor or the ticket agent must have lost it, but neither will admit it.
> Doubtful: There are three vacant lots in the block, either of which can be had cheaply.
> Right: There are three vacant lots in the block, any one of which can be had cheaply.

EXERCISE 15

Correct the following sentences: 1. The air this morning tells you that spring is near. 2. We learned that you must buy seats two weeks before the performance. 3. He is the kind of man that tries at once to put you on the defensive. 4. If they put many more billboards along this road you will not be able to see the country at all. 5. We were there when they said the car would leave, but it had already gone. 6. The city has many fine parks but they do not give them the proper care. 7. On our road map it says to turn here. 8. We read with great interest the passage in which it told of the rescue of all on board the sinking ship. 9. The meeting would have been more largely attended if it had not rained. 10. She came to the party in one of those old fashioned dresses. 11. He spoke in that tiresome sort of way for an hour.

12. I think he lost his life on one of those Arctic exploration trips. 13. It would have been courteous for them to invite yourself and family to the meeting. 14. Please have all letters on that subject sent to myself. 15. He would have been in favor of the idea if himself and brother had been consulted. 16. I cannot come on either Monday, Tuesday, or Wednesday. 17. He would accept neither of the several offers he received. 18. She took neither of her three children with her.

Rhetorical Ornament

Triteness

14. Avoid trite rhetorical expressions. Language should be fitted to its subject; if the subject is simple matter of fact, the language should be without ornament. Of the following list of phrases, many were originally inappropriate and others have lost their force through frequent repetition.

Over-worked formulas

all too soon
sigh of relief
beat a hasty retreat
the commercial world, the social world, etc.
favor with a selection
render a vocal solo
rendition
discourse sweet music
hungry as bears
repast
do justice to a dinner
toothsome viands
sought his downy couch
vast concourse
never in the history of
news leaked out
dull, sickening thud
those present
in evidence

working like Trojans
herculean efforts
wended their way
enjoyable occasion
in a pleasing manner
untiring efforts
all in all
it goes without saying
bolt from a clear sky
some one has said
specimen of humanity
had the privilege
replete with interest
undercurrent of excitement
last sad rites
tonsorial parlor
checkered career
last but not least
tired but happy
cheered to the echo

abreast of the times
was the recipient of
everything went along nicely
the student body
doomed to disappointment
was an impressive sight
made a pretty picture
completed the scene
nestled among the hills *or* among the trees
like sentinels guarding
sumptuous repast
all nature seemed
all nature clothed in a robe
each and every
on this particular day
long-felt want
it seems (in narrative)
fair maidens

breathless silence
speculation was rife
tiny tots
along . . . lines (e.g., along agricultural lines)
along the line of
along these lines
as luck would have it
the proud possessor
in touch with
social function
in the last analysis
waited in breathless suspense
order out of chaos
those with whom we come in contact
imbued with
mother earth
breakneck speed

Hackneyed quotations, allusions, and proverbs

15. Avoid hackneyed quotations, literary allusions, and proverbs, such as the following:

The light fantastic toe
Truth is stranger than fiction
Teach the young idea how to shoot
Method in his madness
Sadder but wiser
Cupid has been busy
Variety is the spice of life
The best laid plans of mice and men, etc.
All work and no play, etc.
Never put off till tomorrow, etc.
Make hay while the sun shines
All is not gold that glitters
When ignorance is bliss, etc.
Music hath charms, etc.

Newspaper mannerisms

16. Certain hackneyed newspaper mannerisms are especially to be avoided. These have arisen through the effort of writers to adorn their style where no ornament was needed, or to introduce a forced humor, or to avoid repetition of the same word. The style books of good newspapers advocate simplicity of diction, and specifically condemn these mannerisms. Repetition of the same word is to be preferred to the invention of artificial epithets. (See Rule 129.) The following offenses against good usage are especially to be avoided:

(*a*) **The designation of states and cities by their nicknames,** as, " the Buckeye State," " the Sunflower State," " the Gopher State," " the Cream City," etc.; and the dragging in of these nicknames where no name at all is needed.

Nick-names of states and cities

> Bad: He arrived in Boston yesterday. Many citizens of the Hub were gathered to meet him.
>
> Right: He arrived in Boston yesterday. Many citizens were gathered to meet him.

(*b*) **The regular employment of verbal ornaments,** such as "fatal affray," "fistic encounter," "struggling mass of humanity," " scantily attired," " knights of the pen " (for *reporters*), " the officiating clergyman," " equines " (for *horses*), " canines " (for *dogs*), " felines " (for *cats*), " fair sex," " well-known clubman," " breakneck speed," " city bastile," " milady."

Current newspaper rhetoric

(*c*) **Obtrusive straining for novelty of phrase.**

Straining for novelty of phrase

> Bad: The football warriors of the Badger State will play the Windy City's squad of pigskin chasers this afternoon.
>
> Right: The Wisconsin football team will play the Chicago team this afternoon.
>
> Bad: The guests spent the evening in doing the "light fantastic" act.
>
> Right: The guests spent the evening in dancing.
>
> Bad: Indefatigable knights of the pen dogged his steps as far as the hostelry.
>
> Right: Reporters followed him to his hotel.

Affectation

High-flown
language

17. Do not use high-flown language for plain things.
Straining for high-sounding expressions to replace
plain English makes a style weak rather than strong.
For instance, say leg, not limb; letter, not kind favor;
house, not residence; body, not remains; flowers, not
floral offerings; funeral, not obsequies or last sad
rites; " I went to bed," not " I retired "; " I got up,"
not " I arose." Such attempts at " fine writing "
are in bad taste.

> Bad: To keep the horse healthy you must be careful
> of his environment.
> Right: To keep the horse healthy you must be careful
> of his stable.

Poetic and
legal
diction

**18. In prose avoid the use of words suited only to
poetry.** Examples are *dwelt, oft, oftentimes, ofttimes,
morn, amid, 'mid, 'midst, o'er, 'neath, 'tis, 'twas. Here-
tofore, therein, thereof, thereby,* are awkward substitutes
in good natural writing for *before this event, in it,* and
of it.

The
historical
present

**19. In narrative relating past events, prefer the
past tense to the so-called " historical present."** The
latter is a device intended to produce the effect of
strong emotion, but is more likely to seem affected
than to create the desired impression. (For awkward
shifting of tenses in narrative, see Rule 136.)

> Affected: He shouted to attract her attention, but
> she went on toward the danger, not heeding his
> warning. Lashing his horse and riding swiftly
> toward her, he shouted again. This time she hears.
> She stands still and awaits him. He lifts her to
> his saddle and rides frantically toward the hut.
> [Throughout this passage the past tense should be
> used.]

20. Designate persons, places, and dates in a story by complete names and dates. The custom of using initials and dashes, and of representing dates in a similar manner, is obsolete; it suggests affectation.

Initials and blanks in place of names

> Objectionable: In the year 18—, when my father was a young man in the little town of B——, he formed a strong friendship with a wealthy farmer, Mr. M——.
>
> Preferable: In the year 1892, when my father was a young man in the little town of Bristol, he formed a strong friendship with a wealthy farmer, Mr. McManus.

NOTE. — In narrative composition, definiteness, clearness, and smoothness are gained by calling the characters by name as soon as they are introduced.

Names for characters in a story

> Awkward: One afternoon this winter two friends of mine called at my home and suggested that we go ice-boating. Now one of these men had never been to ride in an ice-boat. The other man was warmly dressed for the occasion, but the man who had never had the experience, as it afterwards turned out, was dressed rather less warmly than usual. When we reached the lake, the first friend and I were busy getting up the sail, and did not notice that the teeth of the other man had begun to chatter as soon as the chilly breeze struck him. It happened, moreover, that this man who was dressed so lightly was selected to sit on the end of the runner-plank, while my first friend and I managed the tiller and the sheet.
>
> Improved: One afternoon this winter two friends of mine called at my home and suggested that we go ice-boating. Now one of these men, Tom Lamont, had never taken a ride in an ice-boat. The other man, Bert Pryor, was warmly dressed for the occasion, but Tom, as it afterwards turned out, was dressed rather less warmly than usual. When we reached the lake, Bert and I were busy getting up the sail, and did not notice that Tom's teeth had begun to chatter as soon as the chilly breeze struck him. It happened, moreover, that Tom, in spite of his thin clothing, was selected to sit on the runner-

plank, while Bert and I managed the tiller and the
sheet.

"The
writer"
and "we"
for *I*

**21. In mentioning yourself, avoid the expressions
we and *the writer*.** Use *I*, *my*, and *me*, and guard
against unnecessary reference to yourself. The use of
we in an editorial which purports to be the utterance
of a board of editors is entirely proper, but as designating an individual speaker or writer it is an affectation.

> Bad: We have selected for our text the second verse
> of the Epistle of Jude.
> Right: I have selected for my text, etc.

Mixed Figures of Speech

Incongruity
with what
precedes

**22. Do not use a simile or metaphor which is in-
congruous with the expression preceding.**

> Incongruous metaphor: The officers must enforce
> discipline among the raw material.
> Right: The officers must enforce discipline among
> the new men.
>
> Incongruous metaphor: We got some oil for the
> wheel at a farmhouse, and thus our hotbox was
> nipped in the bud.
> Right: At a farmhouse we got some oil for the wheel
> and thus prevented a hotbox.
>
> Incongruous metaphor: He must conduct his busi-
> ness on an honest foundation.
> Right: He must conduct his business in an honest
> manner; [or] He must build his business on an
> honest foundation.
>
> Bad: The probe of the Fond du Lac grand jury has
> netted five corrupt officials.
> Right: The probe of the Fond du Lac grand jury
> has revealed five corrupt officials; [or] The drag

net of the Fond du Lac grand jury has caught five
corrupt officials.

Bad: With his fortune blown to the four winds, all
his ambition was crushed.

Right: All his ambition was, like his fortune, blown
to the four winds; [or] In the ruin of his fortune
his ambition was crushed.

**23. When a simile or metaphor has been used, the
expression following it should carry out the figure —
should not (1) embody an incongruous figure or (2) be
incongruously literal.** Figures not carried out

Bad: The freshman algebra course is a rocky and
difficult road to travel. But whether we like it or
not we are required to wade through it. [The
figure embodied in "rocky road" is not carried out
by the figure embodied in "wade through."]

Right: The freshman course in algebra is a rocky
and difficult road to travel. But whether we like it
or not, we are required to travel it.

Inferior: It made a deep impression on my mind
which I shall never forget. [The figure embodied
in "impression" is not carried out by the literal
expression "forget."]

Right: It made a deep impression on my mind, which
will never be effaced.

EXERCISE 15a

Mixed Figures

Rewrite the following sentences, eliminating the incongruity in the figures of speech: 1. Richelieu used the
bishop's robe only as a stepping-stone to political power.
2. All the pent-up venom of his evil heart rushed to the
front. 3. Let our object be to educate and bring to the
front the laboring men — the backbone of our nation.
4. The student is here prepared to go forth and meet
without difficulty any burdens that may be placed upon
him. 5. If there was a trace of good in his character,
it was stifled by his selfishness. 6. Young man, if you
have a spark of genius, water it.

Incongruity between figures

Figures not
carried out

Rewrite the following sentences, eliminating the incongruities. 1. The sunlight is the mainspring of the photographer's business; it should be admitted through a skylight or a north window. 2. The high tariff is the mother of trusts, and the next Congress should repeal it. 3. Pig iron is the foundation-stone of the iron industry. From it kettles and stoves are made directly, and from it steel and wrought iron are manufactured. 4. Accidents to tires are an annoyance that may occur at any time. We all enjoy sitting by the roadside waiting for a tire to be patched. This experience tries the patience of the most good-humored.

STRUCTURE OF SENTENCES

Some Fundamental Errors

Subordinate
elements
mistaken
for sen-
tences

24. Subordinate sentence-elements should not be capitalized and punctuated like complete sentences. This error, the " period fault," is one of the most serious the writer can commit, because it breaks up a complete thought into incomplete fragments.   An incomplete sentence is to be distinguished from those brief expressions which are the abbreviated forms of complete ideas as in the following cases:

1. Questions and answers to questions, especially in conversation.

> Why not?
> Because it is too late.

2. Exclamations.

> A pretty situation!
> At last!

3. Transitions

> Now for the next objection.
> To consider the next point.

In determining whether an expression is a *complete sentence*, it is dangerous to rely upon your judgment as to whether it expresses a complete thought, for a subordinate member may appear to you complete in thought. Rely instead upon grammatical definitions as the guide to correct punctuation. Distinguish carefully between a *complete sentence*, a *phrase*, and a *subordinate clause*. A complete sentence contains a subject and a predicate, and is not dependent on any words outside itself. A phrase is a group of words not containing a subject and a predicate. A subordinate clause is introduced by (and usually begins with) a relative pronoun or a subordinating conjunction. The relative pronouns are *that, who, what, which, whoever, whatever,* and *whichever*. The principal subordinating conjunctions are *if, as if, even if, though, although, whether, lest, unless, than, as, that, in order that, so that, because, since, when, whenever, while, after, where, whereas, wherever, provided, provided that, before, how, however, until*. Simple conjunctions and conjunctive adverbs, which do not subordinate the subjects and predicates following them, should be carefully distinguished from relative pronouns and subordinating conjunctions. (See *Conjunction* in Appendix A.)

> Wrong: It offers a course for those who wish to study painting. At the same time affording opportunity for literary study. [Participial phrase lacking subject and predicate.]
>
> Right: It offers a course for those who wish to study painting, at the same time affording opportunity for literary study.
>
> Wrong: Among her suitors were two she favored most. One a college student, the other a capitalist. [Phrases in apposition with "suitors."]
>
> Right: Among her suitors were two she favored most; one a college student, the other a capitalist.

Wrong: The care of oil lamps requires every day
some untidy and disagreeable labor. While electric
lights give the housekeeper no trouble. [Subor-
dinate clause, marked by "while."]

Right: The care of oil lamps requires every day some
untidy and disagreeable labor, while electric lights
give the housekeeper no trouble.

Substan-
tives and
participles
for
sentences

**24a. Do not use a substantive and a participle for a
subject and predicate.**

Wrong: The weather being pleasant today.
Right: The weather is pleasant today.

Exercise 16

Complete
and incom-
plete
sentences

Analyze the following, indicating whether the sentence
can be considered a complete sentence. State the reason
for your decision. 1. Further north is a big lake, where
I keep my boats. My bilge-board sloop, my racing power
boat, and my big launch. 2. As you go up the drive,
you see at the right a little summerhouse which is one
mass of vines. While on the other side is a large stable.
3. For after all there is much pleasure to be found in
life. 4. How could you be so thoughtless! 5. I suspected two fellows in particular. Buck Joslin, whom I
had seen hiding near the shed, and Bill Arnold, the pink-
eyed delivery boy. 6. I came to the conclusion that a
musical life was not a fit life for a man who had not the
most extraordinary genius. That it was poorly recom-
pensed and might not bring me the bare necessities of
life. 7. "Into one of these establishments (among the
earliest) near Bow-street, there came one morning as I
sat over my houseless cup, pondering where to go next,
a man in a high and long snuff coloured coat, and shoes,
and, to the best of my belief, nothing else but a hat,
. . . " — Dickens. 8. "No mother?" "No. Dead
many years." 9. The pots are usually made of plum-
bago and German clay. Each pot being used only two
or three times. 10. There were two books on the table.
One a small gilded volume, and the other a commercial
ledger. 11. It was in the winter that the reclamation

of the land began. That time of the year being the
dry season.   12. What chance was there of escape?
13. "What a dead thing is a clock, with its ponderous
embowelments of lead and brass, its pert or solemn dull-
ness of communication, compared with the simple, altar-
like structure and silent heart-language of the old dial!"
— Lamb.

EXERCISE 17

Write the following passage, putting a period at the
end of every complete independent predication, and capitalizing the word following every period:

The topman who had hold of the upper corner of the
topsail lost his balance he was seen to totter the crowd
on the quay uttered a cry he turned around the yard but
caught hold of the footrope as he passed it and remained
hanging by it the sea was below him at a dizzy depth and
the shock of his fall had given the footrope a violent
swinging motion the man swung at the end of the rope
like a stone in a sling to go to his assistance would be
running a frightful risk not one of the sailors dared to
venture it all at once a man could be seen climbing up
the shrouds with the agility of a tiger cat his red clothes
showed that he was a convict in a second he was upon
the yard he stood an instant looking around him the crowd
then saw him run along the yard on reaching the end he
fastened to it the rope he had brought let it hang down
and then began going down hand over hand ten thousand
eyes were fixed on the two swinging men not a cry not a
word could be heard every person held his breath as if
afraid of increasing in the slightest degree the wind that
swung the two men the convict managed to get close to
the sailor then clinging to the rope with one hand and
working with the other he fastened the rope around the
sailor at length he was seen to climb back to the yard and
haul the sailor up he supported him there for a moment
to let him regain his strength and then took him in his
arms and carried him along the yard to the cap and thence
to the top where he left him with his comrades the convict began to descend immediately to rejoin his gang all
eyes followed him at one moment the spectators felt afraid
for they fancied they saw him hesitate and totter all at

once the crowd uttered a terrible cry the convict had fallen into the sea four men hastily got into a boat the crowd encouraged them all felt anxious again the convict did not come to the surface he disappeared without making a ripple as if he had fallen into a tank of oil they dragged for him but in vain they searched till nightfall but did not find his body.

Sentence-elements omitted

25. Do not omit a word, phrase, or clause essential to a clear understanding of the structure and meaning of the sentence.

Bad: The resonator responds in a manner analogous to that *which* one tuning fork responds to another.

Right: The resonator responds in a manner analogous to that *in which* one tuning fork responds to another.

Wrong: There were some people whom I could not tell whether they were English or American. ["Whom" has no construction.]

Right: There were some people about whom I could not tell whether they were English or American.

Confused structure

25*a*. Make the grammatical construction consistent throughout each sentence.

Bad: That's all I want, is a chance to test it thoroughly. ["Is" has no subject.]

Right: That's all I want — a chance to test it thoroughly [see Rule 236 *e*]; [or] All I want is a chance to test it thoroughly.

Sentences or sentence-elements left uncompleted

26. Do not begin a grammatical construction and leave it unfinished.

Bad: The fact that I had never before studied at home, I was at a loss what to do with vacant periods. [The noun "fact" with its appositive modifier "that . . . home" is left without any construction.]

Right: The fact that I had never before studied at home made me feel at a loss as to what to do with vacant periods.

Bad: The story tells how a young German, who, having settled in Dakota, returns to Wisconsin and there marries an old schoolmate. [The clause beginning "how a young German" is left unfinished; "German" (modified by the clause "who . . . schoolmate") has no construction.]

Right: The story tells how a young German, having settled in Dakota, returns to Wisconsin and marries an old schoolmate.

Wrong: Any man who could accomplish that task, the whole world would think he was a hero. ["Man," with its modifier "who . . . task," is left without any construction.]

Right: Any man who could accomplish that task the whole world would regard as a hero.

27. Do not use a sentence (except a quoted sentence) as the subject of *is* or *was*. *Sentence as subject or predicate complement*

Bad: I was detained by business is the reason I am late.

Right: I was detained by business; that is the reason I am late.

A similar fault is the use of a sentence (except a quoted sentence) as a predicate substantive after *is* or *was*. This fault may be corrected by changing the sentence to a substantive clause.

Bad: The difference between them is De Quincey is humorous and Macaulay is grave.

Right: The difference between them is that De Quincey is humorous and Macaulay is grave.

28. Do not use a *when* or *where* clause in place of a predicate noun; use a noun with modifiers. This error is likely to occur in definitions. (See also Rule 117.) *When or where clause for predicate noun*

Bad: Cribbing is where you copy somebody's answer in an examination.

Right: One form of cribbing is copying somebody's answer in an examination.

> Bad: Intoxication is when the brain is affected by the action of certain drugs.
>
> Right: Intoxication is a state of the brain, caused by the action of certain drugs.

28a. Do not use a *because* clause in the predicate instead of a noun clause. (See *Cause* and *Reason* in the Glossary.)

> Wrong: The reason why I failed was because I had not studied my lesson.
>
> Right: The reason why I failed was that I had not studied my lesson; [or] I failed because I had not studied my lesson.

EXERCISE 18

Elements without construction; uncompleted constructions

The following sentences contain elements without construction, or uncompleted constructions; state the fault in each, and correct and rewrite each. 1. Her hair is almost the same color as yours. 2. My afternoons are spent motoring. 3. The football games are played in the same field that the baseball diamond is located. 4. He is like all boys of his age. 5. In the east wall was one window the size of those in the north wall. 6. That wrench will not be any use. 7. I feel just the same way you do. 8. I spent most of the time fishing. 9. The machine is no good. 10. She did not know which direction to go. 11. The removal of the ammonia, which, like the removal of the tar and naphthalin, is one of the most important operations of the gas works, because of the high price which ammonia brings. 12. My first opinion of hazing was when I learned that freshmen must wear green caps. 13. It is one of those stories which you can tell how the plot will turn out after reading one page. 14. One happy event that occurred daily was when the mail arrived. 15. Prize-fighters are brutal, and some people think that football-players are the same way. 16. A buyer is likely to be prepossessed in favor of a man whose clothes fit well, his hair trimmed, his shoes well polished, and a Derby hat set jauntily on the back of his head. 17. There was an orchard near the place that we went swimming. 18. If every man who tries to be good, helping his friends and being kind to every one, it seems to me that this man is a true Christian. 19. Our forests, at the rate that they are now disappearing, will soon be extinct. 20. Hawthorne illustrates the general tendency of people to try to make an impression on others — that is, trying to appear better than they really are. 21. He was very busy, holding meetings, making speeches, and other ways. 22. He made many voyages to Guinea, plying the black ivory trade; one voyage, he ran into a storm, which destroyed the lives of two hundred of his freight. 23. Gaunt was a man about forty years old, a black beard, a hooked nose, and a deep voice. 24. A launch should be broad and deep and as much seating-room as possible. 25. There are men in college who never meet girls other than in the class-room. 26. I love to go places and see things. 27. As a whole, I think I have worked pretty hard. 28. I was surprised the other day when after receiving back several themes which were marked "poor" on account of misspelling but all of which contained favorable comments about the thought and diction, to find one theme marked "fair" because the substance was poor.

Grammatical Agreement [1]

29. A verb should agree in number with its subject.

(*a*) **Be careful not to make a verb agree with a word between it and the subject, instead of with the subject.**

> Wrong: A new order of ideas and principles have been instituted.
> Right: A new order of ideas and principles has been instituted.

> Wrong: You, the chairman, is the one to present the case.
> Right: You, the chairman, are the one to present the case.

Agreement of subject and verb

Intervening words

[1] For definitions of grammatical terms, see Appendix A.

NOTE. — The last example resembles the others in principle, although "one," the word which attracts the verb out of the plural into the singular, precedes the subject instead of following it.

Number of the subject not affected by *with*, etc.

(b) **Words joined to a subject by *with, together with, including, as well as,* or *no less than,* do not affect the number of the subject.**

> Wrong: The captain, as well as the mate and the pilot, were frightened.
> Right: The captain, as well as the mate and the pilot, was frightened.

Subjects joined by *or* or *nor*

(c) **Two or more singular subjects joined by *or* or *nor* require a singular verb.**

> Wrong: Neither he nor she are here.
> Right: Neither he nor she is here.
>
> Wrong: One or the other of those fellows have stolen it.
> Right One or the other of those fellows has stolen it.
>
> Wrong: Every young man or woman is taken for what they really are.
> Right: Every young man or woman is taken for what he or she really is.

Singular and plural substantives

(d) **When a subject is composed of both plural and singular substantives, joined by *or* or *nor,* the verb agrees with the nearer.**

> Wrong: Neither Jack nor the Smiths plays well.
> Right: Neither Jack nor the Smiths play well.

There is and there are

(e) ***There is* should be followed by a singular noun; *there are,* by a plural noun or nouns.**

> Wrong: There is too many people in this room.
> Right: There are too many people in this room.

(f) **A collective noun takes a singular verb when the group is thought of and a plural verb when the individuals are thought of.**

Right: The audience was gathering slowly.

Right: The audience were of different opinions about the play.

Right: The class has voted to increase its dues.

Right: The class have been consulted by letter regarding the proposed increase of dues.

(*g*) **In expressions like *one of the men who, one of the things which, one of the people that,* the relative pronoun refers not to *one* but to the plural object of *of.* The relative pronoun is therefore plural.**

Wrong: He is one of those men who talks much and thinks little.

Right: He is one of those men who talk much and think little.

30. A verb agrees with its subject, not with its predicate noun.

Incorrect agreement with a predicate noun

Wrong: The main part of this machine are the large rollers.

Right: The main part of this machine is the large rollers.

Wrong: Oak, brass, and steel is the material of the structure.

Right: Oak, brass, and steel are the material of the structure.

EXERCISE 19

Write the following sentences, filling the blanks in each sentence with one of the words bracketed after the sentence. In parentheses after each sentence, state the reason why the word chosen to fill the blank ought to be used. 1. The formal statement of the teachings and rules —— set forth in the constitution [is, are]. 2. The distinction between economic and social causes often —— arbitrary [seems, seem]. 3. In my opinion his attentions to the postmaster's daughter, after she had shown him she did not like him, —— very presumptuous [was, were]. 4. The strain of all the difficulties and vexations and anxieties —— more than he could bear [was, were].

Agreement of verb and subject

5. Only a few papers of this edition, which is printed at two P.M., ——— to the newsdealers [goes, go]. 6. In spite of all obstacles, the construction of the three hundred trestles and the twenty scaffolds ——— completed [was, were]. 7. His manipulation of the keys, stops, and pedals ——— miraculous to a novice [look, looks]. 8. One of the arguments he made to the delegates ——— to me especially convincing [seem, seems]. 9. The exact meaning of such words as *inspiration, prophecy,* and *orthodox* at first ——— the laymen [puzzle, puzzles]. 10. His diligent study of explosives, especially of such as might be used to destroy battleships, ——— at last rewarded [were, was]. 11. The manner in which he uses mixed metaphors, split infinitives, and dangling participles ——— lack of training [show, shows]. 12. His use of the various machines, especially of the lathes, the presses, and the forges, ——— him a born mechanic [prove, proves].

Exercise 20

Verb and subject

Correct and rewrite the following ungrammatical sentences and give a reason for each change made: 1. What a contrast does Othello and Cassio present! 2. Among this group of pilgrims was Standish and Alden. 3. Standing in the front row was Helen and her mother. 4. In this little churchyard side by side lies two graves marked by iron crosses. 5. Up the quiet street marches Hubert and his squad. 6. Foremost among the sports I delight in is skating and swimming. 7. There in the ring, the center of all attention, stand Johnson, and Jeffries. 8. At last, just when all hope seems gone, in walks Sherlock Holmes and Dr. Watson. 9. Look! there goes the bride and groom. 10. Throughout the history of this nation there has always been, and always will be, two parties. 11. There seems to be innumerable lights blazing yonder. 12. The formation of the companies to which I have referred were completed in 1909. 13. The great increase in the prices of food, clothes, and building material are caused by the tariff. 14. These attacks are made by men whose political existence depend on their capacity for misrepresentation. 15. Boyd, with three assistants, were sent to the wreck. 16. My uncle, together with his wife and children, were found working in the garden. 17. The north half of the house, including the kitchen and the dining room, were destroyed. 18. Dr. Lincoln, as well as many other physicians, advise abstinence from meat. 19. Good English, no less than good manners, are necessary to your success. 20. His house, with its stables, its tennis courts, and its beautiful grounds, were known for miles around. 21. Mary, or one of the other maids, have disturbed my desk. 22. Either your voice or the telephone are out of order. 23. I was sure that the captain or the mate were drunk. 24. Neither my father nor any other member of my family have any interest in the bill. 25. One of the books which has influenced me most is *Romola*. 26. He is one of those men who is entertaining but has no character. 27. She is one of those mothers who demands that her daughter shall know how to cook. 28. The story of Balaam is one of the Biblical stories that has interested me most. 29. I am not one of those who pretends to be pious and breaks the law. 30. She has one of these new sewing machines that is worked by hand.

31. *Each, every, either, neither, some one, somebody, any one, anybody, every one, everybody, no one, nobody, one,* and *a person* are singular.

> Wrong: Every one opened their window.
> Right: Every one opened his window.

> Wrong: Each of the suspected men were held.
> Right: Each of the suspected men was held.

This rule holds, even with a compound subject.

> Wrong: Each branch and twig were still.
> Right: Each branch and twig was still.

32. In correcting violations of Rule 31, recasting is often advisable.

> Wrong: Everybody there objected and declared they thought it barbarous.
> Right: All the people there objected and declared they thought it barbarous.

34 STRUCTURE OF SENTENCES

Exercise 21

Concord of *each, every,* etc.

Copy the following sentences, filling each of the blanks with a pronoun or with one of the words *is, are, was, were, has,* and *have:* 1. Each of the conspirators went quietly to —— own home and not one of them —— suspected by —— neighbors or by the police. 2. Every one there declared —— in favor of the measure. 3. It makes no difference whether it was Tracy or Reid; neither of those men —— worthy to raise —— eyes to my daughter. 4. A person never feels sure that —— themes will be charitably read by either of those teachers; either one of them —— likely to be severe. 5. No one had any idea what —— fate would be; every student from the best to the poorest —— in anxious suspense. 6. —— either of the boys at home? 7. —— every one here received —— money? 8. —— each of you fully determined to abide by —— promises? 9. —— neither of my assistants yet brought —— tools? 10. Everybody put on —— holiday clothes. 11. If anybody makes a motion to resist, arrest —— at once.

Matters of Case

Nominative case for subject

Who not affected by *he says,* etc.

33. The subject of a verb (except of an infinitive; see Rule 35) should be in he nominative case.

(*a*) **A parenthetical expression like *he says* intervening between the pronoun *who* and its verb does not change the case of the pronoun.**

> Wrong: The man whom I thought was my friend deceived me.
> Right: The man who I thought was my friend deceived me. ["Who" is the subject of "was"; "I thought" is a mere parenthesis.]

> Wrong: Whom did they say won?
> Right: Who did they say won?

> Right: The chairman whom they elected has resigned.

(*b*) **The pronoun *who* or *whoever,* when it is the subject of a finite verb, is sometimes wrongly put into the objective case, because it appears to be the object of a preceding verb or preposition.** *Who or whoever not affected by preceding words*

> Wrong: Send whomever will do the work.
> Right: Send whoever will do the work. ["Whoever" is the subject of "will do," not the object of "send." The object of "send" is the clause "whoever will do the work."]
>
> Wrong: The question of whom should be leader arose.
> Right: The question of who should be leader arose. ["Who" is the subject of "should be," not the object of "of." The object of "of" is the substantive clause "who should be leader."]

34. A predicate substantive completing a finite verb should be in the nominative case. *Predicate substantive with finite verb*

> Right: It is I. — The beneficiaries are she, they, and we. — Is it we that you accuse? ["It is me" is a colloquialism.]

35. The subject of an infinitive and the predicate substantive completing an infinitive should be in the objective case. *Subject and predicate complement of an infinitive*

> Right: The gazette reported him to be dead. ["Him" is the subject of the infinitive "to be," and not the object of "reported."]
> Right: She imagined the burglar to be me. ["Me" is the predicate substantive completing "to be."]
> Right: The man whom I thought to be my friend deceived me. ["Whom" is the subject of "to be." Cf. the first two examples under Rule 33 *a*.]

36. The object of a verb or of a preposition should be in the objective case. *Object of verb or preposition*

> *Whom* do you mean? [not *who*. "Who do you mean?" is an accepted colloquialism.]

When she said that to sister and *me*, we couldn't help laughing [not sister and *I*].

Does that rule apply to *us* upperclassmen? [not *we* upperclassmen.]

EXERCISE 22

Nominative or objective case of *who*

Write the following sentences, filling each blank with *who* or *whom*. State in parentheses after each sentence the construction of the word inserted. 1. They sent invitations to all —— they thought would accept. 2. This money comes from Boyle, —— you know is very liberal. 3. He refused to pardon Mackey, —— he had every reason to believe the police had caught red-handed. 4. The bookkeeper, ——, I cannot doubt, committed these errors, must be discharged. 5. The vacancy was filled by Clayson, —— the manager said ought to be promoted. 6. The vacancy was filled by Clayson —— the manager thought worthy of promotion. 7. An instance is furnished by Saint Paul, ——, the New Testament tells us, was at first an opponent of Christianity. 8. The throne was held by a king —— historians believe to have been insane. 9. The throne was held by a king —— historians say was insane. 10. —— did he say the architect was? 11. —— did he say the board chose as architect? 12. —— do you believe this impostor to be? 13. —— do you think will preside? 14. —— do you consider to be the fastest runner? 15. —— do you think is the fastest runner?

Appositives

37. An appositive should be in the same case as the noun with which it is in apposition.

Right: All are going — he, she, and we two.

He spoke to some of us — namely, her and me.

We all met — she, the officer, they you mentioned and I.

Substantive after *than* or *as*

38. The case of a single substantive following *than* or *as* is nominative or objective, according to its use in the incompleted clause of which it is a part. It is not the object of a preposition, because *than* and *as* are not prepositions, but conjunctions introducing subordinate clauses.

> Right: He is happier than I. ["Than I" = "than I am."]
> Right: I can do it as well as they. ["As they" = "as they can do it."]
> Right: I should help him more willingly than her. ["Than her" = "than I should help her."]

NOTE. — The expression *than whom* is ungrammatical, but well established as an idiom.   *Than whom*

> " . . . when Beelzebub perceived, — than whom,
> Satan except, none higher sat, — with grave
> Aspect he rose. . . ."
> — *Paradise Lost*, Book II.

EXERCISE 23

Write the following sentences, filling the blank in each with one of the words bracketed after the sentence. State in parentheses after each sentence the construction of the inserted word.   1. He stopped —— he met [whoever, whomever].   2. It will greatly assist —— lives in the country [whoever, whomever].   3. —— brings me the cup I will make my son-in-law [whoever, whomever].   4. For —— loves his country I have a message [whoever, whomever].   5. Even food and shelter are withheld from —— the pope has excommunicated [whoever, whomever].   6. Every door is shut against —— the count has said is objectionable to him [whoever, whomever].   7. A discussion followed as to —— should steer [who, whom].   8. There was no doubt as to —— the speaker meant [who, whom].   9. They were anxious about —— the victim would be [who, whom].

Nominative or objective case of who or whoever

EXERCISE 24

Write the following sentences, filling each blank with one of the words bracketed after the blank.   State in parentheses after each sentence the construction of the inserted words.   1. She is not so clever as —— [he, him].   2. She hated both of —— [we fellows, us fellows], but —— [I, me] more than —— [he, him].   3. Are they

Elliptical than and as clauses

better qualified than ——— [we, us] to judge? 4. No one could regret it more than ——— [I, me]. 5. She is so deceitful that I would trust a convict sooner than ——— [she, her]. 6. O king, no man is so wise as ——— [thee, thou]. 7. Her hasty action injured herself more than ——— [I, me]. 8. The others suffered more than ——— [we, us] who were expelled. 9. The conspirators plotted shrewdly, but the detective was shrewder than ——— [they, them]. 10. For a brief time no one was so famous as ——— [I, me]. 11. My lord, thy power wanes; the king favors thy rival more than ——— [thou, thee]. 12. Though the queen protested, the statesman, stronger than ——— [her, she], prevailed. 13. Sir, we are less worthy than ——— [they, them]; we ask that they be promoted rather than ——— [we, us]; honor them rather than ——— [we, us].

EXERCISE 25

General exercise in the use of cases

Write the following sentences, filling each blank with one of the words or groups of words bracketed after the blank. State in parentheses after each sentence the construction of the inserted word or words. 1. She prepared a lunch for my brother and ——— [I, me] to take with us. 2. All ——— [us, we] fellows met to consider the question of ——— [who, whom] should be sent. [What is the subject of "should be sent"? What is the object of the preposition "of"? See *Substantive Clause* in the Grammatical Vocabulary.] 3. It is a question of veracity between ——— [he, him] and ——— [I, me]. 4. She did not refer to ——— [we, us] girls at all. 5. It is unjust to expect ——— [she and I; her and me] to do all the work. 6. Henceforth all is over between you and ——— [I, me]. 7. That was ——— [I, me] ——— [who, whom] you heard last night. 8. It is not ——— [us, we] who are to blame; it is ——— [they, them]. 9. I am at a loss ——— [who, whom] to depend on. 10. Was this my old comrade? I could not believe that this ragged beggar was ——— [he, him]. 11. First he spoke of Jezebel and Athaliah; ——— [them, they] he said were types of depravity. Then he considered Jael and Miriam; ——— [them, they] he apostrophized as patriots. 12. To you Englishmen as well as

to —— [we Americans; us Americans] his name is dear.
13. Hetherington and I thought it was necessary that the
messengers chosen should be —— [us, we] rather than
—— [them, they] who were secret traitors.   14. The
cause so dear to you and —— [me, I] has failed.   15. All
the responsibility rests on Jane and —— [I, me].   16. He
wanted —— [my father and I; my father and me] to
invest in a corporation managed by —— [he and his
father; him and his father].   17. —— [him, he] and all
his associates I repudiate.   18. A large estate was left to
—— [she and her sister; her and her sister].   19. You
ought not to be burdened with —— [he and his family;
him and his family].   20. Do I know Raycroft? Why, I
used to visit —— [he and his wife; him and his wife]
every Sunday.   21. The landlord was inexorable with the
poor widow; he drove —— [she and her children; her
and her children] into the street.   22. Let —— [he that
is without sin; him that is without sin] cast the first stone.
23. —— [they that are negligent; them that are negli-
gent] he admonishes; —— [they that are faithful; them
that are faithful] are commended.

39. In certain cases it is awkward to attribute possession to inanimate objects.

Possessive
case:
Nouns not
designating
persons

Awkward: The porch's roof.
Improved: The roof of the porch.

Awkward: The store's management.
Improved: The management of the store.

NOTE. — Good usage justifies many exceptions, including expressions designating time or measure, as *a day's
journey, a stone's throw, five minutes' walk, a month's wages;*
and expressions implying personification, as *for pity's sake,
duty's pleadings, the law's delay.*

Permissible
exceptions

40. Do not use the possessive case of a noun to indicate the object of an action; use an *of* phrase.

Possessive
case in
objective
sense

Wrong: Lincoln's assassination.
Right: The assassination of Lincoln.

Wrong: Mankind's benefactor.
Right: The benefactor of mankind.

Possessive
with
gerund

41. Put the substantive modifying a gerund in the possessive case. Distinguish a gerund, a verbal noun, from a participle; as " His writing is poor " [gerund] and " I found him writing a letter " [participle].

EXERCISE 26

Use of
possessive
case

Some of the following sentences contain errors or awkward uses of the possessive case. Rewrite the sentences correctly. 1. The book's title is misleading. 2. The tree's shadow concealed me. 3. I am sure of him being able to do the work. 4. I do not like your cigar's odor. 5. She could not understand any one wanting to read it. 6. The fireman climbed upon the church's roof. 7. We rowed along, following the shore's curve. 8. She talked unfavorably of John going. 9. I had not heard of you being ill. 10. She would not permit me going alone.

Adjectives and Adverbs

Adverb or
predicate
adjective

42. In such expressions as *he looks sad, he looks sadly, he stands firm, he stands firmly,* the word following the verb should be an adjective if it describes the subject; if it designates the manner of action of the verb, it should be an adverb. Such verbs as *appear, be, become, seem, smell, sound, taste,* etc., either commonly or invariably require an adjective.

Right: He appears good [*i.e.*, appears to be a *good man*].

Right: He appears well in public [*i.e.*, makes his appearance in a creditable manner].

Right: The music sounds loud [*i.e.*, has the characteristic of *loud music*].

Right: The bugle sounded loudly through the ranks [*i.e.*, sounded in a loud manner].

Right (poetic): Loud through the ranks sounded the bugle [*i.e.*, the loud bugle sounded].

Right: It stands immovable. It smells sweet. It tastes sour. Your hand feels cold. She looks dainty. That statement sounds queer.

NOTE. — In such expressions as *I am well* and *I am ill*, *well* and *ill* are adjectives (see these words in a dictionary). An expression like *I am nicely*, *I am poorly*, is ungrammatical.

"Nicely" and "poorly"

43. In such expressions as *he holds it steady, he holds it steadily, he filled it full, he filled it fully,* the modifier should be an adjective if it designates the condition of the object; if it designates the manner of action of the verb, it should be an adverb.

Adverb or factitive adjective

Right: He kept it safe [*i.e.*, through his keeping, it was safe].
Right: He kept it safely [*i.e.*, he performed in a safe manner the act of keeping].
Right: He wrapped it tight ["tight" designates the condition of the object].
Right: He wrapped it tightly ["tightly" designates the mode of wrapping].
Right: Sweep it clean. Hold it motionless. Shoot him dead. Nail it solid. Bury it deep. Raise it high.

Matters of Voice

44. Avoid awkward use of the passive voice. The active voice is usually clearer, terser, and more forceful than the passive.

Misuse of passive voice

Bad: Your letter was received and carefully read by me.
Right: I received and carefully read your letter. (See Rule 336.)

Bad: That was a crisis in my life which will never be forgotten.
Right: That was a crisis in my life which I shall never forget.

Matters of Mode

45. Most educated and intelligent writers use the subjunctive mode for a wish, volition, or a condition

The subjunctive

improbable or contrary to fact. *Be* and *were* are practically the only special subjunctive forms in modern use.

> Right: If this *were* [not *was*] Wednesday, I could go with you.
> Right: Don't you, John, wish you *were* [not *was*] in his place?
> Right: I insist that he attend to the matter today.
> Right: Everybody stand up.
> Right (less common): If he *be* guilty, let him suffer the consequences. "If he *is* guilty" implies less doubt.

EXERCISE 27

Correct the following sentences and give reasons for corrections: 1. If I was older, I should be going to work. 2. If he was steadier in his habits, he would be a good student. 3. The work was done very hastily by him. 4. The meal was prepared and quickly eaten by us. 5. There were such bad roads that the town was rarely visited by travelers. 6. If it was a matter of great importance, the doctor was to be summoned by me. 7. The wood was chopped and the fire was started by the campers. 8. A night attack should be made upon the enemy if it is desired to catch them unaware. 9. I wish I was grown up. 10. That was my resolution which was made after careful consideration.

Shall and *will*

Expectation

Matters of Tense (including **shall** and **will**)

46. To represent simple expectation on the part of the speaker, use *shall* (or *should*) in the first person, and *will* (or *would*) in the second and third persons. Memorize the following formula:

I shall (should)	we shall (should)
you will (would)	you will (would)
he will (would)	they will (would)

Wrong: I don't believe I will be able to go.
Right: I don't believe I shall be able to go.
Right: I don't believe he will be able to go.

Wrong: We will be glad to hear from you further.
Right: We shall be glad to hear from you further.
Right: He will be glad to hear from you further.

Wrong: I feared I would fail.
Right: I feared I should fail.
Right: I feared you would fail.

NOTE. — Excepted from the rules governing these auxiliaries are the use of *should* to express obligation — I *should* not have said that — and the use of *would* to express habitual action — I *would* sit by the hour in the parlor waiting for her to come down.

47. To represent determination, desire, willingness, or promise on the part of the speaker, use *will* (or *would*) in the first person, and *shall* (or *should*) in the second and third persons. The following is the formula for such expressions:

Determination

I will (would)   we will (would)
you shall (should)   you shall (should)
he shall (should)   they shall (should)

Right: I will help you; I promise it. You shall not stir; I forbid it. They shall be hanged at sunrise; we, the court, decree it.

48. In a question containing *shall* or *should*, *will* or *would* —

In questions

(*a*) **When the subject is in the first person, use the auxiliary *shall* or *should*, except in repeating a question addressed to the speaker.**

Wrong: Well, what will we do now?
Right: Well, what shall we do now?
Right (exception): Will I help you? Why, certainly.

(*b*) **When the subject is in the second or third person, use the auxiliary that will be used in the answer.**

Right form for a question as to expectations: Shall you be recognized, do you think? [The answer, according to Rule 46, would be either, "I shall be" or "I shall not be"; therefore *shall* should be used in the question.]

Right form for a question as to intention: Will you do the deed? [The answer, according to Rule 47, would be either "I will" or "I will not"; therefore *will* should be used in the question.]

In indirect quotations

49. In an indirect quotation use the auxiliary that would properly be used if the quotation were direct.

Right: He said he thought he should ride. [The direct quotation would be, "I think I shall ride"; therefore *should* (an inflectional form of *shall*) should be used in the indirect quotation.]

Shall and should in contingent statements

50. In subordinate clauses making contingent statements, *shall* and *should* are correctly used for all persons. In other subordinate clauses *shall* and *should* are commonly used in all persons for the simple future; *will* and *would*, for wishing, consenting, and willing.

Right: If they should find it, I should rejoice.
Right: A man who should do that would be hated.

NOTE. — Some of the rules for *shall, will, should,* and *would* are disregarded by many intelligent and educated persons. Therefore, "I will probably come on Thursday," although not the best usage, is correct colloquial English. The rule, however, indicates the practice of most writers.

EXERCISE 28

Shall and will

Write the following sentences, filling each blank in sentences 1–10 with *shall* or *will*, and each blank in sentences 11–20 with *should* or *would*. State in parentheses after each sentence why the auxiliaries you have inserted are preferred. 1. I think I ——— find the study easy. 2. I am the carpenter you engaged. ——— my men begin work today? 3. "——— you see Niagara on your way east?" "No; I don't think I ———." 4. "Oh, Mr. Meyer, the singer I engaged has disappointed me. ——— you sing for me tonight?" "Yes, I ——— sing for you."

5. "Hello, Meyer. ———— you be busy tonight?" "Yes; I ———— sing at Mrs. West's tonight." 6. I ———— probably fail in the examination. 7. I am very anxious. If no one assists me, I ———— starve. But sell my library? No! I ———— never do that. 8. "If you eat this rabbit, ———— you be kept awake all night?" "Probably; but by Jove, I ———— eat it anyway." 9. If I miss another class, I ———— be required to take an extra examination. 10. I ———— probably get a cool reception there, but I ———— go, whatever happens. 11. I ———— not have supposed the price would be so high. 12. I ———— have been surprised if he had failed. 13. Perceiving that I ———— soon need a light, I determined that I ———— buy a lantern. 14. I fully understood that I ———— be censured if I did it. 15. ———— you have supposed that the city would grow so fast? 16. We feared we ———— get caught in the rain. 17. Since the car was so late, I knew I ———— miss my class. 18. It was so warm that we thought we ———— not need our overcoats. 19. ———— you have known him if he had not introduced himself? 20. Yes, even if he had not spoken, I think I ———— have known him.

51. Obscurity, or an effect of incompleteness, arises from the use of a verb in the past tense unaccompanied by a time modifier, when there is in the context no indication of the time of the action.

The undated past tense

> Obscure and incomplete: In accounting for the origin of Lake Wingra, geologists say that a small stream ran through the territory where the lake now lies.
>
> Clear [The necessary time modifier of "ran" is supplied]: In accounting for the origin of Lake Wingra, geologists say that at some remote period a small stream ran through the territory where the lake now lies.

NOTE. — When a sentence introduces a new or additional idea, obscurity is often avoided by the addition of a time modifier, no matter what the tense of the verb may be. Words expressing indefinite time, such as "now and then," "always," "frequently," etc., are at times indispensable. Similarly adverbs and adverbial phrases or clauses expressing place or attendant circumstances should not be omitted when they make the meaning clearer. An example of the first part of this suggestion is found in the use of "at times" in the second sentence of the text of this paragraph.

Past mis-
used for
past perfect

52. The past perfect tense represents action prior to some past time.

> Obscure: Mitchell hired a jockey named Brunt to ride Shackles in the approaching race. *Brunt was injured in a jump-race and gave up racing for a time.* But Mitchell persuaded him to begin again. [The reader supposes that the events stated in the italicized sentence followed the employment of Brunt by Mitchell; whereas the writer intends to say that those events preceded the employment. The use of the past tense in the italicized sentence is thus entirely misleading.]
>
> Clear: Mitchell hired a jockey named Brunt to ride Shackles in the approaching race. Brunt *had been injured* in a jump-race and *had given up* racing for a time. But Mitchell persuaded him to begin again.

Sequence of
tenses

52a. Maintain proper sequence of tenses. The past is not all one, but may be said to consist of the particular time of the main narrative, previous time, and subsequent time down to the present, each time having its appropriate tense.

> Wrong: They informed us that they wrote to Paris for instructions.
>
> Right: They informed us [past time, past tense] that they had written [previous time, past perfect tense] to Paris for instructions, but since then we have not heard [subsequent time, perfect tense] the outcome of their inquiry.

Relation of
sub-
ordinate
verbs:
perfect
infinitive

53. Maintain a proper relation between subordinate verb-forms and the verb of the main clause.

(*a*) **An infinitive should be in the present tense unless it represents action prior to that of the govern-**

ing verb. Guard against its being attracted into the perfect.

> Wrong: It was not necessary for you to have gone.
> Right: It was not necessary for you to go.
> Wrong: I intended to have answered.
> Right: I intended to answer.

(*b*) **A conditional verb-phrase in a dependent clause should be in the present tense unless it represents action prior to that of the governing verb.** Guard against its being attracted into the perfect.

Perfect conditional

> Wrong: I should not have said it if I had thought it would have shocked her.
> Right: I should not have said it if I had thought it would shock her.

(*c*) **Statements permanently true should be put into the present tense.** When they occur in a subordinate clause in indirect discourse, following a verb in past time, guard against their being attracted into the past.

Statements permanently true

> Wrong: He said that oak was the best wood for floors.
> Right: He said that oak is the best wood for floors.
> Wrong: I have always heard that the four years of college were the happiest in a man's life.
> Right: I have always heard that the four years of college are the happiest in a man's life.

54. The past participle represents action prior to that of the governing verb; the present participle, action at the time expressed by the verb.

Anachronous participles

> Wrong: It is old, being founded in 1809.
> Right: It is old, having been founded in 1809.
> Wrong: Starting for London, he arrived there two weeks later.
> Right: He started for London and arrived there two weeks later.

EXERCISE 29

Matters of tense

Correct any errors in tense that you may find in the following sentences and give reasons for the corrections. 1. Coming into the room, he opened the windows. 2. She said that she left before the news came. 3. I hoped to have gone. 4. Turning the corner, he hurried down the street. 5. I fully expected to have finished my work. 6. Being well trained, he won first place. 7. If I had known that you had been going, I should have sent word to my mother. 8. I intended to have made a trip to Chicago. 9. He said that baseball was a good sport. 10. He handed in the composition which he wrote. 11. Coming into his office, he held conferences with his students. 12. By following directions carefully, he learns the method and would have no trouble with the course. 13. If it had rained, we planned to have gone to the theater. 14. He cooked the fish which he caught in the lake.

EXERCISE 30

GENERAL EXERCISES IN THE USE OF VERBS

Lay and lie

I. See *Lay* in the Glossary. Write three sentences containing present indicative forms of the verb *lie* (in the sense of *recline*), three containing the present participle, three containing past tense forms, and three containing perfect forms. Write three sentences containing present indicative forms of the verb *lay*, three containing the present participle, three containing past tense forms, and three containing perfect tense forms.

Lay and lie

II. See *Lay* in the Glossary. Write the following sentences, filling each blank with some form of the verb *lie* or some form of the verb *lay:* 1. The logs are ——ing where they fell. 2. Yesterday I —— it on the grass. 3. I will —— down and rest. 4. They —— still and said nothing. 5. Inmates are not allowed to —— in bed after six o'clock. 6. They let the torpedo —— on the railroad. 7. I have —— all his things in readiness. 8. The scythe —— in the rain so long that it got rusty. 9. ——ing quietly in the grass, he watched. 10. Have they —— their wet hats on the parlor table? 11. Coming from

Florida, I was surprised to find the snow still ———ing on the ground.

III. See *Raise* in the Glossary. Write three sentences *Raise and* containing present indicative forms of the verb *rise*, three *rise* containing the present participle, three containing past tense forms. Write three sentences containing present indicative forms of the verb *raise*, three containing the present participle, three containing past tense forms, and three containing perfect tense forms.

IV. See *Raise* in the Glossary. Write the following sen- *Raise and* tences, filling each blank with some form of the verb *raise* *rise* or some form of the verb *rise:* 1. Don't be embarrassed; ——— up and speak. 2. A man suddenly ——— up and interrupted. 3. I will ——— up and deny it publicly. 4. Slowly the load yielded to the upward force; and little by little it ——— until it reached the desired point. 5. It was too late; the balloon had already ——— ten feet. 6. Has the river ——— at all during the night?

V. See *Set* in the Glossary. Write three sentences con- *Set and sit* taining present indicative forms of the verb *set*, three containing the present participle, three containing past tense forms, and three containing perfect tense forms. Write three sentences containing present indicative forms of the verb *sit*, three containing the present participle, three containing past tense forms, and three containing perfect tense forms.

VI. See *Set* in the Glossary. Write the following sen- *Set and sit* tences, filling each blank with some form of the verb *set* or some form of the verb *sit:* 1. The ink-well doesn't ——— level. 2. I enjoy ——— in the dark. 3. How long we had ——— there I do not know. 4. He brought the little girl in his arms and ——— her in a chair by the fire.

VII. Comment on the use of *set* in each of the following *Set* sentences, correcting all errors: 1. Around the table set four chairs. 2. She left the umbrella setting against the chair. 3. You have set a hard task. 4. He saw the pie setting on the doorstep. 5. With the spirit level, he made the table set exactly horizontal. 6. Did you notice the order in which the cups were set?   7. Ready; get set; go. 8. The bluffs appear to set back some distance from the shore.

Lay, lie, raise, rise, set, and sit

VIII.   See *Lay, Raise,* and *Set* in the Glossary.   Write a short narrative or a series of sentences using the words *lie, lying, lay, lain, laying, laid, rise, rising, rose, risen, raise, raising, raised, sit, sitting, sat, set,* and *setting.*

Done and *seen*

IX.   Remember the principal parts of *do* and *see:*

I do	I did	I have done
I see	I saw	I have seen

Write five sentences each containing past tense forms of the verbs *do* and *see,* and five sentences each containing *done* and *seen* properly used.

Write the following sentences filling the blanks with *did* or *saw:* 1. I —— the damage that the fire ——. 2. There we —— a magician, who —— some tricks. 3. I —— my duty and I —— it.   4. He —— the work with his own hands; I —— him do it.   5. She —— that it would do harm, and so she —— all she could to stop it.

Write, rise, ride, drive

X.   Remember the principal parts of *write, rise, ride,* and *drive:*

I write	I wrote	I have written
I rise	I rose	I have risen
I ride	I rode	I have ridden
I drive	I drove	I have driven

Write sentences containing perfect tense forms and past perfect tense forms of *write, rise, ride,* and *drive.*

Run misused for *ran*

XI.   Remember the principal parts of the verb *run:*

I run	I ran	I have run

Write five sentences containing the verb *run* in the past tense, and five containing the form *run,* properly used.

Began, sang, sprang, rang, drank, ran, swam

XII.   Notice the relation between the past tense and the perfect tense of the following verbs:

I began	I have begun
I sang	I have sung

I sprang	I have sprung
I rang	I have rung
I drank	I have drunk
I ran	I have run
I swam	I have swum

Write sentences containing perfect tense forms and past perfect tense forms of the foregoing verbs.

XIII. Notice the relation between the past tense and the perfect tense of the following verbs:

Broke, froze, tore

I broke	I have broken
I froze	I have frozen
I tore	I have torn

Write sentences containing perfect active, past perfect active, and passive forms of the foregoing verbs.

XIV. Remember the principal parts of *know, throw,* and *blow:*

Know, throw, blow

I know	I knew	I have known
I throw	I threw	I have thrown
I blow	I blew	I have blown

Write sentences containing past tense forms and perfect tense forms of the foregoing verbs.

XV. Remember the principal parts of the verb *go:*

Went for *gone*

I go	I went	I have gone

Write ten sentences using perfect tense forms of this verb.

XVI. See *Ought* in the Glossary. The following sentences are grossly incorrect. Correct and rewrite them. 1. He hadn't ought to refuse. 2. I'd ought to accept, hadn't I? 3. Don't you think she'd ought to have gone? 4. No man ought to endure that, had he? 5. If that house was empty, then he had ought to have gone to the next. 6. We really ought to help him — don't you think we had?

"Had ought"

XVII. See *Ought* in the Glossary. Write ten sentences using *ought* correctly, five of them stating present duties, and five, past duties.

"Had ought"

"You was"   XVIII. See *You was* in the Glossary. Write the following sentences, filling in the blanks with *were:* 1. Where —— you, Harry. 2. I thought you —— lying down. 3. You ——n't to blame, my boy. 4. —— you present, Father? 5. When —— you born, young man?

Reference

Uncertain or ludicrous reference   **55. Do not use a pronoun instead of a noun if there can be doubt even for a moment about its antecedent.**

> Uncertain: Geraint followed the knight to a town, where he entered a castle.
>
> Uncertain: He told his father he would soon get a letter.
>
> Not immediately evident: The ghost of his old partner appeared to Scrooge. He told him he must reform.
>
> Ludicrous: Whistling for Rover, my cousin put a pail in his mouth and we started.

NOTE. — Do not use a plural pronoun referring to a singular noun preceding; make the pronoun singular, or else repeat the noun in the plural. (See Exercise 35.)

> Wrong: The incubator is a modern device for hatching chickens. All poultrymen who do business on a large scale use them.
>
> Right: The incubator is a modern device for hatching chickens. All poultrymen who do business on a large scale use it; [or] . . . use incubators.

Methods of correction   **56. Violations of Rule 55 may sometimes be corrected by repeating the antecedent or using an equivalent noun.**

> Right: Whistling for Rover, my cousin put a pail in the dog's mouth, and we started.

But usually recasting is advisable; thus:

> Right: Geraint followed the knight to a town and there saw him enter a castle.

Right: He said to his father, "You will [or I shall] soon get a letter."

Right: The ghost of his partner appeared to Scrooge and admonished him to reform.

57. The pronouns *this* and *that* are peculiarly liable to be used with what may be called weak reference. In case of such use, the fault may often be corrected by changing the pronoun to a demonstrative adjective and inserting a noun after it. Thus:

Weak reference of *this* and *that*

Weak reference: He asked where Cary was. I could not answer that.

Right: He asked where Cary was. I could not answer that question.

Weak reference: We do oppose the bill; if we did not, we should not publish this.

Right: We do oppose the bill; if we did not, we should not publish this article.

58. Do not use a pronoun to refer to a noun that has not been used for a considerable space; repeat the noun.

Remote reference

59. Avoid reference of a pronoun to a noun decidedly subordinate in thought or syntax. Repeat the noun or recast the sentence. Some more prominent noun is likely to be mistaken by the reader for the antecedent.

Reference to a noun not prominent

Bad: Mrs. Bloodgood will appear at Powers's Theatre in Fitch's play, *The Girl with the Green Eyes*. This piece was written by *him* especially for Mrs. Bloodgood.

Right: Mrs. Bloodgood will appear at Powers's Theatre in Fitch's play, *The Girl with the Green Eyes*. This piece was written by Mr. Fitch especially for Mrs. Bloodgood.

Bad: In Miss Howerth's story of her life she relates this incident.

Right: Miss Howerth in the story of her life relates this incident.

Allowable: Tom's happiness was a joy to see; he literally danced on the pavement. ["Tom" is subordinate in syntax but not in thought.]

Reference to a word not expressed

60. Do not use a pronoun, or a pronominal expression, seeming to refer to a word or phrase that has not been expressed. (See Exercise 34.)

Bad: The cadet must keep his hands out of his pockets; *that* would be very unsoldierly.

Right: The cadet must keep his hands out of his pockets; to put them there would be very unsoldierly.

Bad: Marx is a violinist, the study of *which instrument* he began when a boy.

Right: Marx is a violinist. He began the study of the violin when he was a boy.

Bad: Mink-skins are valuable, because *these animals* are now scarce.

Right: Mink-skins are valuable, because minks are now scarce.

Reference to a whole statement

60a. The relative pronoun *which* should not be used referring to a whole statement if that statement contains nouns to which the pronoun may be erroneously referred. Use a dash and put a noun (*fact, act, operation*, etc.) before the *which;* or recast. (See Exercise 33.)

Ambiguous: He did not hear her cry which was due to his deafness.

Right: He did not hear her cry — a fact which was due to his deafness.

Ambiguous: Unless you steer carefully, the boat may crash into the wharf, which may result in serious damage to the hull.

Right: Unless you steer carefully, the boat may crash into the wharf, seriously damaging the hull.

61. Do not use a pronoun followed by its antecedent in parentheses; use the antecedent alone or recast the sentence.

Antecedent in parentheses

Awkward: If Davis treated Dixon discourteously, there is no objection to his (Dixon's) decision.

Right: If Davis treated Dixon discourteously, there is no objection to Dixon's decision; [or] Dixon is not to be blamed for his decision if he was treated discourteously by Davis.

EXERCISE 31

Rewrite the following sentences, correcting faulty reference: 1. When the sergeant saw that a man was getting too much beer at the Canteen, he was immediately put out. 2. The nurse left some medicine, but Molly secretly resolved not to take it. When she made her next visit, she told her she thought she had greatly improved. 3. The directors offered to reward her liberally, but she begged them to give it to her father. 4. Portia and her maid dressed like lawyers and went to court. She found that Antonio had forfeited the bond. 5. The essay on planets is short and witty. After stating a few thoughts regarding them, he makes a digression. 6. But truth will always come out. In this case it occurred in the following way. 7. When the next man came to bat and knocked the ball to shortstop, he threw it over the first baseman's head. 8. She next removes the furniture from the parlor and sweeps it. 9. She prepares the vegetables for dinner and has it ready when her husband returns. 10. Some parts of the story I found interesting, but this was offset by so much dry, uninteresting reading. The descriptions he gives of the different characters are interesting. 11. The cadets at West Point are appointed by the members of Congress. On graduating, he receives a commission in the army. 12. He attached the hose to the tank and flushed it about once a month. 13. The sugar beet is an easy vegetable to grow; in a good season, a farmer gets

Reference of pronouns

fifteen tons of them from each acre.   14. The dam is not water-tight, but allows it to seep through.   15. I delighted in going away from home; one day father found me about two miles away from home, carrying an old bucket. But I spent most of my time there, when I grew older.   16. Dumont said that Charles had been found, as a new-born child, at his doorstep, and that the only means of identifying his father was a slip of paper pinned to his clothes.   17. The abolition of the training table was wise, for it led to professionalism.   18. The marines then opened fire on the natives. They scattered in all directions and were not seen again until they sailed away from the island.   19. I do not believe that one who has left us would wish us to mourn for them.   20. There was never a graduate of the Minneapolis high schools so lacking in knowledge of their native language as are many upper-classmen I have met in our college.   21. Giovanni noticed an old man tending the flowers. This man was the gardener, but he was astonished to see how cautious he was in touching them.   22. Let me try to state my opinion of the high and noble place occupied at the present time by the art of debate. I wish to emphasize "at the present time"; for I fear that if certain tendencies continue, it will not long remain in its honorable station.   23. My acquaintance with the Bible is limited to a few chapters which I read last summer — the first time I ever had access to one.   24. Then began his brilliant military career in the Civil War, which was terminated by his death.   25. My work was principally at the bench, which consisted of cutting, sewing, and riveting.   26. A big box stood near the stove which served as a seat for two loungers.   27. The lamp of an incubator furnishes the artificial heat to the chicken which takes the place of the natural heat of the hen.   28. Tramps of the kind I have described will work, and when necessity presses, he will work hard.   29. The son of Kamal went back with the Englishman as his bodyguard

EXERCISE 32

It used ambiguously or indefinitely

Be careful of ambiguous, indefinite, and meaningless *it* Rewrite the following sentences, eliminating every bad *it* and give the antecedent of every pronoun used. 1. A sloop is a simple form of sail-boat. It has one mast, and it is set in the forward deck. 2. There is a prohibitory law in Evanston; and though it is easy to get on a car and go to Chicago, yet it is effective because it makes it more difficult to get liquor. 3. The small draught of the boat makes it possible to use it in shallow water. 4. Poe's description of the Maelstrom is very impressive, though whether it is true is doubtful. At any rate, it is a terrific whirlpool. 5. The sickle should be changed at noon for a sharp one as it makes it easier for the horses and it also cuts the hay better. 6. If there were two classes in chemistry, it would bring better results. As it is now, the students get little good from the lectures. 7. Toward the end of the essay a marriage feast is described. It tells of the illustrious guests who were present. 8. The incident you speak of occurs in *Romeo and Juliet;* it tells how a friar assisted in an elopement. 9. It was difficult sometimes to get permission to go swimming. Yet often it was an advantageous way for our parents to get odd jobs done. If it was to mow the lawn, the work would be finished in a remarkably short time when a swim was to be the reward. 10. A block in which crushed stone is used is more durable than one in which only sand is mixed with the cement; and it is also the cheaper method.

EXERCISE 33

Correct the ambiguous use of *which* in the following sentences and tell the antecedent of every *which* used: 1. The reference books are used a great many times, which necessitates an unlimited amount of handling. 2. I have driven a motor for many hundreds of miles and have had no accidents which I attribute to the scrupulous care I have always taken. 3. One day he was ransacking a house which the army often did at that time. 4. He did not hear her cry which was due to his deafness. 5. I was tardy at the opening exercise which resulted in a lecture from the principal. 6. My Christmas vacation was spent in camping on the shore of a lake, which people do not usually do for a week in winter. 7. The throttle can be opened any desired amount, which will raise the

Which without antecedent

speed of the boat proportionately. 8. Unless you steer carefully, the boat may crash into the wharf which may result in serious damage to the hull.

EXERCISE 34

Reference
to words
not
expressed
Correct and rewrite the following sentences: 1. He is intellectually powerful, as may be seen in his many keen and pithy comments on life; but he uses it for malicious purposes. 2. Debating was a popular amusement in our county, and most of the farmers attended these debates. 3. Farm machinery is very fascinating to me, and I greatly enjoy using them. 4. The doctor had a country patient who required his presence every day. On one of these visits the doctor's motor broke down. 5. Curtis speaks of his interest in Spanish affairs, telling of his estates there and of how he longs to see them. 6. Anders and his brothers were accustomed to fish at a point near the whirlpool, because the fish were plentiful there. While they were taking one of these trips, they were overtaken by a storm. 7. For several centuries England and France were at war almost constantly. One of these wars began in 1450. 8. It is a pleasure to go to my German class because I feel there is some possibility of my getting that lesson. 9. I will not attempt to discuss dress from the feminine point of view, for their tastes are too intricate for my comprehension. 10. If the car is dusty, this should be removed with a feather broom. 11. Look at ancient Greece; consider the love of athletic games that prevailed among these people. 12. I took a great fancy to ice-boating, which furnishes sport, exercise, and knowledge of the art of sailing. I made several small ones, which I used on the pond near our home.

EXERCISE 35

Plural
pronouns
referring to
singular
antecedents
In the following sentences make the pronouns agree with their antecedents in number: 1. The Arabs understand the horse and how to train it. They train them so that it brings out their noblest traits. 2. I should hardly say that a salesman must smoke in order to succeed, and yet most of them do. 3. As a vermin-killer the cat is very useful; were it not for them, rats and mice would

abound in our houses. 4. The horse is the most useful animal employed by man. Their usefulness should make us grateful to them. 5. The gasoline launch is coming more and more into use. These boats are used chiefly for pleasure. 6. When you go duck-shooting, use decoys; throw out your decoys, and wait for them to come within shooting distance. 7. It is harder to get a duck after it is wounded than when it is flying, because when they are wounded they dive. 8. Even when you see which tree your squirrel went up, you are likely to lose him, because they are so clever at hiding themselves. 9. The incubator is a modern device for hatching chickens. All poultrymen who do business on a large scale use them. 10. The life of an engineer demands that they be able to endure hardship. 11. An electric car, no matter how many people are jammed into it, can go, and usually does go, very rapidly; consequently it is often uncomfortable and even dangerous to ride in them.

EXERCISE 36

Correct the obscure reference in the following sentences. 1. A college graduate loves to recall the friends he met there. 2. When you fill the gasoline-tank, always strain it through a chamois-skin. 3. On the counter was the usual cheese-case, with a knife lying near, for the convenience of any who wished to taste it. 4. Since my fishing-rod is broken I am deprived of that sport. 5. If the coffee-mill is out of order we can't have any tonight. 6. The members of the suicide club used various means for accomplishing that gruesome object. 7. Since the chapel bell was silent, few people came to that building. 8. He came into the senate-chamber and insulted that body. 9. The Baltimore *Sun* is the cleverest paper of that city. 10. The sophomore point of view is different; they think the practice is beneficial. 11. The freshman yell could be heard about a block away, but none of them were seen to pass the house. 12. I did not care to contract the habit of cigarette-smoking because I had heard so much about their bad effects. 13. Bass-fishing is not much fun unless you catch a big one. 14. When a large bass is hooked, do not be hasty in drawing in your line,

Obscure reference

for they make a desperate fight for freedom. 15. The school I attended was inferior to most city schools; their English department was especially poor.

Dangling Modifiers

Dangling participles

62. Place a participle near the word it modifies.

Wrong: Every morning I take a run followed by a shower bath.

Right: Every morning I take a run and immediately afterward a shower bath.

Wrong: He was deaf, caused by an early attack of scarlet fever.

Right: (a) He was deaf, as the result of an early attack of scarlet fever; or (b) His deafness was caused by an early attack of scarlet fever. ["Caused," a participle, must modify a noun.]

Participle introducing a sentence or clause

63. A participle should not introduce a sentence or clause, unless it logically modifies the subject of the sentence or clause.

Wrong: Having come of age, I took my son into partnership with me.

Wrong: There we landed, and having eaten our lunch the steamboat departed.

Method of correction

64. Violations of the foregoing rule may be corrected either (a) by changing the participial phrase to a clause, or (b) by using as the subject the noun which the participle modifies.

Right: (a) When my son came of age, I took him into partnership; [or] (b) Having come of age, my son entered into partnership with me.

Right: (a) There we landed, and after we had eaten our lunch the steamboat departed; [or] (b) There we landed, and having eaten our lunch we saw the steamboat depart.

65. Do not end a sentence with a participial phrase of result which is not related to any noun preceding. Such phrases frequently begin with *thus* or *thereby*. The error may be corrected by changing the participial phrase to an independent clause or to a subordinate clause.

Participial phrase of result (thus or thereby)

> Wrong: He was well acquainted with the best literature, thus helping him to become an able critic.
>
> Right: He was well acquainted with the best literature; this helped him to become an able critic, [or, so that he was helped].

> Wrong: He has to stand still until the rod man comes up, thus giving him no chance to move about and keep warm.
>
> Right: He has to stand still until the rod man comes up; thus he has no chance to move about and keep warm; [or, so that he has no chance].

> Wrong: The little ship was very light, causing it to ride the waves easily.
>
> Right: The little ship was very light; thus it rode the waves easily; [or, so that it rode the waves easily].

EXERCISE 37

Complete the following sentences: 1. Arriving there late ———. 2. Stepping upon the platform ———. 3. Checking his horse as he neared the two straying children ———. 4. Having thus accidentally disclosed her identity to the policeman ———. 5. Having heard that you are a skillful portrait painter ———.

Dangling participles

EXERCISE 38

Revise the following sentences and tell what each participle used modifies: 1. Looking toward the east, the harbor presents the appearance of a crescent. 2. Looking at these trees from the west, they appear very close together. 3. Looking toward the north, the walls of the valley rise high and steep. 4. Viewing the Troy schoolhouse in summer, the foliage of the surrounding trees

Participle introducing a sentence or clause

seems almost to bury it.   5. Not being a spring switch, care must be taken to open and close it rapidly.   6. "Now for this packet of papers!" said the squire.   Tearing open the envelope a map fell out.   7. Having twice before been a candidate for the presidency, a third nomination indicates a substantial growth in the principles for which I have contended.   8. A large crowd of spectators watched Mr. Wright's trip around the drill ground in his aeroplane. Rising, descending, turning sharp angles, the sight was marvelous.   9. Having bought my gun from a reliable dealer, and having used it carefully for five years, it shoots as accurately and looks as well now as it did when I first got it.   10. Having been in America only a few months her English is very broken.   11. Never having seen the house, it is naturally hard for me to describe it.   12. Going up the north shore, the wind was against us.   13. Having eaten no breakfast and therefore feeling somewhat faint, the motion of the ship soon brought on a distressing nausea.   14. Arrived at the hospital a consultation was held, to determine whether I should be operated on. 15. Being in need of a pair of suspenders my mother extemporized a pair for me, using some strong tape. 16. Pondering on this contrast, my respect for my compatriots increased.   17. We looked back for a last view of the little group of cottages; then turning a bend in the road, they were hid from our view.   18. Taking into consideration all the good that football does, the game should not be abolished.   19. I felt very sick caused by the motion of the boat.   20. I could not recognize him caused by his beard.   21. He displeased several of the audience caused by his frivolity.   22. The larger boats cannot land here caused by the shallowness of the water.

Dangling gerund phrases

66. Place a gerund phrase (*e.g., in speaking, after going*) close to the word it modifies. The same remark may be made with respect to infinitives. (See the examples under Rule 67. For a discussion of the gerund, see Appendix A.)

> Bad: He assumed a curious pose unusual for him in speaking.

Right: In speaking, he assumed a curious pose unusual for him.

NOTE. — This rule and Rule 67 do not apply when the gerund designates general action, not the action of any special agent. Thus:

Right: In swimming, the head should not be lifted too high.

67. A gerund phrase should not introduce a sentence or clause unless it logically modifies the subject of the sentence or clause.

Gerund phrase introducing sentence or clause

Wrong: In talking to Smith the other day, he told me about the race.
Wrong: After pointing out my errors, I was dismissed.
Wrong: After flunking three times, the professor reproved me.
Wrong: After singing hymn 523, Mr. Barnes will lead in prayer.

NOTE. — An error similar to the dangling gerund is the dangling infinitive. (See also Rule 76.)

Dangling infinitive phrases

Wrong: To enjoy a walking trip, the feet should be in good condition.
Right: To enjoy a walking trip, take care that your feet are in good condition.
Wrong: To appreciate pictures, they should be studied.
Right: To appreciate pictures, study them; [or] If pictures are to be appreciated, they should be studied.

68. Violations of the foregoing rule may be corrected either (a) by changing the gerund phrase to a clause, or (b) by using as subject the noun to which the gerund phrase is related in thought.

Method of correction

Right: (a) As I was talking to Smith the other day, he told me about the race; [or] (b) In talking to Smith the other day I learned about the race.
Right: (a) When he had pointed out my errors, I

was dismissed; [or] (*b*) After pointing out my errors he dismissed me.

Right: (*a*) When I had flunked three times, the professor reproved me; [or] (*b*) After flunking three times, I was reproved by the professor.

Right: (*a*) After we have sung hymn 523, Mr. Barnes will lead in prayer; [or] (*b*) After singing hymn 523 we shall be led in prayer by Mr. Barnes.

EXERCISE 39

Dangling gerund phrases

Complete the following sentences: 1. Without denying your statement ———. 2. Upon questioning his sister as to the truth of the report ———. 3. In removing the chimney of his lamp that evening ———. 4. Upon examining the letters that I found in the injured man's pocket ———. 5. After setting the vase in this very insecure position, naturally ———.

EXERCISE 40

Dangling gerund phrases

Correct the following sentences: 1. Instead of gluing the top in place, it was fastened with nails. 2. After opening the champagne bottle it was found to contain only water. 3. In talking to old Romulus he does not answer as if he were intelligent, but he is so, really. 4. After seeing that the tires are in order, the engine may be started. 5. While traveling through a small town not long ago, the general store attracted my attention. 6. Upon arriving at the station our train had not yet been made up. 7. After being borne forward some distance, the roar of a cataract announced greater danger. 8. The horse now became utterly ungovernable; and after dashing madly through the crowded street, knocking down several pedestrians, and kicking the dash-board to pieces, I decided to get out of the buggy. 9. After looking at the high bluffs, the green valley attracts one's attention. 10. After mixing the cement and the sand in the right proportions the mixture is put into moulds. 11. By moving the clutch half-way, it will become disengaged. 12. By letting a gun stand for several days without cleaning, it will usually rust. 13. He gave an antidote so powerful that any poison was made harmless after taking it. 14. A mixture of sand and gravel is used for filling the holes; after being dumped into the holes, water is poured upon the mixture.

EXERCISE 41

Dangling infinitives

Revise the following sentences which contain dangling infinitives: 1. To enjoy a walk thoroughly, it should be taken early in the day. 2. To make a farm profitable, it must be managed by an expert. 3. To appreciate pictures, they should be studied. 4. In order to save the railroads from bankruptcy, they must increase their rates. 5. To make a horse a good roadster, it should be trained while it is a colt. 6. In order to enjoy the full value of a horse, he should be well cared for. 7. To make a dog come home, his feet may be greased. 8. To make the linen stiff, it is usually dipped in starch. 9. In order to make a politician popular, he need only abuse the corporations. 10. In order to protect the children, they were sent into the cellar. 11. The wheels should be oiled regularly to keep them in good order.

Dangling elliptical clauses

69. An elliptical clause (a clause from which the subject and predicate are omitted; *e.g., while going* for *while I was going, when a boy* for *when he was a boy*) should not be used unless the omitted subject is the subject of the governing clause.

Wrong: When six years old, my grandfather died.
Wrong: You must not cut the cake until thoroughly cooked.

Method of correction

70. A violation of the foregoing rule may be corrected by supplying the subject and predicate of the elliptical clause.

Right: When I was six years old, my grandfather died.
Right: You should not cut the cake until it is thoroughly cooked.

33813

Elliptical clauses in titles

71. Rule 69 forbids such titles as *An Accident while Hunting, Things Learned while Canvassing*. Write rather *An Accident in a Bear Hunt, Things Learned by a Canvasser*.

EXERCISE 42

Dangling elliptical clauses

Complete the following sentences: 1. When a mere boy (he was certainly no more than ten years old at the time), ———. 2. Although a very instructive book, ———. 3. While moving about in disguise among his subjects, ———. 4. If in doubt as to what college you had better attend, ———. 5. When engaged in this work, if any friends come to see him, ———. 6. While thoroughly in sympathy with the plans you have told me about ———.

EXERCISE 43

Dangling elliptical clauses

Rewrite the following sentences which contain dangling elliptical clauses: 1. When making a landing, great care should be taken not to jam the boat. 2. While inflating the tire, the air-tube of the pump broke. 3. When a small boy my summers were spent at Nantasket Beach. 4. When about half way to his destination, a storm overtook him. 5. When a boy, many were the hours I spent in boating. 6. Last winter while on a hunting expedition, my first chance to bag a deer came to me. 7. One dark night, while keeping a herd of steers in corral on my uncle's ranch, a stampede occurred. 8. While on my way to church, the Sunday quiet was suddenly broken by a shriek. 9. While leaning against the door, it suddenly opened, and he found himself in the vestibule. 10. While spending my vacation at home, my father took me on a long ride in the country. 11. While working in the garden one day, cultivating the blossoming shrubs, a lizard crawled across the path. 12. I have said little about my life while in the high school. 13. The injured man was quickly placed in the ambulance: but while on the way to the hospital, a blood vessel burst. 14. While still in the high school, thoughts of college life roused my enthusiasm. 15. When a young man, people spoke of him as a reckless spendthrift.

Unity

72. A sentence should be so composed that the reader feels it to be a unit. If it contains more than one statement, these should be so related as to express a single thought.

73. Statements conspicuously lacking connection with each other should not be embodied in the same sentence. Defects in unity may be corrected by one of the following means:

(*a*) **By placing the unrelated statements in different sentences.**

> Wrong: Mathematics is my hardest subject, and comes at eleven in the morning.
> Right: Mathematics is my hardest subject. It comes at eleven in the morning.

> Wrong: Ruskin was a famous English critic, and was born in 1819.
> Right: Ruskin was a famous English critic. He was born in 1819.

> Wrong: I have received your letter of May 6, and the shirts referred to were shipped yesterday morning.
> Right: I have received your letter of May 6. The shirts referred to were shipped yesterday.

(*b*) **By subordinating one statement to another, when their logical relationship can be made clear by this means.**

> Right: Mathematics, my hardest subject, comes at eleven in the morning.
> Right: Ruskin, the famous English critic, was born in 1819.
> Right: The shirts referred to in your letter of May 6 were shipped yesterday.

Unity
secured by
recasting

(*c*) **By filling up the gaps in thought, subordinating properly, and using connectives which show the precise relationship of statements.**

> Wrong: Engineering has always interested me, but last winter I heard a talk by a famous engineer. Then I decided to take an engineering course.
>
> Right: Although engineering has always interested me, I did not decide to take up an engineering course until I heard last winter a talk by a famous engineer.
>
> Wrong: The scenery along the banks is very pretty, but the river is too shallow to be navigated by large boats.
>
> Right: The scenery along the banks is very pretty, but few people have seen it, because the river is too shallow to be navigated by boats large enough to carry passengers.
>
> Wrong: The operation of an incubator is simple, but no machine will work well unless it is watched.
>
> Right: An incubator is simple in operation, but, like any other machine, it will not work well unless it is watched.

Stringy
compound
sentences

74. Long compound sentences consisting of many statements strung together with *and's*, *but's* and *so's* are especially bad violations of unity. Proper division and subordination, with the use of the right connectives, provide the remedy. (See Rules 97–98.)

> Wrong: The aircraft production program was badly delayed, and a good many people think we did nothing in building airplanes, but the government reorganized the work, and put capable production specialists in command, and these men corrected the faults in the planes and increased production, and before the end of the war they were turning out planes faster than the government could supply pilots to man them.
>
> Right: It is true that the aircraft production program was badly delayed, so that it is no wonder

many people think we accomplished nothing in building airplanes. As a matter of fact, however, after the government reorganized the work and put capable production specialists in command, not only were the faults in the planes corrected, but production was increased. Before the end of the war, airplanes were being turned out faster than the government could supply pilots to man them.

NOTE. — It is rarely advisable to begin sentences with *and* or *also*. Practise instead the use of a variety of connectives, and note that it is often advantageous to place them within the sentence rather than at the beginning (see Rule 83).

75. Long, straggling sentences written without grammatical plan and covering either too many ideas or too many periods of time to make a definite impression on the reader's mind are a palpable violation of unity.

Straggling sentences

Narrative

Wrong: That night we camped near the outlet, and the next morning we packed our equipment and took down the tents and put them into the canoes and started down the outlet with our canoe in the lead, but we had not gone more than a few miles when we came to a fallen tree right across our way, and as the banks were soft mud it would be hard to carry around it, so we held a council of war and decided to cut through the trunk, which was not very large, so after much splashing and nearly upsetting the canoe we succeeded in disposing of the obstacle, after which we proceeded on our way.

Right: That night we camped near the outlet. The next morning after stowing our tents and equipment in the canoes, we started down the stream, our canoe leading. After we had paddled a few miles, we came to a tree which had fallen right across our way. As the banks were soft mud, to carry around the tree would have been difficult; accordingly, holding a council of war, we decided to cut through the trunk, which was not very large. After much splashing, and nearly upsetting the canoe, we succeeded in disposing of the obstacle, and proceeded on our way.

Summary

Wrong: Tennyson's poem *Lady Clara Vere de Vere* is the speech of a young country fellow to a young lady of high birth who is beautiful but a heartless coquette, having attempted to ensnare the young man and then cast him off merely to amuse herself, as she has done with a number of other young fellows, one of whom, as the young man who is speaking reminds her, committed suicide from grief at her cruelty, which makes the young man who is speaking despise the lady, for he tells her that he cares neither for her beauty nor for her high birth, since she has no goodness of heart, and he solemnly tells her she ought to cease amusing herself by her coquetry and to "pray Heaven for a human heart."

Right: Tennyson's poem *Lady Clara Vere de Vere* is the speech of a manly young country fellow to a beautiful but heartless young lady of high birth, who has attempted to amuse herself by breaking his heart, — a speech expressing disdain for charms beneath which there is no goodness of heart, and contempt for hereditary rank of which the possessor lacks true virtue and honor; reminding the lady of the suicide of another country lad, whom she had enticed by feigned affection and then cruelly repudiated; and solemnly adjuring her to cease her unworthy and injurious diversion, to turn her leisure to some good end, and to "pray Heaven for a human heart."

NOTE. — A sentence may be long without violating unity. The first of the two foregoing sentences violates unity because it is straggling, lacking grammatical plan. The second does not violate unity; it has a definite organization of which parallelism is an important factor (see Rule 111). This parallelism may be made clear by the following diagram:

$$
\text{Tennyson's poem } \dots \text{ is}
\dots \text{ a speech}
\left\{
\begin{array}{l}
\text{1. expressing } \left\{ \begin{array}{l} a.\ \text{disdain} \\ b.\ \text{contempt} \end{array} \right. \\
\text{2. reminding} \\
\text{3. adjuring her } \left\{ \begin{array}{l} a.\ \text{to cease} \\ b.\ \text{to turn} \\ c.\ \text{to pray} \end{array} \right.
\end{array}
\right.
$$

76. Avoid unnecessary changing of the subject or of the voice, mode, or tense of the verb.

Unnecessary change: We passed over the road quickly and soon the camp was reached.

Right: We passed over the road quickly and soon reached the camp.

Bad: In order to clean the chain, it should be removed and soaked in kerosene.

Right: In order to clean the chain, remove it and soak it in kerosene; [or] In order that the chain may be thoroughly cleansed, it should be removed and soaked in kerosene.

Bad: First stir in the flour and then you should add the butter and salt.

Right: First you should stir in the flour and then you should add the butter and salt.

Right: You should first stir in the flour and then add the butter and salt.

EXERCISE 44

Rewrite the following sentences: 1. If you buy this car, it will give you good service. 2. Turn to the right at the cross road and it will be easy to find the house. 3. A bright gleam of lightning illuminated the landscape and a loud clap of thunder was heard. 4. Because we started very late, no lunch was taken. 5. If you hurry with the message, much trouble will be saved you. 6. I arrived in Milwaukee at one o'clock and soon my aunt's house was reached. 7. Although at first the whole family objected to my plan, yet it was finally approved by them.

Order of Members — Coherence

77. Every modifier should be so placed that the reader connects it immediately with the member it modifies, and not with some other member. A phrase or clause that modifies the main clause may very often be placed with advantage at the beginning of the sentence.

Bad: The storm broke just as we reached the shore with great violence.

Right: Just as we reached the shore, the storm broke with great violence.

Bad: The ball is thrown home by a player stationed in the middle of the square called the pitcher.

Right: The ball is thrown home by a player called the pitcher, who is stationed in the middle of the square.

Position of the adverbs *only, almost,* etc.

78. As a rule, place the adverbs *only, merely, just, almost, ever, hardly, scarcely, quite, nearly,* next to the words they modify, not elsewhere. If they are to modify only a part of the predicate, place them before that part.

Colloquial: I only want three.
Better: I want only three; [or] I want three only.

Colloquial: Do you ever expect to go again?
Better: Do you expect ever to go again?

Wrong: It is the handsomest vase I almost ever saw.
Right: It is almost the handsomest vase I ever saw.

Wrong: I never remember having met him. [Here "ever" is misplaced and made to modify the wrong word, for *never = not ever*.]

EXERCISE 45

Position of *only, almost,* and *ever*

Rewrite the following sentences, placing the adverbs as close as possible to the words modified: 1. The manufacture of sugar is only profitable in a large factory. 2. I only saw him once after that. 3. The office is only open in the forenoon. 4. I only need a few dollars. 5. He only succeeded in stopping the horse after it had collided with an electric car and demolished the buggy. 6. He had almost got to the top when the rope broke. 7. I never expect to see the like again. 8. Do you ever remember to have seen the accused before?

Misplaced clauses

79. A modifying clause should not be so placed that a verb following it may, in reading, be erroneously

joined with the verb of the clause instead of with the
verb preceding the clause. Observe that in some instances the difficulty is remedied by placing the time
modifier first.

> Ill arranged: I walked out into the night as the moon
>   rose and wandered through the grounds.
> Clear: As the moon rose, I walked out into the night
>   and wandered through the grounds.
> Ill arranged: He sprang to the platform on which the
>   dead man lay and shouted.
> Clear: Springing to the platform on which the dead
>   man lay, he shouted.
> Bad: A terrible wind and thunder storm visited the
>   Fourth Regiment camp Thursday night, shortly
>   after taps were sounded, playing havoc on all sides.
> Right: On Thursday night, shortly after taps was
>   sounded, a violent wind and thunder storm visited
>   the Fourth Regiment camp, playing havoc on all
>   sides.

**80. As a rule, arrange a sentence containing a rela-
tive clause so that the clause immediately follows its
antecedent.** *Position of relative clauses*

> Awkward: I had many pleasant experiences while I
>   was there, some of which I shall always remember.
> Better: While I was there, I had many pleasant ex-
>   periences, some of which I shall always remember.
> Awkward: The correspondence began just one month
>   later which led to the surrender.
> Better: Just one month later began the correspon-
>   dence which led to the surrender.

NOTE. — It may happen that a sentence containing a
relative clause cannot be arranged according to the foregoing rule. In such a case it is often necessary, for clearness, to use two separate sentences or two coördinate
clauses.

> Bad: The police are looking today for the persons
>   last in company with Clara Belinfant, the daughter

of Abraham Belinfant, a rich New York merchant, who has been missing since July 18.

Right: The police are looking today for the persons last seen in company with Clara Belinfant, the daughter of Abraham Belinfant, a rich New York merchant. The girl has been missing since July 18.

EXERCISE 46

Sentence-order

Rewrite the following sentences, improving the arrangement; make no changes except in the order of the members; if you change the position of a member tell what the member modifies: 1. The top is a cylinder on the surface of which a number of strips one sixteenth of an inch thick and one inch above the surface, called knives, are placed. 2. These pulleys are connected with another set of pulleys of ten inch diameter at the lower part of the machine by belts. 3. He sometimes tried to discuss subjects that interested him with the Autocrat. 4. I judged that the fellow was a monk who had fled from the monastery by his gown and his air of trepidation. 5. He finally succeeded in drawing the spoon hook up close to the boat, on which he found a turtle. 6. Every one felt sure that Beiler had no chance of winning soon after he began to speak. 7. He tore up the tender letter which his mother had written him in a fit of peevish vexation. 8. Lamb playfully pretends to prove that the art of roasting pigs originated in China by an old manuscript. 9. The author here makes a digression proving that devil-fish actually exist and that they have been known to devour men, to make the story more real. 10. In a village on the Wisconsin River just above the point where it joins the Mississippi on a cold February afternoon I first saw the light of day. 11. There are two ways of chiseling at present in use among machinists that are equally effective. 12. The light causes a chemical action on the plate in the camera which is imperceptible to the eye. 13. The yacht is drawn up out of the water after every race on a small railway. 14. There was a pilot house just in front of the engine room which looked like a watchman's box. 15. He was taken out to the transport which was anchored off the coast in a row boat. 16. Keeping his opponent covered with his six-shooter, he collected all the money that was lying on the table in his hat.   17. How can a man write a theme when he has the problem of finding the equation of the common tangent to a hyperbola and an ellipse on his mind?   18. He adds the amounts of all checks received during the day on an adding machine.   19. I was able to save the motor car that had broken away from destruction by a happy accident.   20. Sometimes you will see an alligator lying in the sunshine on the bank eight feet long.   21. Members will please inform the steward of their intention to dine at the club upon their arrival to insure good service.   22. We demand the suppression of the traffic in liquors to be used for beverages by every lawful means.

81. Do not place between two members of a sentence a modifier applicable to either member. Do not trust to punctuation to show the application of the modifier; recast the sentence.

Squinting modifiers

> Defective: The person who steals in nine cases out of ten is driven to it by want.
>
> Right: In nine cases out of ten, the person who steals is driven to it by want.
>
> Defective: Since a canoe cannot stand hard knocks when not in use it should be kept out of the water.
>
> Right: Since a canoe cannot stand hard knocks, it should be kept out of the water when not in use.
>
> Defective: The coroner's jury which has been investigating the death of the girl today brought in a verdict of suicide.
>
> Right: The coroner's jury which has been investigating the death of the girl brought in today a verdict of suicide.

Exercise 47

Recast the following sentences to place modifiers where their relationships cannot be mistaken: 1. Studying the style of a master in a certain way improves the style of a student. 2. When Samson came of age, much to his parents' displeasure, he married a Philistine woman. 3. Since a canoe cannot stand any hard knocks when not in use it should be kept out of the water. 4. Although it

seems illogical, to my mind, at least, it is very pathetic.
5. As he reached Randolph Street by a lucky throw a
policeman tossed his club into the rear wheel of the
bicycle.   6. Dawes who led the party after the passage
of the ford saw an antelope in the distance.   7. If a man
who is anxious about business matters after his work is
over will play a game of tennis or handball, his cares will
vanish.   8. Though we think there will be much to talk
about when our guests are with us we stare at each other
and can think of little to say.   9. That disregard of law
has a bad effect in most cases is self-evident.   10. When
the villain Pew sees that he will be discovered by base
methods he tries to throw the guilt on his innocent companion.   11. When I arrived in Chicago for the first time
in my life I was left to take care of myself.   12. When a
boy is sent to college, as a rule, he wishes to be popular.
13. To live in a well-kept house without doubt affords
much comfort to every one.

Parenthetic
position of
modifiers

**82. For the sake of emphasis and clearness a modi-
fier of a clause may often with advantage be inserted
within the clause it modifies rather than placed before
or after.**

> Clear and forcible: If, after all that has been said,
> you still hesitate, I despair of persuading you.

Parenthetic
position of
therefore,
however, etc.

**83. For the sake of beginning the sentence with
words that deserve distinction, it is often advantageous to place *however, therefore, nevertheless, moreover, also,* and the like, within the sentences they
introduce rather than at the beginning.**   Such words
should be placed early in the sentence, so that their
qualifying effect is seen at first glance.

> Less emphatic: His master was always very kind to
>   him.   However, his master's wife was altogether
>   too parsimonious.
> Better: His master was always very kind to him.   His
>   master's wife, however, was altogether too parsi-
>   monious.

Inferior: The study of birds is fascinating. It requires a great deal of patience, however.
Better: The study of birds is fascinating. It requires, however, a great deal of patience.

NOTE. — This caution includes such expressions as *I think* and *it seems to me*. Do not, however, place these particles and expressions at the ends of clauses.

Bad: There is another use for this machine, I think.
Right: There is, I think, another use for this machine.

84. Two phrases or clauses modifying the same sentence-element and of parallel form and function should not be placed one before and one after that element; they should be put together. *Separation of coördinate modifiers*

Awkward: When he has once made up his mind, you may be sure he will never draw back when he has got fully started.
Right: When he has once made up his mind and got fully started, you may be sure he will never draw back.

85. Do not put an adverb or a phrase between an infinitive and its sign *to*. *Split infinitives*

Inelegant: I went there in order to personally inspect it.
Right: I went there in order to inspect it personally.
Inelegant: It is impossible to in any way remove them.
Right: It is impossible in any way to remove them.

NOTE. — Though the split infinitive is usually to be avoided, it can be justified when used to avoid awkwardness or loss of clearness.

EXERCISE 48

Rewrite the following sentences to avoid split infinitives: *Split infinitives* 1. A considerable period is required to properly heat the eggs. 2. The acid is allowed to slowly percolate. 3. The glare of the fire seemed to completely light the city. 4. He reefed his canvas in order to better weather the storm.

5. Because of the confusion he was able to easily make his escape.   6. She was seen to slowly and steadily sink into the quicksand.   7. Are you willing to in any way assist us?   8. It is advisable to always keep the tank full.

Smooth order

86. Arrange the members of a sentence so that the sentence reads smoothly, unless this arrangement impairs clearness.

> Awkward: He, instead of acting as my guide, followed me.   [Awkwardness caused by needless separation between subject and verb, throwing false emphasis on "he."]
>
> Right: Instead of acting as my guide, he followed me.
>
> Awkward: Fishing was not good, and they, becoming impatient, decided to quit.
>
> Right: Fishing was not good, and becoming impatient they decided to quit.

Pause after preposition

Note. — This principle is violated by interposing a number of words between a preposition and its object, so that an awkward pause occurs after the preposition.

> Awkward: He submitted to, though he did not fully approve of, the rules.
>
> Better: He submitted to the rules, though he did not fully approve of them.

See also the first *Right* example under Rule 90 e.

Such a construction may be used, for the sake of brevity, in statutes, contracts, and the like, in which smoothness of style is of little consequence.

> "The Congress shall have power to dispose of, and make all needful rules and regulations respecting the territory . ˙. . belonging to the United States." — *The Federal Constitution.*

Except in such a context, the harshness of the construction more than offsets the gain in compactness.

Ordering a sentence with reference to the preceding sentence

87. Arrange the members of a sentence so as to form close connection with the preceding sentence.

> Inferior: He wished to examine the planet Mars, then in the western part of the sky.   He began to turn the telescope in order to do this.

Better: He wished to examine the planet Mars, then in the western part of the sky. In order to do this, he began to turn the telescope.

Order of Members — Emphasis

88. For force, close sentences strongly; put unimportant phrases elsewhere than at the end. Transforming a loose sentence into a periodic sentence — one in which the main clause is not completed until the end — is an effective means of securing emphasis.

Strong close

Inferior: Then he would return to work, whistling a merry tune all the while.

Better: Then he would return to work, all the while whistling a merry tune.

Inferior: He said nothing, but kept looking at my neck for some reason or other.

Better: He said nothing, but for some reason or other kept looking at my neck.

Loose: We were drenched to the skin in spite of our rubber coats before we had gone a hundred yards through the wet grass and underbrush that covered the hillside.

Periodic: Before we had gone a hundred yards through the wet grass and underbrush that covered the hillside, in spite of our rubber coats we were drenched to the skin.

NOTE. — The foregoing rule does not concern a matter of correct or incorrect practice, but merely a matter of greater or less rhetorical effectiveness. The common belief that a sentence ending with a preposition is on that account incorrect is a mistake; such sentences abound in good literature; *e.g.*,

A sentence ending with a preposition

"I will not say that the meaning of Shakespeare's names . . . may be entirely lost sight of." — ARNOLD.

"M. Planche's advantage is . . . that there is a force of cultivated opinion for him to appeal to." — ARNOLD.

Moreover, such sentences, as Professor Hill remarks, "do not contravene the principle which forbids a writer to throw stress on unimportant words; for . . . the stress is thrown, not on the last word, but on the next to the last."

89. A series of assertions or modifiers noticeably varying in strength should be placed in climactic order, unless the writer intends to make an anti-climax for the sake of humor.

> Weak: I think that the characters are well drawn, the diction is stately and beautiful, and the plot is very interesting.
>
> Improved: I think that the plot is very interesting, the characters are well drawn, and the diction is stately and beautiful.
>
> Weak: He proved himself to be mercilessly cruel at times, unforgiving, and discourteous.
>
> Improved: He proved himself to be unforgiving, discourteous, and at times mercilessly cruel.

EXERCISE 49

Rewrite the following sentences for better coherence (arrangement and connections) or emphasis: 1. The rain beat upon his face, but he staggered on although he was intensely cold. 2. Although she was to all appearances perfectly polite and agreeable, I knew that she was longing for a good opportunity to throttle me, however. 3. As soon as they left the ship, the men began on board to prepare for action. 4. The news spread among the boys finally when a beautiful warm day arrived that Ray Hoover had been swimming. 5. Jim McTaggart starving, uncouth, and dirty stood in the doorway. 6. During the past semester I have had considerable trouble with some of my studies. Much attention is paid to detail in these courses. 7. Last night I dreamt that it was an October evening, and that I was driving slowly along a country road, watching the sun setting behind the woods almost in front of me. My attention was drawn to a homestead when the sun was almost hid. 8. He is, to say the least, not trustworthy. 9. As I work ahead, I build new castles in Spain as I see more clearly what is possible.

Incorrect Omissions

90. Avoid the incorrect use of words in a double capacity. A word or a combination of words may often be correctly used in a double capacity if it is perfectly fitted for both the offices it serves. For example, in the sentence, " I can do it as well as you," " can do it " serves as the predicate of both " I " and " you," and does so correctly, since it agrees grammatically with both pronouns. But there are various ways of using words in a double capacity that are incorrect; these are indicated in the following rules:

Words used in a double capacity

(*a*) **Do not supply an auxiliary verb or a copula from one part of a sentence to another if the same form is not grammatically proper in both parts; write the proper form with each part.**

Auxiliaries and copulas in a double capacity

> Wrong: The fire was built and the potatoes baked.
> Right: The fire was built and the potatoes were baked.
> Wrong: He was a patriot, but all the rest traitors.
> Right: He was a patriot, but all the rest were traitors.

NOTE. — The supplying of an auxiliary from one clause to another is likely in most cases to produce an awkward sentence, even when there is no violation of the foregoing principle. As a rule, repeat an auxiliary rather than supply it.

> Awkward: Light was seen through the opening, and the voice of my rescuer heard.
> Better: Light was seen through the opening, and the voice of my rescuer was heard. [See Rule 221*f*.]

(*b*) **Do not make a single form of the verb *be* serve both as a principal and as an auxiliary verb.**

Be as both principal and auxiliary

> Wrong: At first the drill was interesting and liked by most of the men.
> Right: At first the drill was interesting and was liked by most of the men.

Principal verbs in a double capacity

(c) Do not supply a principal verb from one part of a sentence to another if the same form is not grammatically proper in both parts; write the proper form for each part.

> Wrong: He did what many others have and are doing.
> Right: He did what many others have done and are doing.
> Wrong: We ate such a dinner as only laborers can.
> Right: We ate such a dinner as only laborers can eat.

Than or *as* clause in a double capacity

(d) Two expressions of comparison, the one an adjective preceded by *as,* the other an adjective in the comparative degree, should not both be completed by a single *as* clause or a single *than* clause, unless that clause immediately follows the expression of comparison that stands first in the sentence.

> Wrong: Fostoria is as large, if not larger, than Delaware.
> Right: Fostoria is as large as Delaware, if not larger.
>
> Wrong; He is bigger and fully as strong as Buck.
> Right: He is bigger than Buck and fully as strong.

Other modifiers in a double capacity

(e) Aside from the two cases given under *d*, above, two sentence-elements should never be limited by a single modifying phrase or clause unless that modifier is idiomatically adapted to both.

> Wrong: He had no love or confidence in his employer.
> Right: He had no love for, or confidence in, his employer. [The foregoing is correct, but awkward; the following is better:] He had no love for his employer and no confidence in him.
>
> Wrong: I shall always remember the town because of the good times and the many friends I made there.
> Right: I shall always remember the town because of the good times I had and the many friends I made there.

Wrong: He acquired a knowledge and keen interest in chess.
Right: He acquired a knowledge of chess and a keen interest in it.

(*f*) **Two incomplete members of a sentence, the one requiring to complete it a singular noun, the other requiring a plural noun, should not both be completed by one noun, unless that noun immediately follows the incomplete member that stands first in the sentence.** *A noun in a double capacity*

Wrong: One of the greatest, if not the greatest, generals of America.
Right: One of the greatest generals of America, if not the greatest.

(*g*) **When *as to, in regard to,* or *in respect to* is used as a single preposition to govern a clause, the *to* should not be made to govern a substantive within the clause.** *To (in as to, in regard to, etc.) used in a double capacity*

Wrong: A dispute arose *as to* [= *concerning*] whom the honor should belong.
Right (awkward): A dispute arose *as to* [= *concerning*] whom the honor should belong to.
Preferable: A dispute arose *as to* [= *concerning*] who should receive the honor. See Rule 33 *b*

(*h*) **Do not omit the subordinating conjunction *that* at the beginning of a substantive clause which follows a verb of *saying, thinking, feeling,* etc., when to do so causes awkwardness.**

Bad: Silas Marner was brought back to church interests because he felt to do the right thing by Eppie he must have her christened.
Right: Silas Marner was brought back to church interests because he felt *that* to do the right thing by Eppie he must have her christened.

Note. — For the faulty omission of *that* after *so*, see the Glossary. *That after so*

Exercise 50

Omission of auxiliaries

Rewrite the following sentences, supplying the necessary auxiliaries: 1. All the men were assembled and the paper signed. 2. She was shown into the parlor and the light turned on. 3. The garret was ransacked but no clothes found. 4. The envoy was socially agreeable and welcomed by the aristocracy. 5. The bear was very ferocious and therefore carefully guarded. 6. She was anxious and tearful and pitied by all who met her. 7. The machine is put in place and the rollers connected. Later the rollers are stopped and a wide board substituted for them. 8. Her adventure was related at the hotel and the police informed. 9. A large dam is built and the mill operated by water-power. 10. The stock is soaked again and more chemicals added. 11. The date for the game was set and our men given the privilege of two nights' practice. 12. I was elected president and the installation ceremonies performed. 13. I think that for every temptation to which a man may be exposed a parallel case may be found in the Bible and the proper way to act learned from the example. 14. After all these details have been attended to and the boat painted and varnished, your work is done. 15. Next the armature was wiped clean and the oil-cups taken out.

Exercise 51

Omission of principal verb

Rewrite the following sentences, supplying the principal verbs: 1. I hope you will not find the room so disagreeable as I have. 2. At the decisive moment he weakened, as I suppose I shall too when my time comes. 3. The sun rose just as splendidly and brilliantly as it had on the day before. 4. I have and I hope I always shall call Milwaukee my home. 5. The agricultural experiment stations have and will continue to be a great aid to farmers. 6. We were brought into closer companionship than we could have in any other circumstances. 7. Will the game continue to hold the high place it has in the past? 8. Who then will perform this labor? Why, the same man who has been, all these years. 9. History has seldom and perhaps will never again record such an act. 10. Football will continue to be the leading American sport in the future as it has in the past.   11. On my trip I saw one of the saddest sights I ever expect to.   12. The state of a man's linen often tells more about his character than a long conversation could.

EXERCISE 52

Correct and rewrite the following sentences: 1. Bacon was not so brilliant, but much more learned, than Shakespeare.   2. The climate here is warmer, but not so agreeable to me, as the climate of the north.   3. My crayons are whiter, and just as strong, as my competitor's.   4. Rubies are just as costly, if not more so, than diamonds.   5. The Whig candidate was not so conscientious, but far more effective, than his rival.   6. The price of meat is as high, if not higher, than it was last year.   7. Lake Erie is as treacherous, if not more so, than the ocean.   8. Prairie hay fattens horses as well if not better than timothy does.   9. My work in the drawing class was just as successful, though it cost a little more effort, than my work in the shop.

Omission of than *and* as *clauses*

EXERCISE 52a

Correct and rewrite the following sentences: 1. Their love and devotion to their father is remarkable.   2. He showed a distrust and opposition to his adviser.   3. She was in a constant state of discontent and rebellion against her lot.   4. I feel a perfect love and confidence in my king.   5. He expresses complete approval and satisfaction with our plan.   6. I am not only thoroughly familiar, but exceedingly fond of the game.   7. He is not only different but far more admirable than his cousin.   8. Though he endeavored, he did not succeed, in convincing me.   9. I cannot consent — in fact I most heartily disapprove — of the measure.   10. He acted not in accordance, but contrary to my instructions.   11. They were willing to comply, but not disposed to respect, our orders.   12. Are you willing in all matters to comply and yield to our wishes?

Omission of modifying phrases

EXERCISE 53

Correct and rewrite the following sentences: 1. Goethe possessed one of the greatest, if not *the* greatest mind of

Omission of plural nouns

his era.   2. This battle brought one of the severest, if not *the* severest defeat of the war.   3. Sowles was one of the mildest, if not *the* mildest curate in Sussex.   4. *Markheim* is one of the strangest, if not *the* strangest story I ever read.

EXERCISE 54

Omission of
that after *so*

Rewrite the following sentences inserting *that* where it is necessary.   See *Note* under 90 (*h*) and also *so* (1) in the Glossary.   1. It was so hot I had difficulty in eating it.   2. He was so weak he could not stand.   3. The lamp was hung so high I could not reach it.   4. This pen is so rusty it is useless.   5. It moves so fast you can hardly see it.   6. It became so interesting I forgot my engagement.   7. The surgeon was so deft he gave me no pain.   8. The cars are so slow I prefer to walk.   9. He was so rude she became angry.

Omission of
articles and
possessives

91. As a rule, repeat an article or a possessive adjective before each noun in a series, unless all the nouns designate the same thing.

> Wrong: Near by are a grocery, drug store, barber shop, and garage.
>
> Right: Near by are a grocery store, a drug store, a barber shop, and a garage.
>
> Wrong: She watched her grandmother, aunt, and mother sewing.
>
> Right: She watched her grandmother, her aunt, and her mother sewing.
>
> Wrong: I asked what were the names of her puppies and kitten.
>
> Right: I asked what were the names of her puppies and her kitten.
>
> Right: For that summer I was day clerk, night clerk, bell boy, and porter, all in one.

Omission of
prepositions

92. In certain instances, a noun used to indicate the time, place, or manner of an occurrence should be accompanied by a preposition.   Some uses of the noun without the preposition are distinctly wrong; some others are better suited to informal composition than to formal composition. (See Rule 1 *b*.)

Wrong: Friendships made that way will never last.
Right: Friendships made in that way will never last.

Wrong: He is living some place in Arizona.
Right: He is living in some place in Arizona. [Observe that ordinarily the writer who uses the incorrect expressions *any place, some place,* etc., means to use the adverbs *anywhere, somewhere,* etc. See Glossary.]

Wrong: You may sit any place you wish.
Right: You may sit in any place you wish.

Informal (not incorrect): The armistice was signed the eleventh of November.
More formal: The armistice was signed on the eleventh of November.

Right: Last year, last month, last night, last Saturday, next year, next day, next Tuesday, some day, one day, any day, that day, this day, this afternoon.

NOTE. — The expression "He is home" is bad idiom when used to mean location in a place; as, "Where is your sister this afternoon?" "She is home"; [should be, "at home"]. It is good idiom when used to mean arrival at a place; as, "He is safe home at last";

"Home is the sailor, home from sea,
    And the hunter home from the hill." — STEVENSON.

A fault similar to those noted under this head is the omission of the article from the phrases *all the morning, all the afternoon, all the week, all the evening,* etc. *All day* and *all night* are established idioms.

EXERCISE 55

Rewrite the following sentences: 1. August 21 I went to Chicago. 2. Our team will play Friday. 3. Lincoln died April, 1865. 4. Did Selma wash Monday? 5. I wrote June 2: he answered July 3. 6. Saturday night the tenor was reported sick and a substitute was engaged to sing Sunday. 7. The Rockford nine won Tuesday but lost

Time expressions with preposition omitted

Wednesday. 8. I was in a hospital the time of the
World's Fair. 9. All the hydrants froze the day of the
fire. 10. Let us meet Christmas day. 11. His first book
appeared 1845. 12. Is the meeting to be Monday? In
order to attend that day, I must travel Sunday.

93. Do not make comparisons leaving the standard of comparison not indicated or only vaguely implied; let the standard be definitely stated or implied.

> Incomplete: Manufacturers have come to see the
> greater economy of the electric motor.
> Right: Manufacturers have come to see the greater
> economy of the electric motor as compared to
> steam power.

NOTE. — When *such* and *so* are used for *very* — as,
"We had such a good time"; "I am so tired," — a comparison is vaguely implied. (See Glossary.)

Coördination

Misuse of
coördinat-
ing conjunc-
tions

94. Do not introduce by *and, but,* or *or* an expression which is not grammatically and logically coördinate with any preceding expression. Either omit the
conjunction and make the expression properly subordinate, or recast one expression so as to make it
coördinate with the other.

> Wrong: He put up signs to keep people off the grass
> and thereby improving the appearance of the
> campus.
> Right: He put up signs to keep people off the grass,
> thereby improving the appearance of the campus,
> [or] and thereby improved the appearance of the
> campus.
> Wrong: The gun barrel is then sent to be chambered
> and slots to be cut in.
> Right: The gun barrel is then sent to be chambered
> and to have slots cut in it.

EXERCISE 56

Correct and rewrite the following sentences: 1. I regard any such action as dishonorable and by no means does credit to one who proposes it.   2. He brought in some wood with the intention of building a fire and make the room more cheerful.   3. As many students desire to dispose of their books, and not wishing to purchase unsalable stock, we should like to know what books will be used next year.   4. Many people commit suicide simply for the purpose of getting their names in the paper and thus win a brief renown.   5. In a large city dogs are useless, because the conditions of a city prevent them from herding, from hunting, and even as companions, to some extent.   6. It would have been better had such people either waited until they were certain what profession they desired to follow, or else have taken a general college course.   7. We seemed to know each other better, and brought into closer fellowship.   8. The oats, being a heavier grain than the barley and would become heated much sooner, had to be piled in long shocks pointing north and south.   9. Some men have had bones broken, eyes blinded, and otherwise seriously injured.   10. I heard the sound of footsteps and voices growing fainter and fainter and then cease entirely.   11. I saw a gentleman approach a friend and with great show of cordiality grasped his hand and said, "Hello, old fellow!"   12. They joined their forces for the express purpose of breaking through the line and so be able to reach Baden.

Ungram-matical coördina-tion

95. In accordance with Rule 94,

(*a*) **Do not join a relative clause to its principal clause by *and, but,* or *or*.**

"And which" construc-tion

Wrong: He came home with an increase in weight, but which hard work soon reduced.

Wrong: On the way we met a Mr. Osborn from the neighborhood of Denver and who had the typical Western breeziness.

(*b*) **A predicate in a relative clause should not be joined by *and* or *but* to a second predicate if the**

"Which and" construction

second predicate is unfit to stand alone. The test of correct coördination is to omit the first predicate.

> Wrong: In this river are some large fish which the people regard as sacred and allow no one to catch them. [Test, "which the people allow no one to catch them."]

> Wrong: It is subjected to severe strains, which it must withstand and at the same time work easily and rapidly. [Test, "which it must work easily and rapidly."]

> Wrong: Next day I went to Cleveland where I stayed for a week and then returned home. [Test, "where I then returned home."]

Method of correction

96. Violations of the foregoing rules may be corrected in the following manner:

(*a*) Violations of (*a*) may be corrected by (1) omitting the conjunction, (2) changing the relative clause to a principal clause, or (3) inserting a relative clause before the conjunction.

> Right: (1) He came home with an increase in weight, which, however, hard work soon reduced; [or] (2) He came home with an increase in weight, but hard work soon reduced it.

> Right: (1) On the way we met a Mr. Osborn from the neighborhood of Denver, who had the typical Western breeziness; [or] (3) On the way we met a Mr. Osborn, who came from the neighborhood of Denver, and who had the typical Western breeziness.

(*b*) Violations of (*b*) may be corrected by (1) changing the second predicate so that it could stand alone, (2) changing the relative clause to an independent assertion, or (3) omitting the *and* or *but*, and using a subordinate element instead of the second predicate.

Right: (1) In this river are some large fish, which the people regard as sacred and allow no one to catch; [or] (2) In this river are some large fish. The people regard these as sacred, and allow no one to catch them.

Right: (2) It is subjected to severe strains; it must withstand these, and at the same time must work easily and rapidly; [or] (3) It is subjected to severe strains, which it must withstand, at the same time working easily and rapidly.

Right: (2) Next day I went to Cleveland. There I stayed a week, and then returned home.

EXERCISE 57

Correct each of the following sentences by one of the methods shown in § 96; consider which of those methods is best for each sentence, and according to your choice write (1), (2), or (3) after each sentence: 1. North of the house was a beautiful lawn and on which several apple trees grew. 2. On a Sunday evening I took the steamboat *City of St. Louis* for Minneapolis, and which brought me to my destination on Tuesday. 3. There was once in Germany an independent principality, Grünewald, but which was weak and insignificant. 4. The radiators vary in size according to the volume of power necessary for heating, and which power may be either hot water or steam. 5. I formed a lasting friendship with a fellow named Banks, but who could make no headway in school. 6. It was an excellent town to bring up children in, but the advantages of which did not end there. 7. I soon went to San Francisco, where my friend Pinkerton had settled, and who thought I could make a fortune there. 8. Macaire is the most interesting character of the play, and about whom the whole action centers. 9. The tramp often lightens a housewife's work by sawing wood or drawing water, which her husband has forgotten to do, and who is in that case worse than the tramp. 10. I met some pleasant companions on the journey — all good fellows and whose friendship I still prize. 11. About 1762 Goldsmith wrote *The Vicar of Wakefield*, but which was not published until three years later.

"And which"

"Which
and"
Correct and rewrite the following sentences; consider which of the three methods of correction shown above is best for each sentence, and according to your choice write (1), (2), or (3) after each sentence: 1. I supplied him with a pair of pumps which he wore to the ball but resumed his shoes later. 2. I then entered the Hainsville Academy, which I planned to attend for four years and then go into partnership with my father. 3. It is subjected to severe strains, which it must withstand and at the same time work easily and rapidly. 4. A well-dressed woman avoids picture-hats, flying veils, and other things which she can dispense with and still be attractively clad. 5. In this river are some large fish which the people regard as sacred and allow no one to catch them. 6. I am looking for a man from South Africa whom I used to know well but do not know what has become of him. 7. He has the responsibility for a piece of work which he must take sole charge of and see that all the details of that work are properly attended to. 8. Last autumn I entered the academy in my town, where I hope to graduate in 1928 and to be successful in my subsequent professional career. 9. Next day I went to Cleveland, where I stayed for a while, and then returned home. 10. They then went to Junction City, where they were to spend the night and on the following day go to Philadelphia. 11. He then went to Boston, where he sold the jewels and then returned to Washington.

97. Avoid illogical and excessive coördination; put subordinate thoughts into subordinate form. (See also Rule 125.) Endeavor to reduce predication; *i.e.,* express an idea in a minor form of predication — subordinate clause, phrase, or single word — instead of a major form of predication — sentence or independent clause — when doing so does not interfere with clearness or force. The untrained writer does not perceive differences of importance between ideas, but places each in an independent clause and joins them by *and, but,* or *or.* The skilled writer endeavors to express these differences by exactness and variety of subordination.

Inferior: [First clause over-emphasized.] I came into class and found I was five minutes late.

Predication reduced: [Subordinate clause.] When I came into class I found I was five minutes late; [or, participial phrase] On coming into class I found I was five minutes late.

Inferior: There were three big maple trees beside the house, and under them in the shade was a sand-pile, and in this we children used to play.

Predication reduced: Beside the house in the shade of three big maples lay a sand-pile, in which we children used to play.

Inferior: It was a fine frosty morning and two seniors were walking toward college.

Predication reduced: One fine frosty morning two seniors were walking toward college.

Bad: The time comes, and the student is unprepared to choose a major study, but yet he must choose.

Predication reduced: When the time comes, the student must choose a major study, even though he is unprepared to make the choice.

Illogical coördination: I have seen many pumps that were defective and gasoline leaked out around the piston-plunger. ["I have seen many pumps" and "gasoline leaked out around the piston-plunger" are not logically coördinate.]

Right: I have seen many pumps so defective that gasoline leaked out around the piston-plunger.

Illogical coördination: They did not recognize him, his hair having become snow-white, and the expression of his face was entirely altered. ["They did not recognize him," and "the expression of his face was entirely altered" are not logically coördinate.]

Right: They did not recognize him, his hair having become snow-white, and the expression of his face being entirely altered.

EXERCISE 59

Illogical coördination

The coördination in the following sentences is conspicuously illogical. Recast the sentences, making the grammatical relations correspond to the logical relations. 1. *Mrs. Dane's Defense* is a play in four acts and was written by Henry Arthur Jones. 2. The collapse was due to the undermining of the stratum and the vibrations caused by the cars had dislodged the walls. 3. The essay tells about chimney sweeps, and the author writes in his usual delightful style. 4. Alfalfa thrives in a high soil, which becomes too dry to nourish other plants, but alfalfa sends its roots down sometimes thirty feet for water. 5. A board fence surrounds the plant to keep stragglers from wandering about the dangerous machinery, and besides many secret processes are used which the company does not wish to become known to outsiders. 6. He showed me some marbles which looked as if they had once been white but now they seemed to have been dropped into an ink bottle. 7. It undergoes here a process similar to the preceding one but the quantity of lime added is in this case smaller. 8. The seeds are planted in long beds, which are boarded in and a muslin cover is stretched over them. 9. The trouble began at Loper's restaurant which was completely wrecked and all the furniture thrown into the street and burned. 10. My attention was attracted by a door which every now and then opened and a nurse walked noiselessly out. 11. No one could pass through and I not see him. 12. The poem teaches us to be kind to our inferiors, and we shall always have their help in time of need.

EXERCISE 60

Practice in securing variety of subordination

Study the note under Rule 97. Recast the following sentences, using as many varieties of subordination as possible: 1. The name of this bar is the whiffletree and to it the traces are attached. 2. He ate his breakfast and then he went to his office. 3. It had a fine outlook and so we thought it would be a good camping ground. 4. It had not been watered for a week and it looked dry and wilted. 5. An electric bell is a form of motor and a motor is a machine for transforming electrical energy into power.   6. In the box is a battery and the poles of the battery are connected to binding posts.   7. The tube widens out at the end and is called the speaking trumpet. 8. The second tube is shorter than the first and is called the receiver.   9. I didn't want the paper at all, but I wanted to please the editor and I subscribed.   10. He is quicker and more capable than his rivals and he is sure to get the best of them.   11. The foundry is a low brick building and projecting above the roof is a huge chimney. 12. Presently she met a lady and asked her the way to the Hall.   13. The material was brought to the nearest station by rail and it was drawn to the mine by horses. 14. In the corner was a bureau and a mirror hung over it. 15. There was a big kettle of water on the stove and he turned quickly around and accidentally struck it and it was upset.

98. Good usage does not sanction the general habit of joining coördinate verbs in a sentence by *so, then,* or *also*. It is preferable either to recast, subordinating one member, or to use a conjunction, *and* or *but*, in addition to the adverb.

So, then, and also used to join verbs

> Inferior: He was only one among many so was not observed.
> Preferable: Being only one among many, he was not observed; [or] He was only one among many and so was not observed.
> Inferior: I paddled the boat for a while, then fell into a reverie.
> Preferable: After paddling the boat for a while, I fell into a reverie; [or] I paddled the boat for a while, and then fell into a reverie.

99. Avoid the habit of compounding clauses with *so*. Ordinarily, subordinate the preceding clause and omit the *so*. If the preceding clause is too important to allow subordination, the best practice is to place a semicolon (or a period, if the connection is not close) between the clauses. (See Rule 231 *b*.)

The so habit

Wrong: His wife thought he would be thirsty so she brought a pitcher of water.

Right: His wife, thinking he would be thirsty, brought a pitcher of water.

Inferior: The people were opposed to him for some unknown reason, so he had to accomplish his purpose through secret agents.

Correct but undesirable: The people were opposed to him for some unknown reason. So he had to accomplish his purpose through secret agents.

Preferable: Since the people were, for some unknown reason, opposed to him, he was compelled to accomplish his purpose through secret agents.

Inferior: I decided it was high time we camped, for it would soon be dark, so I turned the canoe toward shore.

Right: I decided it was high time we camped, for it would soon be dark; so [or, "accordingly"] I turned the canoe toward shore.

NOTE. — The problem of the *so* sentence is one of excessive coördination rather than of wrong punctuation. The student fails to perceive that the relations between various ideas which he loosely indicates by a single connective may be expressed by a variety of connectives, and by logical subordination. (For a list of subordinating conjunctions, and of conjunctive adverbs other than *so*, see page 300, Appendix A.)

EXERCISE 61

The *so* habit

Recast the following sentences, using as many varieties of subordination as possible: 1. She wished to make a good appearance so she borrowed a necklace. 2. He feared she would be corrupted by the court, so he kept her close at home. 3. This is a difficult piece of work so great care is necessary. 4. The cups did not match, so she sent them back. 5. He needed some little shoes as a model for his picture so his mother found for him the shoes that he himself had first worn. 6. I felt very tired and jaded so I could not listen very attentively. 7. The stalks of the wheat must be bent back, so a large reel like a paddle-wheel is provided. 8. He wished to show deference to the strong religious principles of his host so he attended mass on Sunday.   9. He wanted it to be legible and permanent so he wrote in ink.   10. His eyes were still unaccustomed to the dim light so he did not notice the change.   11. He was in his shirt sleeves as usual so the servant asked the visitor to wait a minute.   12. That old signboard was one of the landmarks of the town so they hadn't the heart to remove it.   13. The boarders are beginning to fall upon the toothpicks so we shall soon have the room to ourselves.   14. The rusty hands of the clock marked half past four so the editor laid down his pencil.   15. This throe of oratory was particularly violent so the speaker took a swallow of water before proceeding.

100. Two consecutive statements should not both be introduced by *but* or *for*.   (See Rule 106.)

> Bad: Iago became fond of Desdemona but she paid no attention to him but seemed to favor Cassio.
>
> Bad: He suddenly paused, for it seemed wonderful that he could speak so easily, for usually he was bashful.

101. Violations of the foregoing rule may usually be corrected by omitting the first *but* or *for*.

> Right: Iago became fond of Desdemona. -She paid no attention to him but seemed to favor Cassio.
>
> Right: He suddenly paused; it seemed wonderful that he could speak so easily, for usually he was bashful.

102. For the sake of clearness, coördinate sentence-members that are long or complex should be introduced in a similar or identical manner.   Otherwise the reader may associate the wrong members.

> Obscure coördination: Then I learned how he had run away from his father, a gypsy vagabond who professed to be a horse-trader and was in reality a thief, dressed in some clothes that he found on a scare-

crow in a cornfield, learned the way to my home through the map in an old railway time-table, and come all the way on foot. [This sentence is well constructed; its defect is that the relation between the coördinate members is not shown by similar beginnings.]

Clear coördination: Then I learned how he had run away from his father, a gypsy vagabond who professed to be a horse-trader and was in reality a thief; how he had dressed in some clothes that he found on a scarecrow in a cornfield; how he had learned the way to my home through the map in an old railway time-table, and had come all the way on foot.

The foregoing principle has many different applications. The four following are worthy of special mention:

Repetition of auxiliary verbs

102a. An auxiliary verb introducing several principal verbs should be repeated with each if the coördination would otherwise not be immediately clear.

Obscure coördination: The captain must be quick to see just what movement will get his company out of close quarters and give the order clearly.

Clear coördination: The captain *must be quick* to see just what movement will get his company out of close quarters and *must give* the order clearly.

NOTE. — When the verbs stand close together, repetition is usually unnecessary; *e.g.*, —

Right: You must line up quickly and march downstairs.

Right: The sheep may stray and be lost.

But when other verbs intervene between the coördinate verbs, clearness usually demands repetition of the auxiliary.

Repetition of prepositions

103. A preposition governing several objects should be repeated with each object after the first, when the

construction of those objects would otherwise not be immediately clear.

A. Not immediately clear: The place is often visited by tourists who are fond of rugged scenery, and especially amateur photographers.

   Right: The place is often visited *by* tourists who are fond of rugged scenery, and especially *by* amateur photographers.

B. Not immediately clear: With the refusal of Mr. Goggins to accept the office left vacant by the resignation of Mr. Barnes and the presence of Governor Davidson in the city, the friends of Mr. Roemer were kept busy yesterday.

   Clear: *With* the refusal of Mr. Goggins to accept the office left vacant by the resignation of Mr. Barnes, and *with* the presence of Governor Davidson in the city, the friends of Mr. Roemer were kept busy yesterday.

NOTE. — When the objects stand close together, repetition is usually unnecessary; *e.g.*, —

   Right: He had lived in Cuba, Panama, and Barbadoes.
   Right: It was exposed to the wind, the rain, and the scorching sun.

But when the objects are separated by intervening modifiers, as in sentences *A* and *B*, clearness usually requires that the preposition be repeated.

104. An infinitive-sign (*to*) introducing several coordinate infinitives, should be repeated with each infinitive after the first, when the construction of those infinitives would otherwise not be immediately clear. Repetition of the infinitive-sign

A. Not immediately clear: Here nature has done her best to enchant those that can see and feel, and make them her lifelong worshipers.

   Right: Here nature has done her best *to enchant* those that can see and feel, and *to make* them her lifelong worshipers.

NOTE. — When the infinitives stand close together, repetition of the *to* is usually not necessary; *e.g.*, —

> Right: Has he learned to dance, converse, and make himself agreeable?

But when the infinitives are separated by intervening adjuncts, as in sentence *A* above, repetition of the *to* is usually necessary to clearness.

Repetition of subordinating conjunctions

105. A subordinating conjunction introducing several coördinate assertions should be repeated with each assertion after the first, when the coördination of those assertions would otherwise not be immediately clear. This is especially important with clauses in indirect discourse introduced by *that*.

> Obscure coördination: The registrar told him that he could not have credit for his half year of German and he must be put on probation because of his poor grades in English.
>
> Clear coördination: The registrar told him *that* he could not have credit for his half year of German and *that* he must be put on probation because of his poor grades in English.
>
> Obscure coördination: When they saw the excellent structure which, though handicapped by the strike and the difficulty of getting materials, he had yet completed in less than the required time, and considered how valuable such a man would be to them, they gave him a permanent position.
>
> Clear coördination: When they saw the excellent structure which, though handicapped by the strike and the difficulty of getting materials, he had yet completed in less than the required time, and when they considered how valuable such a man would be to them, they gave him a permanent position.

NOTE. — When the coördinate assertions are very short, repetition of the conjunction is usually not necessary; *e.g.* —

Right: He seems to be pretty well, though he takes no exercise and neglects his diet.

It is only when the assertions are complex that repetition of the conjunction is necessary.

EXERCISE 62

Rewrite the following sentences making the coördination clearer. 1. The amount of care he takes can be judged by the amount of milk he brings day after day to the creamery and the price he gets for his cattle. 2. We could make the same argument regarding baptism, which makes the sinful child pure and holy, or the miracles. 3. My respect for the Bible is due to its vast influence in the progress of civilization; to the new vigor and refinement it has given to nations and individuals originally outside the zone of its influence; and not only these things, but the constant evidence of its present power for whatever is good and high. 4. I succeeded in going through the high school without very much trouble and graduating at the end of four years. 5. We both took much pleasure in such sports as that country afforded, especially hunting and fishing. 6. I was occupied for several years, I am told, in playing with my sister's discarded dolls because I was sorry for them and bringing home bugs and worms for my mother to pet. 7. She was a great favorite with all the children who lived in the neighborhood, and in fact whomever she met. 8. The required shape is obtained by clamping a piece of one-inch oak, which has been bent previously into the standard form, to one side of the runner and following the outline of this oak piece with knives. 9. His faithfulness is shown by his encountering so many dangers for the sake of Macaire and the manner in which he clung to Macaire through thick and thin. 10. Lamb tells of his dislike for all kinds of music, such as opera-singing and organ-playing, and the pleasure he gets from the noises of the street. 11. The lens should be kept free from dust, which scratches the surface, and also spots of grease. 12. All meetings are held in a large hall, decorated with the school colors at all times, and on certain occasions the colors of the various classes and the trophies won in class contests.

Long coördinate elements to begin similarly

Subordination

Overlap-
ping de-
pendence

106. Do not put a series of similar clauses or a series of similar phrases in an overlapping construction, — *i.e.*, with the second depending on the first, the third on the second, the fourth on the third, etc. Recast the sentence. (Cf. Rule 100.)

Awkward: I never knew a man who was so ready to help a friend who had got into difficulties which pressed him hard.

Right: I never knew a man so ready to help a friend who found himself hard pressed by difficulties.

Awkward: I was so uncomfortable that I rolled up my sleeves so far that my arms got sunburned, so that I could hardly sleep that night.

Right: Feeling very uncomfortable, I rolled up my sleeves so far that my arms got badly sunburned. The pain of my smarting skin kept me awake most of that night.

Awkward: This was the first of the entertainments of the senior girls of the dormitory.

Right: This was the first entertainment given by the senior girls of the dormitory.

Coördinate
dependence

107. Note, on the other hand, that a series of similar clauses or phrases all depending on the same sentence-element gives rise to no awkwardness. (Cf. Rule 75, note.)

Right: I rise to nominate a man who has ever been stanch in his loyalty, who has long been a trusted counselor in the policies of our party, who has demonstrated his fitness for his office by the efficiency of his administration in others, whose honor has never been assailed save by calumnious envy, whose fame is destined to echo down the coming ages, who . . . etc.

Right: His face has come down to us marked with all the blemishes put on it by time, by war, by sleepless nights, by anxiety, perhaps by remorse.

108. A *when* clause is properly used only to fix the time of an event stated in the principal clause. Hence:

109. A statement of primary importance in a narrative should not be embodied in a *when* clause; it should be embodied in an independent clause or sentence.

> Bad: The thoughts of the engineer turned toward the home he was approaching when suddenly he saw the glare of fire on the track ahead.
>
> Right: The thoughts of the engineer turned toward the home he was approaching. Suddenly he saw the glare of fire on the track ahead.
>
> Bad: Having finished their work, they began to talk about former good times when one of the fellows suggested that they haze Nicholson.
>
> Right: Having finished their work, they began to talk about former good times. Presently one of the fellows suggested that they haze Nicholson.

110. To put a logically principal statement in a subordinate clause and the logically subordinate statement in the principal clause is especially objectionable, unless there is some good reason for such inversion.

> Bad: I was walking down State Street yesterday when I came upon a crowd of people gathered about a horse that had fallen down.
>
> Right: As I was walking down State Street yesterday I came upon a crowd of people, etc.

Exercise 63

Correct and rewrite the following sentences: 1. On my first evening in Beloit I was sitting in my room when I heard a commotion outside. 2. Jim was standing in the doorway one morning when he saw a blind man come along

the road.   3. Dodd continued his studies for two years
when his father failed in business and he was obliged to go
to work.   4. We presently came to some particularly deep
drifts of snow.   Jim was wading through one of these
when he suddenly gave a yell of surprise and terror, and
sank from sight.   5. I was busily studying one night when
two freshmen rushed into the room and asked for my
waste-paper basket.   6. I was sitting at my open window
last night when I saw a big tomcat catch a sparrow.   7. I
was engaged in a game of football one November day when
I broke my collar-bone.   8. I walked west for about a
mile when I came to a stream forming a right angle with
the road.   9. The three fishermen were returning home
one evening when they were caught in a violent squall.
10. They expected to be submerged at any moment when
suddenly the wind entirely subsided.   11. They were
silent for a while, when Baglioni suddenly produced a
small stiletto.   12. At first Mauprat emphatically refused
to take part in the conspiracy, when Baradas, by dwelling
on the Cardinal's insult, succeeded in persuading him to
join.

Parallelism

Parallel forms for analogous elements

**111. As a rule, two or more sentence-elements that
have the same logical office should be made grammatically parallel; *i.e.,* if one is an infinitive, the other
should be; if one is a relative clause, the other should
be; if one is an appositive, the other should be; and
so on.**

> Bad: The crowd began to wave handkerchiefs and
> shouting good-byes.   ["To wave" and "shouting,"
> both objects of "began," are awkwardly dissimilar
> in form.]
> Right: (*a*) The crowd began to wave handkerchiefs
> and to shout good-byes; [or] (*b*) The crowd began
> waving handkerchiefs and shouting good-byes.
> [The two objects of "began" are made parallel;
> in (*a*) they are both infinitives, in (*b*) they are both
> gerunds.]

Bad: I met many people there whom I had seen before but did not know their names. ["Whom I had seen before" and "did not know their names," both qualifiers (logically) of "people," are awkwardly dissimilar in form.]

Right: I met many people there whom I had seen before but whose names I did not know. [The two qualifiers of "people" are made parallel; both are relative clauses.]

Bad: I delight in a good novel — one which portrays strong characters and in reading the book you are thrilled. [The two qualifiers of "one" are awkwardly dissimilar; the first ("which portrays strong characters") is a relative clause, the second ("in reading the book you are thrilled") a sentence.]

Right: I delight in a good novel — one which portrays strong characters and which thrills the reader. [The two qualifiers are made parallel; both are relative clauses.]

Bad: Two courses are open to us: first, to have the missionary society transfer to us a missionary now in the field; second, one of our own members has volunteered to go, and we may send him. [The two logical appositives to "two courses" are awkwardly dissimilar; the first ("to have . . . field") is a grammatical appositive, the second ("one of our own members . . . him") a sentence.]

Right: Two courses are open to us: first, to have the missionary society transfer to us a missionary now in the field; second, to send one of our own members, who has volunteered to go. [The two logical appositives are made parallel; both are grammatical appositives to "courses."] [Or] Two courses are open to us. First, we may have the missionary society transfer to us a missionary now in the field; second, we may send one of our members, who has volunteered to go. [The two logical appositives are made parallel; both are sentences.]

Bad: I have lived in many states, some for only a short time, while in others I have lived a year or more. [The two qualifiers of the main clause are awkwardly dissimilar; the first ("some for only a short time") is an incomplete modifier of "lived," the second ("while . . . more") a complete subordinate clause.]

Right: I have lived in many states, — in some for only a short time, in others for a year or more. [The two qualifiers of the main clause are made parallel; both are prepositional phrases modifying "lived."]

Bad: I was asked to contribute to the church, Christian Association, and to the athletic fund. [The three modifiers of "contribute" are awkwardly dissimilar in form; the first is a complete phrase, the second a noun with both the preposition and the article lacking, the third a complete phrase.]

Right: I was asked to contribute to the church, to the Christian Association, and to the athletic fund. [The three modifiers of "contribute" are made parallel in form; each is a complete phrase.] [Or] I was asked to contribute to the church, the Christian Association, and the athletic fund. ["To" is made to govern three objects parallel in form, — each consisting of "the" and a noun.]

EXERCISE 64

Analogous thoughts to be cast in the same grammatical form

Rewrite the following sentences, making parallel the members that should be parallel. Separate the parallel members from the remainder of the sentence; write them side by side; mark them *a* and *b*, or *a*, *b*, and *c*; and after the sentence state why they are parallel, thus:

1. The old man was kept ignorant
   | (*a*) of the true state of affairs
   and | (*b*) of the fact that his son was a prisoner.
   Members *a* and *b* are parallel; both are *of* phrases modifying "ignorant."

2. Since
   | (*a*) it was getting late
   and | (*b*) the night air was chilly
   we set out homeward.
   Members *a* and *b* are parallel; both are clauses dependent on "since."

1. The old man was kept in ignorance of the true state of affairs and that his son was a prisoner. 2. Since it was getting late, and the night air being chilly, we set out homeward. 3. Take your time, letting him go when he makes a plunge, reeling him in when he relaxes, but slack should never be allowed him. 4. They told me that I might attend Cornell University and to select my course. 5. Most employers demand that their employees keep their good health and must not spoil it by dissipation. 6. He noticed several barrels, boxes, logs, and spars near him and that the barrels seemed to be empty. 7. They were of different nationality, different in breeding, different men entirely. 8. It is argued that women's minds are different from men's, either naturally or made so by environment. 9. It is important that he be given every opportunity to learn what he needs to know, and not waste time on elegant but useless studies. 10. The binder can be protected from storms by a canvas cover, or if no canvas is available, take bundles of oats and cover the metal parts. 11. The muskrat must take time to stop and breathe, allowing the air to come up to the surface, and then breathe the same air after it has been purified. 12. Although we had made ourselves hobos for the time, and our companions being also hobos, yet I do not think the experience did us any harm. 13. I was fond of games — not those of the rougher sort, like football, but running games, games of skill, and also very fond of baseball. 14. The most important measures are the laying aside of worn-out garments and also to keep fresh garments free from spots. 15. It is necessary that he take things as they come and to make the best of them. 16. The cause of my trouble in college was the fact that my preparation was very poor, my high school instructors being negligent in regard to the details of the students' work. Also, I made no effort to do good work in high school. 17. Remember these things: to avoid the company of Fenella, not to delay unnecessarily on the road, and whatever occurs, do not part with the dispatch. 18. A salesman should have a pleasing appearance, be courteous and agreeable, and he should have a persuasive tongue. 19. The establishment consists of an engine

room, boiler room, casting house, and a stack. 20. In
the yard the pig iron is weighed, the grade of iron marked
on it, and then loaded upon cars. 21. Some have gained
fame by portraying human character, others the life of
animals, and others by writing of inanimate forces.
22. You may go fishing, boating, bathing, or take a drive.

Correlatives   **112. Correlative conjunctions should be followed
by coördinate sentence-elements; if a predicate fol-
lows the first, a predicate should follow the second; if
a modifier the first, a modifier the second; and so on.**

> Wrong: They would neither speak to him nor would
> they look at him. ["Neither" is followed by
> "speak," a part of a compound verb; "nor" by
> "would they look," a subject and complete predi-
> cate.]
>
> Right: They would neither speak to him nor look
> at him. ["Neither" and "nor" are each followed
> by an infinitive completing "would."]
>
> Wrong: He is not only discourteous to the students
> but also to the teacher. ["Not only" is followed by
> an adjective, "but also" by a phrase modifying the
> adjective.]
>
> Right: He is discourteous not only to the students but
> also to the teacher. [The correlatives are each fol-
> lowed by a phrase limiting "discourteous."]

Exercise 65

Correlation   Rewrite the following sentences, placing the correlative
conjunctions in each before coördinate members: 1. It
may either be read for pleasure or systematic study.
2. The bees had not only stung my brother, but my friend
and me also. 3. I intend to assist him, both for the sake
of his mother and himself. 4. Neither the fear of the
king nor any one else retarded him. 5. I will neither
give you money nor favor. 6. The crew was discouraged
both on account of the prevalence of sickness and the bad
weather. 7. Either he has not been here at all, or only
for a few minutes. 8. They are neither permitted to
read the newspapers, nor even old magazines. 9. He not

only spoke all the principal languages of Europe, but of Asia also. 10. He could not be persuaded either by promises of money or promotion. 11. The trustees invite full investigation not only relative to the charges made but any other matters concerning the college. 12. The new truck can be used either for carrying a load up or down stairs. 13. Athletics not only develop the muscles but also the mind. 14. He not only endangers his own life but also the lives of the passing pedestrians. 15. It is not valued either from the standpoint of religious reverence or æsthetic appreciation. 16. Our Christmases are either spent in Minneapolis or Boston. 17. Not only did he win laurels in his studies but also in athletics. 18. Articles to be drilled are either bolted to the base or table. 19. At first I was very much surprised not only at my marks but the method of teaching. 20. The lake, being situated so near the college, affords to the students an opportunity not only for swimming, but boat crews can be formed and rowing contests can be held. 21. I was not allowed to either ride or drive. 22. For only two years was the Democratic party in a position to either enact or repeal a law. 23. The engine should never be allowed to run hot either through stoppage of oil or water.

113. Do not make a sentence-element similar in form to a preceding element with which it is not coördinate. Incorrect parallelism

> Misleading: He is a blunt, manly fellow, who admires a soldier and despises an effeminate fop, who struts about affectedly and dresses daintily.
>
> Right: He is a blunt, manly fellow, who admires a soldier and despises an effeminate, affected, daintily dressed fop.

114. Do not join by *and* and put in the same grammatical construction, two substantives or substantive clauses widely differing in logical function. Junction of incongruous substantives

> Bad: The story tells of the bravery and promotion of a private. ["Bravery" designates a quality, "promotion" designates an experience.]

Right: The story tells of a private's bravery and of his promotion.

Bad: He tells in vivid language how dangerous to a vessel is the breaking loose of a cannon on wheels, and how a ship's gunner captured an escaped cannon. [The substantive clause "how dangerous to a vessel is the breaking loose of a cannon" designates a general truth; the substantive clause "how a ship's gunner captured an escaped cannon" designates a specific event.]

Right: He tells in vivid language how a cannon on wheels broke from its fastenings on a ship (explaining the perils that attend such an accident), and how it was captured by a gunner.

Series form for dissimilar elements

115. The formula *a, b,* and *c* should not be used for sentence-elements not coördinate.

Bad: He was tall, slim, and wore a black coat. [Here *a* and *b* are adjectives, and *c* is a verb.]

Bad: We denounce the act as cruel, barbarous, and sincerely regret that it occurred. [Here *a* and *b* are adjectives and *c* is a verb.]

Method of correction

116. Violations of the foregoing rule may be corrected (1) by inserting *and* between *a* and *b,* or (2) by conforming *c* to *a* and *b.* Thus:

Right: (1) He was tall and slim, and wore a black coat; [or] (2) He was a tall, slim, black-coated fellow.

Right: (1) We denounce the act as cruel and barbarous, and sincerely regret that it occurred; [or] (2) We denounce the act as cruel, barbarous, and worthy of condemnation by all right-thinking sophomores.

Exercise 66

False parallelism

Rewrite the following sentences, correcting the false parallelism: 1. Among the books I first read were Dickens's *Oliver Twist*, Scott's *Ivanhoe*, and I have a very vivid remembrance of *Ben Hur*. 2. The Gulf Stream is 50 miles wide, 2000 feet deep, and flows 90 miles a day.

[See, regarding the figures in the preceding sentence, Rule 272 *a*.]   3. He had curly black hair, dark blue eyes, and wore glasses.   4. Coal burns brightly, slowly, and throws out much heat.   5. The incubator must be thoroughly cleaned, ventilated, and the inside apparatus put into good order.   6. On the west side are the offices of the president, treasurer, auditor, and the draughting room.   7. He said that the Russian peasants were dull, unprogressive, and that farm machinery is almost unknown to them.   8. Every man must have a military suit, a gun, and must report promptly at four.   9. Hazlitt tells of his experience on the way to the fight, at the fight, and of his return home.   10. The new elephant is six years old, five feet high, and it may be stated incidentally that his rail road fare was $130.   11. The first few pages contain a brief account of the last commencement, new appointments, and the president's annual report is reprinted entire. 12. By means of the clutch one can send the boat ahead, backward, or allow the engine to run free.   13. He had blue eyes, dark brown hair, and weighed two hundred pounds.   14. He must have a knowledge of the English language, some foreign language, and an acquaintance with economics.   15. The bank was covered with trees, wild gooseberry bushes, and not far away was a spring of cold water.   16. We saw a sledge draw up, stop, and heard a hearty voice say, "Whoa! Charlie."   17. The use of tobacco, alcohol, and other injurious habits must be stopped by candidates for the team.   18. Tyndall tells of the formation of snow crystals, their power of uniting under pressure, and explains how glaciers are formed. 19. I found that a messenger was expected, that this person would be a stranger, that he would identify himself with the password "Tuxedo," and then I decided to personate the messenger.   20. The horse is naturally intelligent, quick to learn, gentle, and quickly becomes attached to one who treats him kindly.

Logical Agreement

117. Every sentence-element should be in logical accord with the rest of the sentence. (In connection

Logical
agreement
of sentence-
members

with this rule, see Rules 27 and 28.   See also *Subject,
Cause,* and *Reason* in the Glossary.)

> Bad: Of these names sixteen were chosen to be mem-
> bers.   ["Sixteen (names)" does not agree logically
> with "were chosen to be members."]
>
> Right: Of the persons named, sixteen were chosen
> to be members.
>
> Bad: The life of a hod-carrier is sometimes happier
> than a prince.   ["The life" does not agree logically
> with "is happier than a prince."]
>
> Right: The life of a hod-carrier is sometimes happier
> than that of a prince.
>
> Illogical: He hated to submit to the rules — *viz.,*
> church attendance and not smoking.   [Church
> attendance and abstinence from tobacco are not
> rules.]
>
> Right: He hated to submit to the rules — namely,
> those requiring attendance at church and abstinence
> from smoking.
>
> Illogical: A fireman seldom rises above an engineer.
>
> Right: A fireman seldom rises above the position of
> engineer.
>
> Illogical: The comedy *Love's Labour's Lost,* written
> by Shakespeare, is supposed to have occurred in
> Navarre.
>
> Right: The events related in Shakespeare's comedy
> *Love's Labour's Lost* are supposed to have occurred
> in Navarre.
>
> Illogical: Nothing looks more untidy than to see an
> expensive motor coming out of the garage covered
> with mud.
>
> Right: Nothing looks more untidy than an expensive
> motor coming out of the garage covered with mud.
>
> Illogical: As a question of economy, it is advanta-
> geous to use water-power.
>
> Right: For the sake of economy, it is advantageous
> to use water-power.
>
> Illogical: He had to choose between signing away his
> inheritance or being hanged.

Right: He had to choose between signing away his inheritance and being hanged.

Illogical: There is no place to hang it only in the hall.

Right: There is no place to hang it except in the hall; [or] The hall is the only place to hang it.

Illogical: I sat on the opposite side from which Charlie was sitting.

Right: I sat opposite Charlie; [or] I sat on the side opposite to the one on which Charlie was sitting.

EXERCISE 67

Study Rules 117 and 28; and see *Subject, Cause,* and *Reason* in the Glossary. The following sentences are illogical. State briefly in what respect each one is illogical, and rewrite each one, correcting its defects. 1. I jumped off the car in the opposite direction from which it was going. 2. The efforts of the militia were as futile as the police had been. 3. The subject of the first paragraph tells how the mail coaches carried the news of English victories. 4. The topic of the fifth paragraph is where the author told a mother of the death of her son. 5. *Discord* means that sounds are lacking in harmony. 6. Exclusiveness is when a person likes to remain aloof. 7. The outward appearance of an ordinary telephone consists of a box-like structure. 8. *Aërial* means to be moving in the air or flying. 9. The fact that caused this chemical change was due to the hot weather. 10. The topic of the essay deals with the value of a technical education. 11. The cause of the current is attributed to the continuous winds. 12. The only use to which the farm is now put is for pasturing sheep. 13. His aim in taking a college course is simply for general culture. 14. The reason I dislike the study is on account of the numerous statistics that must be learned. 15. Draughting as practiced nowadays is far different from the old method. 16. The material of drawing pencils is much finer than the ordinary commercial pencils. 17. He was soon promoted to vice-president of the company. 18. The style of architecture employed in this church resembles very closely an old cathedral. 19. The sugar beet is rapidly taking the place of cane sugar, and in the past few years has grown to be an extensive business.   20. The greatest fault I have against drill is the trouble of changing clothes.   21. The story tells of the breaking loose of a cannon on board a ship and a description of the weather at the time of the accident.   22. Why I should have an aversion to Saturday classes any more than any other day is due to habit.

Other or *else* in a *than* or *as* clause:

118. When comparing a thing to other members of its own class, exclude from the group the thing compared.

When correct

> Illogical: Lead is heavier than any metal.
> Right: Lead is heavier than any other metal.
>
> Illogical: Shakespeare is greater than any English poet.
> Right: Shakespeare is greater than any other English poet.

When incorrect

119. When comparing a thing to the members of a class to which it does not belong, in the *than* or an *as* clause, do not restrict the standard of comparison by *other* or *else* or any equivalent word.

> Illogical: That little word *home* means more to me than any other word of twice its length.
> Right: That little word *home* means more to me than any word of twice its length.

The *of* phrase limiting a superlative

120. In the *of* phrase limiting an adjective or an adverb in the superlative degree, —

(*a*) **The object of *of* should be a plural noun or a collective noun, not a noun designating an individual person or thing.**

> Illogical: He is the tallest of any man in the regiment.
> Right: He is the tallest of all the men in the regiment; [or] He is the tallest man of the regiment.
> (Right: He is taller than any other man in the regiment.)

(b) **The object of** *of* **should designate a class to which the subject of comparison belongs, not a class to which it does not belong.**

Illogical: Blackbirds make the best pie of all birds.
Right: Blackbirds make the best pie of all game pies.
(Right: Blackbirds make better pie than any other birds.)

(c) **The object of** *of* **should not be restricted by** *other* **or** *else* **or any equivalent word.**

Illogical: Shakespeare is the greatest of all other English poets.
Right: Shakespeare is the greatest of all English poets.

Negation

121. Double negative (*i.e.,* **the use, in a sentence, of two or more negative words not coördinate — as "I could not find it nowhere") is forbidden by modern usage.** — Double negative

EXERCISE 68

The following sentences are incorrect. Correct and rewrite them. 1. I can't find it nowhere. 2. They didn't find no treasure. 3. There isn't no one here who knows. 4. I didn't see no fire; my opinion is that there wasn't no fire. 5. There hasn't been no panic since 1907. 6. I haven't written no theme. 7. I haven't done no reading. 8. I haven't studied no lesson. 9. She hasn't never missed a class. 10. She isn't .never late. 11. Haven't you had no breakfast? 12. Didn't you get no pay? 13. I don't want no dispute. 14. Don't break no dishes here. — Double negative

122. *Hardly, scarcely, only,* **and** *but* **used in the sense of** *only* **are often incorrectly joined with a negative.** (For *cannot help but,* see Glossary, *Help.*) — Incorrect negative with *hardly,* etc.

Wrong: It was so misty that we couldn't hardly see.
Right: It was so misty that we could hardly see.

Wrong: For a minute I couldn't scarcely tell where I was.
Right: For a minute I could scarcely tell where I was.

Wrong: They are not allowed to go only on Saturdays.
Right: They are allowed to go only on Saturdays.

Wrong: There isn't but one store.
Right: There is but one store.

Exercise 69

Incorrect
negation
with
hardly, etc.

The following sentences are incorrect. Correct and rewrite them   1. It will not take but a minute. 2. I didn't see but two men there. 3. I can't hardly believe it. 4. I did not feel hardly strong enough. 5. She couldn't stay only a week. 6. He said angrily that he wouldn't give only forty cents. 7. You wouldn't scarcely believe the real story. 8. I hadn't scarcely passed by when the stone fell. 9. There didn't seem to be hardly any chance of success. 10. I can't hardly see it so far away. 11. I can't understand hardly anything in the chapter. 12. He doesn't appear to be hardly master of himself. 13. You haven't been here hardly an hour; don't go yet. 14. They didn't seem hardly near enough to hear my gunshot. 15. He isn't hardly as big as a derringer. 16. Six feet! Why, you aren't hardly five feet five. 17. I don't hardly see the difference.

Redundance

Tautology

123. Avoid tautology — *i.e.*, the useless repetition of an idea, in part or entire.

Bad: If I had abundant wealth and plenty of resources . . .
Right: If I had abundant wealth . . .

Bad: Will you please repeat that again?
Right: Will you please repeat that?

Bad: The autobiography of my life.
Right: My autobiography.

124. Avoid pleonasm — *i.e.,* the use of words which do not involve repetition of thought, but which are structurally unnecessary. Beware of clumsy circumlocutions such as *along the lines of, of the nature of, of the character of,* etc.

> Bad: There were two hundred students went.
> Right: Two hundred students went.
>
> Bad: It has no relation as to time or place.
> Right: It has no relation to time or place.
>
> Bad: They went through with the formalities.
> Right: They went through the formalities.
>
> Bad: He took work along the lines of banking.
> Right: He took work in banking; [or] He studied banking.

125. Avoid burdening a statement with too many **words.** Avoid the similar fault of embodying in a series of scrappy sentences what could be more fitly embodied in one sentence. Put subordinate thoughts into subordinate forms — not into separate independent assertions. (See also Rule 97.) Independent assertion in excess not only gives to prose the style of a primer but wastes words. Observe the number of unnecessary words in the passage below marked *Primer style.*

> Wordy: Yesterday I had occasion to be witness of a very interesting incident.
> Right: Yesterday I saw an interesting incident.
>
> Wordy: At midnight the physician made a statement saying that the governor was better.
> Right: At midnight the physician stated that the governor was better.
>
> Wordy: In the house in which we used to live when we were in Winstead was a large play-room, which was located just at the head of the stairs.
> Predication reduced: Just at the head of the stairs in our house in Winstead was a large play-room.

Primer style: As you approach the island from th
west, you get a view of a high cliff. This cliff i
about six miles in length. It is of sandstone, an
rises about perpendicularly from the water. Nu
merous cracks and crevices can be seen in the clif
. . . 45 words.

Predication reduced: Approaching the island from
the west, you get a view of a high, sandstone cli
about six miles in length, rising almost perpendicu
larly from the water, its face seamed with crack
and crevices. . . . 33 words.

125*a*. Use forceful predicate verbs.

Weak: A mountain was seen looming up in the dis
tance.
Stronger: A mountain loomed up in the distance.
Weak: There is a horse eating grass in our yard.
Stronger: A horse is eating grass in our yard.

EXERCISE 70

Was seen

Strengthen the following sentences by using some othe
verbs than *was seen:* 1. Just around the turn the cottag
was seen nestling in a clump of trees. 2. When we reache
the wharf the vessel was seen leaving the harbor. 3. W
had heard no sound during the night, but next mornin
footprints were seen beneath the window. 4. Although
storm was seen in the distance, we started on our trip.

EXERCISE 71

Independ-
dent predi-
cation to be
reduced

Embody the substance of each of the following passage
in one sentence containing only one independent clause
After each sentence write the number of words saved i
the sentence as compared with the original passage
1. Prospect Farm is situated at the junction of two roads
One road extends east and west, and the other north an
south. 2. On each side of the road is a row of trees. Th
trees in each row are about thirty feet apart. 3. There i
a small grove of trees north of the cottage. A drive ca
be seen winding among the trees. 4. Far to the north i

a lighthouse, very substantial and solid in appearance.
This lighthouse warns the lake vessels of dangerous reefs
in the vicinity.   5. At the south end of the island a camp
is situated.   This camp is called Camp Stella.   It is
famous as a resort for sufferers from hay fever.   6. Running up from the shore is a road of red clay.   This road
winds in and out up the high hill.   It finally disappears
behind the trees.   7. As I stood at one of the front gates,
I saw that the drive encircled the house.   It had the shape
of a great inverted U lying before me.   I could see all of
the U except the round part.   This lay behind the house,
as I have said.

Embody the substance of the following passage in four
sentences, each containing only one independent clause;
write at the end of the number of words saved in your
version as compared with the original: On the north side
of the road was a large white gate.   A winding path led
from the gate to a beautiful house.   The house was about
fifty yards from the road.   Between the road and the house
was a large lawn.   About the lawn were scattered several
flower-beds.   Many large trees were irregularly placed
about the lawn.   The house was a large white structure.
Its architecture was of the colonial style.   Along its entire
front was a spacious veranda.   The veranda was about
three feet above the ground.   The main entrance was at
the middle of the front side of the house.   One large door
closed the entrance.   On each side of the door was a large
window.   Each window was about half-way between the
door and the nearest side of the house.   The windows
were four feet wide and ten feet high.   Their lower edges
were level with the floor of the veranda.

Repetition of Words

**126. Do not use a word in two senses in the same
sentence or within a short space.**

Bad: Since several years passed since the death of his
   wife . . .
Right: Several years having passed since the death
   of his wife . . .

Bad: I couldn't get up courage to get up and investigate.

Right: I couldn't summon courage to get up and investigate.

Awkward repetition

127. Avoid awkward and needless repetition of a word or phrase.

Bad: MacArthur was to speak on that day; hence we selected that day for our trip.

Bad: He said that the orders said that uniforms must be worn in future.

Method of correction

128. Violations of the foregoing rule may be corrected by a judicious use of pronouns, by the use of synonyms, or by recasting the sentence.

Right: That was the day on which MacArthur was to speak; we therefore selected it for our trip.

Right: He said that the orders required the wearing of uniforms in future.

Awkward avoidance of repetition

129. Prefer repetition, however, to labored and awkward avoidance of it.

Awkward: If it has this effect on a healthy skin, it will have a worse result on an inflamed cuticle.

Preferable: If it has this effect on a healthy skin, it will have a worse effect on an inflamed skin.

Straining for synonyms

NOTE. — A constant straining for conspicuous synonyms to use in referring to something previously mentioned is a characteristic mannerism of newspaper writers (cf. Rules 20 and 16). Avoid this practice; repeat the noun, or else choose an inconspicuous synonym.

Bad: At the faculty meeting yesterday the question of football was again discussed. Those of that learned aggregation who opposed the gridiron game succumbed at the final vote. (See Rule 125.)

Improved: At the faculty meeting yesterday the question of football was again discussed. The opponents of the game were defeated at the final vote.

Bad: The extreme warm weather during the past several weeks has not exactly been conducive of producing record-breaking scores at the Y. M. C. A. bowling alleys. In fact it has almost been too warm for even the most ardent lovers of the tenpin game, and enthusiasm has for some time been at a rather low ebb. (See Rule 125.)

Right: The extremely warm weather of the past several weeks has discouraged the production of high scores at the Y. M. C. A. bowling alleys. It has been almost too warm for even the most enthusiastic bowlers, and the general interest in the game has been slight.

130. When the conjunction *that* is separated by intervening words from the subject and predicate which it introduces, guard against the careless repetition of *that*.

Careless repetition of the conjunction that

Wrong: It is pleasant to reflect that after all this work has been done and all these difficulties have been conquered, that we shall get a good rest.

Right: It is pleasant to reflect that after all this work has been done and all these difficulties have been conquered, we shall get a good rest.

Euphony

131. For euphony, avoid a succession of like sounds. Avoid rhyme in prose.

Concurrence of like sounds

Not euphonious: The chilling blasts blowing with cutting force.

Bad: Then came the time for the heart-breaking leave-taking.

Bad: The fountains were kept playing night and day to keep up the display.

NOTE. — This rule is not intended to object to the sparing use of alliteration in prose, as a means of increasing the force of passages designed to produce an emotional appeal.

Absolute phrases:

132. Absolute phrases are often a useful aid to proper subordination and to smoothness of style. But there are two kinds of absolute phrases which, being conspicuously awkward, are best avoided; *viz.,*

Absolute pronoun

(*a*) Absolute phrases in which the substantive is a pronoun.

> Clumsy: He gave up the task, it being too difficult.
> Better: He gave up the task as too difficult.
> Clumsy: I being unacquainted with the road, my party got lost.
> Better: Since I was unacquainted with the road, my party got lost.

Note. — Such an absolute phrase is particularly objectionable when the pronoun refers to the subject of the sentence. In such cases wordiness is added to awkwardness, since the pronoun is pleonastic (see Rule 124).

> Bad: I made a trip to Catalina Island in 1902, I being then in my tenth year.
> Better: I made a trip to Catalina Island in 1902, being then in my tenth year.
> Bad: The furnace could not be repaired immediately, it being red-hot.
> Better: Being red-hot, the furnace could not be repaired immediately.

Latinistic phrases

(*b*) Absolute phrases in which the substantive is modified by a perfect participle, especially a passive perfect participle. Such phrases are clumsy, unidiomatic, and suggestive of elementary Latin exercises.

> Clumsy: His horse having been fed, Macy continued his journey.
> Better: When his horse had been fed, Macy continued his journey.

Variety

Forms of expression noticeably frequent

133. Do not make many sentences in a composition or a passage monotonously alike in construction. This principle is often violated (*a*) by beginning many sentences near each other with *after*, with *this* or *these*, or with *there is* or *there are;* (*b*) by using with noticeable frequency a compound sentence with two members of about equal length joined by *and* or *but;* (*c*) by using participial or absolute phrases with noticeable frequency; and (*d*) by the habitual use of *so* as a connective (cf. Rule 99).

STRUCTURE OF LARGER UNITS OF DISCOURSE

Unity of a Composition

134. A composition should treat a single subject and should treat it throughout according to a self-consistent method. *The general principle*

The following composition is an example of the violation of unity by failure to hold to one subject:

OUR TRIP UP SPRUCE CREEK

While I was in Port Orange, Mr. Doty, the proprietor of the hotel there, took some of his guests five miles up Spruce Creek on a launch. It was the third of February. As the boat steamed up the creek, we stood on the deck, some of us taking pictures and others shooting at alligators with revolvers. The alligators are of all sizes. Sometimes you will see one seven or eight feet long, lying on the bank in the sunshine. As the boat goes past, he slides into the water and swims away with only his head above the water. When we have gone a little farther, we see another alligator about four feet long, with ten or twelve little ones crawling over her back.

When the launch has gone about five miles, it stops at the wharf of an orange grove. Here the passengers are allowed to take all the oranges they want. After they have walked about the grove for a while, they have a picnic dinner, and then start back.

The writer of the foregoing composition keeps to his subject — a trip which he took up Spruce Creek on

February 3 — for only three sentences. He shifts to a different subject after the third sentence — the Spruce Creek trips in general — and throughout the rest of the composition forgets all about " our trip." Unity may be given to this composition (*a*) by making it entirely a narrative, dealing with the trip of February 3; or (*b*) by making it, throughout, a general discussion of the Spruce Creek picnics provided by Mr. Doty.

Too big a subject

135. A very small composition on a very large subject — such as Character, Patriotism, Selfishness, Advertising, The Waste of Energy — usually violates the principle of unity. It usually consists of a number of brief scraps of discussion, each dealing with a different division of the subject. The divisions of so large a subject are themselves large; the composition therefore reads like a fragmentary and disconnected treatment of a number of distinct subjects, not like a connected treatment of a single subject.

When a short composition is to be written on a big subject, it is best to choose some single, well-defined phase of the subject. For example, choose the subjects in the left column rather than those in the right.

Limited	*General*
The Difference between Character and Reputation.	Character
The Work of Patriotic Women During the World War.	Patriotism
Selfishness in the Conduct of Students toward their Parents.	Selfishness
Advertising as a Necessary Measure of Self-Defense.	Advertising
The Value of a Daily Schedule	The Waste of Time
How Students' Adversities aid them toward Success.	Success

136. In reproducing a story (*e.g.,* the story of *Macbeth*) or in composing a story, do not shift carelessly between the present and the past tenses. Decide at the beginning which tense to use, and use it consistently; ordinarily, prefer the past tense. (Cf. Rule 19.)

Shifting the tense in narrative

137. If in a story the narrator tells what he saw or had a part in, the introduction of events or speeches or thoughts which he could not have seen or heard or known, violates unity.

Shifting the point of view in narrative

Thus the italicized part of the following extract violates unity:

> I strolled down to the boat-house at six o'clock yesterday evening. As I got there a row-boat was approaching the wharf containing a man and a girl who I judged must have arrived from the country very recently. *They had started for Picnic Point at two o'clock. On the way the young man had had great difficulty at the unfamiliar work of rowing. Often his oars would slip and send a shower of water into the girl's lap, at which he would say, "Oh, I am so sorry!" and she would reply, "Oh, that's all right."* . . . *As they neared the wharf, he was anxiously wondering whether he could land without accident.* Jimmy, the keeper of the boat-house, stood ready to assist at the disembarkation. . . .

A story in which unity is thus violated may be corrected (*a*) by omitting all events, speeches, and thoughts of which the narrator could not, according to his own account, have been aware at the time they took place (*e.g.,* omitting the italicized passage in the story quoted); (*b*) by introducing all such events, speeches, and thoughts as having been learned by the narrator after they took place (*e.g.,* making the oarsman in the above-quoted story tell the narrator, in a subsequent conversation, what is improperly related in the italicized passage); or (*c*) by omitting all reference to the narrator — telling everything impersonally (*e.g.*, omitting from the above-quoted story all preceding the italicized part and continuing without any reference to the narrator).

Shifting the tense in description

138. In description introduced by narrative in the past tense, maintain the tense throughout the composition. Carelessly shifting to the present tense changes the point of view and violates unity.

Shifting from point of view of one person to that of another

139. Do not change the point of view of a composition or of a passage by shifting carelessly from *I* to *one*, from *we* to *the observer*, from *you* to *a person*, etc. Keep consistently to one point of view unless there is good reason for changing.

> Wrong: You seldom meet such people, but when one does, he should be on his guard against them.
> Right: You seldom meet such people, but when you do, you should be on your guard against them.

Organization of a Composition — Coherence

The general principle

140. To make a composition effective, proceed by a definite plan. Even good thoughts and interesting statements will not be effective if the writer sets them down haphazard, just as they occur to him; they must be organized into a whole. To get good organization, a writer must proceed by a definite plan; that is, he must, before he begins to write, or at least before he puts the composition into its final form, decide on a few topics, and on each topic write a passage (see Rule 142), constituting a unit of the whole composition. As in warfare a band of men, though strong and brave individually, is collectively weak if it is

ot well organized; so a speech, a report, an editorial,
n essay, any composition, though its parts may be
orcible or clever, is weak as a whole if it is not well
rganized.

For example, a composition on Denver consists of
a short paragraph on each of the following topics:

1. Location.
2. History.
3. Local pride.
4. Water supply (derived from mountain snow).
5. Capitol and United States mint.
6. Museums.
7. Principal business.
8. Dwelling houses (none built of wood).
9. Schools.
10. Wealth of citizens.
11. The city as a health resort.
12. Churches.
13. Strange spectacle of men skating in winter in their
shirtsleeves.

This production, however interesting its material, is
as far from being a good composition as two wheels, a
diamond frame, a chain, and a pair of handle bars, all
piled in a heap, are from being a good bicycle. It is
a series of haphazard remarks not organized into a
whole. There is no reason for most of the parts' standing where they are — no reason, *e.g.*, for discussing
public buildings after the water supply, or skaters'
costumes after churches. The material of this composition may be organized into a whole by the method
shown in the following outline. The numbers within
the brackets refer to parts of the preceding outline.

I. History. [2]
II. Location and climate. [Put 1 and 13 here — 13 as
an illustration of the statements about the
climate.]

III. Especially striking peculiarities of the city.
1. Evidences of its being a health resort. [11]
2. Absence of wooden buildings. [8]
3. Public buildings. [5]
4. Water supply. [4]
5. Most striking of all, — local pride. [3]

IV. Conditions of the people's life.
1. Economic: Principal occupations.   General wealth. [7 and 10]
2. Educational and moral: Schools, museum, churches. [9, 6, and 12]

Passages misplaced

141. Material belonging to one part of a composition should not be placed carelessly in another part.

In the following paragraph, the italicized sentence is evidently misplaced:

The physical training department is very good and is constantly improving. *A good gymnasium for the women is greatly needed, to replace the present unsatisfactory make shift.* As I am more acquainted with the work of the girls, I shall confine myself to the physical training provided for them.

The italicized sentence does not belong in this introductory part, but in a subsequent part; *viz.,* that which discusses the equipment for the girls' exercise.

Unity and completeness of each part

142. Make each division of an expository composition a well-organized, well-introduced, well-concluded whole, which would seem rounded and complete if it stood by itself. Each of these passages constituting the major units (see the third sentence of Rule 140) should be somewhat like a distinct composition; just as a military company is a complete organization within itself, as well as a unit in a regiment.

Coherent beginning

143. The opening sentences of a formal composition should be self-explanatory; they should be

clear to the reader without reference to the title of the composition.

Bad:

LAMPS

 They are contrivances for furnishing artificial light. . . .

Right:

LAMPS

 Lamps are contrivances for furnishing artificial light. . . .

Bad:

MY WORK DURING THE PAST TERM

 Latin and German were more difficult than any other studies. . . .

Right:

MY WORK DURING THE PAST TERM

 In my work during the past term, I had more difficulty with Latin and German than with any other studies.

144. The beginning of a new division, either of a whole composition or of a paragraph, should be clearly marked. Otherwise the reader may begin reading the new division supposing that the preceding division still continues. For marking the beginning of a new part, the following are useful means:

Distinct introduction of a new part

(*a*) A transitional sentence or group of sentences, such as the following:

Transition sentence or paragraph

So much for the amount of free time which the student has. It remains to discuss the use he makes of it.

The willingness of the faculty to allow student self-government is, then, unquestionable. But are the students equally willing to govern themselves?

(*b*) Connective words, phrases, and other expressions:

Connective or transitional words and phrases

 Addition: *then, then too, again, next, too, also, further,*

moreover, another cause of, equally important with the
preceding, first, secondly, finally, etc.

Addition with intensification: *even, perhaps.*

Repetition: *in fact, indeed, in other words.*

Exemplification: *for example, for instance, thus.*

Comparison: *similarly, likewise.*

Purpose: *to this end, for this purpose, having this in*
view.

Resumption after a digression: *well, now, thus.*

Placing key words at the beginning

(*c*) Placing near the beginning of the first sentence
of the new division the word or words that indicate
the subject of the new division. For example, after
discussing the abuses of college athletics, to begin a
new division with the words " The remedy . . ." makes
the change of topic immediately evident. After discussing a statesman's foreign policy, to begin a new
division with the words " His internal administration. . . ." makes the change of topic immediately
evident.

Ineffective pronouns

(*d*) It is usually ineffective to use a pronoun in place
of a principal word in the topic sentence of a paragraph.

Coherence of a state-ment of con-sequence

**145. Establish clear connections between a state-
ment of consequence and the preceding statement.**
Unless this relation is immediately obvious, it should
be indicated by some connective word, phrase, or
other expression, such as *therefore, accordingly, hence,*
consequently, in consequence of the foregoing, for this
reason, it follows that, the result is, etc.

EXERCISE 72

Pick out the transitional words and phrases in the
following paragraph and tell what kind of service each
performs:

The word paradox is commonly supposed to be a term of abuse; but there is nothing abusive in its meaning. It means what is contrary to the common opinion, and that may be true or false. The value of a paradoxical saying lies in its truth, not in its relation to what most people think. Yet most people when they have called a saying a paradox think that they have condemned it; as if every discovery in thought were not a paradox, for if it were not a paradox it would not be a discovery. It is no abuse to call an original writer a lover of paradox but a simple statement of fact, for he does not want to discover what everyone knows. The truths that he seeks and delights to find are new and surprising ones, and the surprise which they cause expresses itself in this word paradox.

146. Establish clear connection between a passage making an abatement and the preceding assertion. This relation should usually be indicated by some connective, such as *to be sure; I admit; there is, to be sure, an exception . . .*; etc.

Coherence of an abatement

147. Establish clear connections between a statement of contrast and what precedes. This connection should usually be indicated by some connective, such as *but, yet, in spite of, on the contrary, on the other hand, nevertheless, however*, etc.

Coherence of a contrasting part

148. Lack of connective words or sentences between a statement and a contradiction of it is especially apt to cause incoherence.

Coherence of a contradiction

> Incoherent: Some people think clerking is an easy job and that a clerk ought never to be tired. Clerks stay closely housed day after day, working from six in the morning to ten at night. . . .
> Coherent [the necessary connective is supplied]: Some people think the occupation of a clerk is easy and that a clerk ought never to be tired.

This is not the case. In the first place, clerks stay closely housed day after day, etc.

Emphasis

Emphasis   If a composition is coherently arranged and clearly expressed, emphasis of the more important ideas or expressions will usually follow. But, there are a number of special devices or ways by which emphasis is obtained. For instance, see: 82. Parenthetic position of modifiers; 83. Strong beginning; 88. Strong close; 89. Climactic order; 97. Skillful use of subordination; 109, 110. Independent expression of important statements and vice versa; 202. Sentences made conspicuous by detachment.

II. PUTTING DISCOURSE ON PAPER

Spelling

The way to reform bad spelling is to work at it determinedly, correcting a few faults at a time. In most cases, the bad speller does not *see* the words correctly; his mental photograph of them is wrong, or blurred. Sometimes his vision is defective, and he needs to visit an oculist. In many cases he does not *hear* and *pronounce* the words correctly; he fails to include syllables, he transposes or omits letters, and he confuses one word with another. A misspelling should never be corrected hastily. The student should look up the correct spelling and fix it in memory by careful observation and by writing it out. He should keep a list of words he misspells, and should refer to it regularly.

Careful study of the following rules, and of the list in 162, will aid the student to recognize his misspellings, and will provide him with principles by means of which he can remember more easily the correct spellings.

149. A monosyllable or a word accented on the last syllable, if it ends in one consonant preceded by one vowel, doubles the final consonant when a suffix beginning with a vowel is added. Thus: *bid, bidden; quiz, quizzes; drop, dropped, dropping; glad, gladder, gladdest; man, mannish; tin, tinny.* — Doubling final consonants: General rule

Note 1. — The final consonant in words not accented on the last syllable is not usually doubled before a suffix; — *Benefit*, etc.

Worship,
travel, etc.

thus: *benefit, benefited.* In the words *worship* and *kidna*
and words like *bevel, counsel, quarrel,* etc., the final cons
nant *may* be doubled, but it is better not to double i
e.g., worshiper, worshiping, worshiped; kidnaped; travele
traveling, traveled, etc.

Suffix be-
ginning with
consonant

NOTE 2. — A final consonant is not doubled before
suffix beginning with a consonant. Thus: *fit, fitting, bu*
fitness.

Receding
accent

150. This rule does not apply to words in whic
the accent is shifted to a preceding syllable. Thu:
refer, referred, but *reference; confer, conferring, bu*
conference. But *excel, excellence.* Nor does it affect
chagrin, chagrined; transfer, transferable; infer, infe
able; gas, gaseous.

EXERCISE 73

Doubling
final con-
sonants

Write the infinitive, the present participle, and th
past participle of each of the following verbs (*e.g., stop*
stopping, stopped): *rob, crib, stab, bed, shed, bud, beg, flog*
sprig, rig, hem, ram, hum, plan, skin, shun, pin, rip, drop
stop, grip, tip, equip, dip, whip, slip, scar, mar, debar, occu:
demur, prefer, refer, confer, bat, pet, rot, flit, quit, regre
omit, commit, permit, admit, repel, propel, compel, expe
impel.

Picnicked,
etc.

151. Words ending in *c* add *k* before a suffix be
ginning with *e, i,* or *y.* Thus: *picnic, picnicked*
traffic, trafficking; panic, panicky.

Dropping
final *e:*
General
rule
before
ing

152. Words ending in silent *e* usually drop the
before a suffix beginning with a vowel. Thus: *lov*
lovable; stone, stony. Hence, a verb ending in silen
e drops *e* when *ing* is added. Thus: *shine, shining.*

EXERCISE 74

Dropping
final *e*

Write the following words, together with the adjective
ending in *able* derived from them (*e.g., love, lovable*)
love, excuse, believe, name, tame, sale, deplore, appeas
use, forgive, live, shake.

153. An exception to Rule 152: Words ending in ce or ge do not drop the e when ous or able is added. Thus: *notice, noticeable; outrage, outrageous.*

NOTE. — *C* and *g* in words of French, Latin, and Greek derivation usually have the soft sound before *e, i,* and *y,* as *cede, genial, civil, giant, cyanide, gymnasium;* elsewhere they have the hard sound, as *calendar, Gallic, code, gorgon, acute, gusto.* (*Get, geese, gew-gaw, geld, giddy, gift, gig, giggle, gild, begin, gird, girdle, girl,* and *give* are not of the above-mentioned derivation.) Notice how the principle applies to *accent, accident, flaccid, occiput, accept, accurate, desiccate, except, excuse.* On account of this principle, the *e* must be retained in such words as *noticeable and courageous,* in order to keep the soft sound of *c* and *g.*

EXERCISE 74a

Write each of the following words together with its derivative ending in *ous* (*e.g., courage, courageous*): *courage, advantage, outrage, umbrage.* Write each of the following words together with its derivative ending in *able* (*e.g., notice, noticeable*): *notice, peace, manage, change.*

154. A noun ending in y preceded by a consonant forms the plural in ies; as library, libraries. A noun ending in y preceded by a vowel forms the plural in ys; as valley, valleys.

EXERCISE 75

Write the singular and the plural of each of the following nouns (*e.g., lady, ladies*): *lady, body, buggy, lily, folly, dummy, ninny, company, harmony, copy, berry, library, century, country, courtesy, city, party, frivolity, valley, monkey, chimney, money, pulley, volley, kidney, trolley, donkey, galley.*

155. A verb ending in y preceded by a consonant forms its present third singular in ies and its past in ied. Thus: *rely, relies, relied; marry, marries, married.*

Happiness, etc.

Studying, etc.

155a. Words ending in *y* preceded by a consonant usually change the *y* to *i* before a suffix. Thus: *happy, happiness; beauty, beautiful; busy, business.* But verbs ending in *y* do not drop the *y* before *ing.* Thus: *study, studying; hurry, hurrying.*

EXERCISE 76

Change of *y* to *i:* Verbs

Write the first and third persons, present indicative, and the first person past, of each of the following verbs (*e.g., I cry, he cries, I cried*): *cry, fly, fry, try, apply, supply, defy, deny, satisfy, classify, hurry, marry, carry, tarry, bury.*

Change of *ie* to *y*

156. Verbs ending in *ie* change *ie* to *y* before *ing.* Thus: *lie, lying*

EXERCISE 77

Change of *ie* to *y*

Write the infinitive and the present participle of each of the following verbs (*e.g., lie, lying*): *lie, die, tie, vie.*

Suddenness, etc.

156a. Adjectives ending in *n* do not drop the *n* before *ness.* Thus: *sudden, suddenness; green, greenness.*

Finally, etc.

156b. Words ending in *l* do not drop the *l* before *ly.* Thus: *final, finally; cool, coolly.*

EXERCISE 78

Adverbs in *lly*

Write each of the following words, together with its derivative in *ly* (*e.g., final, finally*): *final, usual, actual, continual, principal, practical, casual, general, oral, original, occasional, special, partial.*

Acci-dentally, etc.

Write each of the following words together with its derivative in *ally* (*e.g., accident, accidentally*): *accident, incident, heroic, poetic, dramatic, prosaic, occasion.*

Plurals in *s* and *es*

157. (*a*) **Nouns ending in a consonant add *es* to form the plural when the plural has an extra syllable;**

when the plural has no extra syllable, they add only *s*.
Thus: *lass, lasses; lad, lads.*

(*b*) Words like *leaf, thief, self,* form the plural in
ves. Thus: *leaves, thieves, ourselves.* Some words
ending in *f* form the plural in *fs*. Thus: *beliefs,
chiefs, griefs, hoofs, scarfs, dwarfs.*

Leaf, thief,
etc.

(*c*) Some nouns ending in *o* add *es* to form the
plural. Thus: *buffaloes, calicoes, echoes, mosquitoes,
negroes, potatoes, volcanoes, dominoes, embargoes, heroes,
jingoes, mulattoes, noes, tomatoes, tornadoes.* Some
add only *s*. Thus: *banjos, dynamos, Eskimos, pianos,
silos, solos, sopranos, zeros.* A few plurals may be
written either *os* or *oes*.

Nouns in *o*

(*d*) The plurals of letters of the alphabet, of numerical symbols, and of a word considered *as a word* are
formed by adding *'s*. (See Rule 255.) Thus: " Mind
your *p's* and *q's*," " His *well's* and his *and's* made up
half his story."

Letters,
symbols,
etc.

(*e*) Observe that certain words of foreign origin
retain their foreign plurals. Note especially *datum,
data; phenomenon, phenomena; analysis, analyses;
parenthesis, parentheses; thesis, theses.*

Foreign
nouns

EXERCISE 79

Write the singular and the plural of each of the following nouns (*e.g., bead, beads*): *bead, road, leak, freak, wheel,
pail, beam, seam, screen, steep, leap, paradox, hiss, heir,
fair, repair, pass, glass, beet, boat, boot, flash, crash, cow,
row, crow, dish, box.*

Plurals in
s and *es*

158. Verbs ending in a consonant add *es* to make
the present third singular form when that form has an
extra syllable; when it has no extra syllable, they
add only *s*. Thus: *miss, misses; proclaim, proclaims.*

Present
third sin-
gular in *s*
and *es*

Exercise 80

Write the indicative present first and third persons singular of the following verbs (*e.g.*, *refer, refers*): *refer, deem, claim, gleam, disdain, feel, squeal, pass, rush, differ, assign, toss, gash, miss, fix, eat, twist.*

158a. There are three verbs ending in *eed: exceed, succeed,* and *proceed.* Other verbs have *ede.*

159. For the sound *ee*, use *ei* after *c* and *ie* after any other letter. If *c* precedes the digraph, *e* follows *c*, as in *Alice.* If another letter precedes the digraph, *i* follows the letter, as in *Alice.* Exceptions: *weird, seize, neither, leisure, financier, obeisance.*

For any other sound of the digraph use *ei.* Exceptions: *friend, view, sieve, mischief, handkerchief.*

Exercise 81

Copy the following:

receive	receipt
believe	belief
deceive	deceit
relieve	relief
conceive	conceit
perceive	

160. In case of doubt whether to use *principal* or *principle*, remember that *principle* is always a noun and that the word which contains *a* (princip*a*l) is the adjective. *Principal* is occasionally a noun: *the principal of the school, both principal and interest.*

Exercise 82

Write the following sentences, filling the blanks with *principal* or *principle*: 1. The —— street runs north 2. The —— of the school was a man of strong ——s 3. The —— involved is what I ——ly object to. 4. I

was against his ——s to use more than the interest; the
—— he kept intact. 5. His —— occupation was to
master the ——s of geometry.

**161. The common interjection is spelled *oh*. It is
capitalized only at the beginning of a sentence, and is
followed by an exclamation point, a comma, or no
mark at all.**   *Oh* and *O*

> Examples: "Oh, no, it is no trouble," "Oh! you ought
> not to do that," "My child! oh, my child!" "I will
> do it — and oh, by the way, where's the key?"

**The sign of direct address (poetic or archaic) is
spelled *O*. It is always capitalized, and is not followed
by punctuation.**

> Examples: "I am come, O Caesar," "O ye spirits of
> our fathers," "O God, we pray thee," "I fear for
> thee, O my country."

GENERAL EXERCISES IN SPELLING
EXERCISE 83

I. Write the following words, observing that in the
great majority the ending is *le*, only a few ending in *el*.
Observe that in most of the words ending in *el*, the final
syllable is preceded by *v*, *m*, or *n*.   *Able, amble, addle, axle,
apple, Bible, babble, bramble, buckle, battle, bubble, bridle,
baffle, cable, cradle, coddle, crackle, candle, castle, dandle,
dazzle, dawdle, double, dwindle, eagle, feeble, fable fondle,
fickle, gable, giggle, goggle, gamble, handle, huddle, ingle,
icicle, juggle, jangle, jingle, ladle, marble, muddle. maple,
middle, noble, nibble, ogle, paddle, poodle, people, quibble,
riddle, rabble, rifle, ripple, stable, sable, sample, staple,
subtle, saddle, sprinkle, sickle, table, tackle, title, topple,
trestle, twinkle, wrinkle, wrestle, whistle, mantle* (a garment).   The endings *le* and *el*

> *Bevel, drivel, gavel, gravel, hovel, level, navel, novel, ravel,
> revel, dishevel, shrivel, snivel, travel. Camel, enamel, trammel.
> Flannel, funnel, panel, tunnel. Babel, label, libel. Angel,
> vessel, chisel, nickel, mantel* (a chimney-piece).

The adjective ending *ful*

II. Write the following adjectives, observing that in all, the ending is not *full*, but *ful*: *useful, beautiful, careful, merciful, joyful, awful, skillful, hopeful, vengeful, mournful, cheerful, wonderful, delightful.*

The adjective ending *ous*

III. Write the following words, observing that in all, the ending is not *us*, but *ous*: *humorous, courageous, plenteous, mischievous, simultaneous, miscellaneous, pretentious, luminous, ridiculous, grievous, glorious, bounteous, outrageous, hideous, heinous, troublous, garrulous, bibulous.*

The adverb prefix *al*

IV. Write the following words, observing that in all, the prefix is not *all*, but *al*: *already, altogether, almost, also.*

Disappear* and *disappoint

V. Write the following words, observing that in each the prefix is not *diss*, but *dis*: *dis+appear, dis+appoint, dis+grace, dis+close, dis+gorge, dis+honor, dis+band, dis+locate, dis+dain, dis+turb.*

***Professor,* etc.**

VI. Write the following words, observing that in each, the prefix is not *prof*, but *pro*: *pro+fessor, pro+fession, pro+fessional, pro+vide, pro+found, pro+voke, pro+tect, pro+bation, pro+nounce, pro+ceed, pro+gress.*

***Precede, proceed,* etc.**

VII. Write the following words, observing the variations in the spelling of the last syllable:

precede	proceed (*but* procedure)	supersede
recede	exceed	
concede	succeed	
intercede		

Business

VIII. Write the following pairs of words:

happy	happi+ness	dizzy	dizzi+ness
rosy	rosi+ness	lonely	loneli+ness
fluffy	fluffi+ness	busy	busi+ness
crazy	crazi+ness		

Lose* and *loose

IX. *Lose* is a verb; *loose* is an adjective. "Lose" is pronounced *looz;* "loose", *loos.* Write the following sentences, filling the blanks with *lose* or *loose:* 1. The screw is ——. 2. Don't —— it. 3. If it gets ——, you will —— it. 4. His coat is ——er than yours, but mine is the ——est of all. 5. By ——ing his —— change, the ——jointed traveler suffered.

X. The principal parts of *lead* are *lead, led, led.* Write the following sentences, filling the blanks with *lead* or *led:* 1. He met me and ―― me in. 2. They will ―― us astray, as our friends were ―― astray. 3. It was this act that ―― to his success. 4. I was ―― to think that this would ―― to misfortune.

Lead and *led*

XI. *Too* is an adverb; it means *excessively* (as "He is too weak") or *also.* *To* is a preposition. *Two* is a number (= 2). Write the following sentences, filling the blanks with *too, to,* or *two:* 1. It is ―― weak ―― withstand ―― winters. 2. He thought the ―― men were ―― harsh, and I thought so ――. 3. ―― say that, is ―― say a thing with ―― meanings. 4. He was ―― miles from home and was hungry ――.

Too, to, and *two*

XII. Write the following sentences, filling the blanks with *accept* or *except; affect* or *effect:* 1. I would ―― the offer, ―― for my religious scruples. 2. He is the best pianist in Europe; I do not ―― even Liszt. 3. Most of the rebels were offered pardon and ――ed it; but the leaders were ――ed from the offer. 4. He burned all the household goods, not ――ing even the heirlooms.

Accept and *except*

1. That statement is true, but it does not ―― the case. 2. The failure of the bank did not ―― his equanimity. 3. The admonition of the dean had a good ――. 4. The generals ――ed a junction, but this action had no ―― on the enemy.

Affect and *effect*

XIII. Regarding *advice, advise, device, devise,* remember the following formula:

Advice, advise, device, devise

Nouns	*Verbs*
advice	advise
device	devise

Write the following sentences, filling the blanks with *advice* or *advise:* 1. I ―― you to buy. 2. He was ――ed not to take the lawyer's ――. 3. A message from his ――er brought important ――es. 4. He ――ed me, and I thought it ――able to follow his ――.

Write the following sentences, filling the blanks with *device* or *devise:* 5. It is an ingenious ――, but can't we ―― a better one? 6. Many ――es were employed.

162. The following list is composed chiefly of ordinary words which are often misspelled. With many of these are grouped — for the sake of comparison and distinction — related words, words not often misspelled, and words of different derivation commonly confused with them. (Numbers refer to rules.)

absence
absorb
absorption
absurd
accept (*receive*)
  except (*exclude, aside from*)
access (*admittance*)
  excess (*greater amount*)
accessible
accident
accidentally
accommodate
accompanying 155*a*
accumulate
accustom
acquainted
acquitted
across
additionally
address
advice (noun)
advise (verb)
adviser
Æneid
æroplane
affect (verb, *to influence*)
  effect (verb, *to produce*)
  effect (noun, *result*)
    (There is no noun *affect*)
aggravate
aghast
aisle (in church)
  isle (*island*)
all right (There is no such word as "alright" or "allright.")

alley (*small street*)
alleys 154
allies 154
alliteration
allotted
allusion (*hint*)
  illusion (*false image*)
ally (*confederate*)
already
all ready
altar (*shrine*)
alter (*change*)
altogether
alumna (feminine singular)
alumnæ (feminine plural)
alumnus (masculine singular)
alumni (masculine plural)
always
amateur
among
analysis
analyze
angel (*celestial being*)
angelic
angle (*corner*)
annual
answer
anxiety
apart
apartment
apiece 159
apology
apparatus
apparent
appearance
appreciate
appropriate

arctic
arguing 152
argument
arise
arising 152
arithmetic
around
arouse
arranging 152
arrangement
arriving 152
arrival 152
article
ascend
ascends 158
ascent
   assent (*agreement*)
assassin
assassinate
association
athlete (two syllables)
athletic
athletics
attack (present)
attacked (past)
attendance
audience
auxiliary
awkward
bachelor
balance
banana
Baptist
baptize
barbarous
bare
barely
baring
barring
based
bearing
becoming
before
beggar 149
believe 159
benefit
benefited

berth (*bed*)
   birth (*beginning of life*)
boarder (*one who boards*)
border (*edge*)
born ("I was born in 1890")
borne ("borne by the
   wind"; "She has borne
   a son")
boundary
breath (noun)
breathe (verb)
bridal (*nuptial*)
bridle (*for a horse*)
brilliant
Britain (*the country*)
Britannia
Briton (*a native*)
Britannica
buoyant
bureaus
burglar
buries 155
bus (*omnibus*)
   Buss means *kiss*
business 155a,
cafeteria
calendar
candidate
can't
canvas (*cloth*)
canvass (*review*)
capital (*city*)
capitol (*building*)
career
carry
carriage 155a
   (*Cf. marry, marriage*)
caucus
ceiling
cemetery
certain
change
changing 152
changeable 153
chaperon
characteristic
chauffeur

chautauqua
choose
choosing 152 } (present)
chose } (past)
chosen }
chord (*of music*)
cord (*string*)
clothes (*garments*)
cloths (*kinds of cloth*)
coarse (*not fine*)
    course (*path, series*)
colonel
column
coming 152
commission
commit
committed 150
committee 149
committing 150
comparative
comparatively
compel
compelled
competent
complement   (*completing
    part*)
compliment   (*pleasing
    speech*)
complimentary (*gracious*)
comrade
comradeship
concede 158*a*. See *precede*.
conceit 159
conceive 159
confidant (noun)
confidence
confident (adjective)
confidently
    confidentially (*secretly*)
connoisseur
conquer
conqueror
conscience (*inner guide*)
conscientious
conscientiousness
conscious (*aware*)
consciousness

considered
contemptible (*worthy o
    scorn*)
contemptuous (*scornful*)
continuous
control
controlled 150
cool
coolly 156*b*
copy
copied 155
copies 151, 155
corps (*squad*)
corpse (*dead body*)
costume (*dress*)
    custom (*manner*)
council (noun, *assembly*)
councilor (*member of a coun-
    cil*)
counsel (noun, *legal advice,
    adviser*)
counsel (verb, *to advise*)
counselor (*adviser*)
country
courteous
courtesy
creep
crept
criticism
criticize
cruelty
cylinder
dealt
debater
deceased (*dead*)
    diseased (*ill*)
deceit 159
deceive 159
decide
decision
deep
defendants
definite
definite
dependant (noun)
dependent (adjective)
depth

descend
descends 158
descent (*slope*)
  decent (*proper*)
    dissent (*disagreement*)
describe
describing 158
description
desert (*waste place*)
  dessert (*food*)
despair
desperate
destroys
develop (preferable to *develope*)
device (noun)
devise (verb)
diary (*daily record*)
  dairy (*milk room*)
dictionary
die
dying 156
difference
different
digging
dining room 152
dinning
diphtheria
dirigible
disappear (dis+appear)
disappoint (dis+appoint)
disaster
disastrous
discipline
disease
diseased. See *deceased*
dissatisfied
dissipate
distribute
divide
doctor
don't
dormitories 154
dual (*twofold*)
duel (*fight*)
dying
ecstasy

effect. See *affect*
eight
eighth
elicit (*to draw out*)
  illicit (*unlawful*)
eliminate
embarrass
eminent
emphasize
encouraging
enemy
enemies 154
equipped
ere (*before*)
  e'er (*ever*)
especially
etc. (*et cetera*)
everybody
exaggerate
exceed
excellence
excellent
except
exceptionally
excess. See *access*
exercise
exhaust
exhilarate
existence
expense
experience
explanation
extraordinary
facilities
familiar
fascinate
February
fiery
finally 156*b*
financier
forbode
foreboding 152
forehead
foreign
foremost
forfeit
formally (*ceremoniously*)

formerly (*at a former time*)
forth (*forward*)
    fourth (*4th*)
forty. But —
    four
    fourteen
    fourth
frantically
fraternities 154
freshman (adjective)
freshman (noun, singular)
freshmen (noun, plural)
friend
fulfill *or* fulfil
furniture
gambling (*wagering*)
gamboling (*frisking*)
gauge *or* gage
ghost
government
grabbing 150
grammar
grandeur
grief 159
grievous
guard
guess
guidance
handkerchief
handsome
harass
having 152
hear (verb)
    here (adverb)
height
heinous
hinder
hindrance
hop
hopping 150
hope
hoping 152
human (*of mankind*)
humane (*merciful*)
humorous
hurried 155

hypnotize
hypocrisy
imaginary
imagining 152
imitation
immediately
impetuosity
impromptu
incident (*occurrence*)
    incidence (*way a thing falls or strikes* — scientific term)
incidentally
incredible
incredibly
independence
independent
indictment
indispensable
infinite
ingenious (*clever*)
ingenuous (*frank*)
innocence
instance (*occasion*)
instant (*moment*)
intellectual
intelligence
intentionally
intercede
invitation
irrelevant
irresistible
itself
knowledge
laboratory
laid
later (*subsequent*)
latter ("the former, the latter")
lead (*metal*)
led (past tense of *lead*)
legitimate
lessen (*make less*)
lesson
liable
library
lightning (noun)

likely
literature
livelihood 155*a*
liveliness 155*a*
loneliness 155*a*
loose (adjective)
lose (verb)
lying
maintain
maintenance
maneuver
mantel (*chimney shelf*)
mantle (*cloak*)
maual
manufacture
manufacturer
marriage 155*a*
marries
mathematics
mattress
meant
metal (*e.g., iron*)
mettle (*spirit*)
millionaire
miniature
minute
mischievous
misspelled
momentous
murmur
muscle
mystery
mysterious
naïve
naphtha
necessary
negroes
neither
nine
nineteen
ninety
ninetieth. But *ninth*
noticeable 153
notoriety
nowadays
nucleus
oblige
obstacle
occasion
occasionally
occur
occurred 150
occurring 150
occurrence 149
officer
omit
omitted
omission
oneself
operate
opportunity
optimism
origin
outrageous
overrun
pageant
paid
pamphlet
parallel
paralysis
parliament
parliamentary
particularly
partner
passed (verb, past tense of *pass*)
past (adjective, adverb, and preposition)
pastime
peace
perceive 159
perform
perhaps
permissible
perseverance
personal (*private*)
personnel (*persons collectively employed*)
persuade
Philippines. But *Filipino*
physical
physician
plan
planned 150

plain (adjective, *clear, simple*)
plain (noun, *flat region*)
plane (adjective, *flat*)
plane (noun, geometric term; *carpenter's tool*)
pleasant
politics
pore (*read intently*)
pour
possess
possible
practically 156*b*
practice (noun and verb)
prairie
precede 158*a*
prece'dence
pre'cedents
preference 150
prejudice
preparation
presence
presents (*gifts*)
principal 160
principle 160
privilege
probably
proceed. See *precede*
professor (pro+fessor)
promenade
pronunciation
prove
pumpkin
pursue
quiet (*still*)
quite (*entirely*)
quiz
quizzes 149
really 156*b*
recede 158*a*. See *precede*
receipt
receive 159
recognize
recommend
reference 150
referred 150
reign (*rule*)

rein (*of a bridle*)
religion
religious
repetition
replies
representative
reservoir
respectfully (*with respect*)
respectively (*as relating to each*)
restaurant
rhetoric
rheumatism
rhyme
rhythm
ridiculous
right
rite (*ceremony*)
sacrificing 152
sacrilegious
safety
sandwich
scene
schedule
secretary
seize
separate
sergeant
severely
shining 150
shone (past of *shine*)
    shown (past participle of *show*)
shriek
siege 159
similar
simultaneous
sincerely
site (*place*)
    cite (*refer to*)
    sight (*view*)
soliloquy
sophisticated
sophomore (three syllables)
specimen
speech. But *speak*

statement
stationary (adjective) *place*
stationery (noun) *writing*
statue (*monument*)
stature (*height*)
statute (*law*)
stopping
stops
stretch
studying 155*a*
succeed 158*a*. See *precede*
suffrage
suit (*of clothes*)
suite (*of rooms*)
superintendent
supersede 158*a*. See *precede*
suppress
sure
surprise
syllable
symmetry
symmetrical
temperament (four syllables)
temperature (four syllables)
tendency
their (possessive of *they*)
there ("here and there")
there (expletive; *e.g.*, "there is no use")
therefor (Cf. *thereof, thereby, therein*)
therefore (*for that reason*)
thorough
thousandths
threw (past tense of *throw*)

through (preposition and adverb)
to ("Go *to* bed")
too ("*Too* bad!" "Me *too!*")
two (2)
together
track (*mark*)
tract (*area*)
tragedy
tries
truly
Tuesday
typical
tyrannically
undoubtedly
unprecedented
until. But *till*
usage
use
using 152
usually
vengeance
village
villain
weather
  whether (*which of two*)
weird 159
who's (*who is*)
whose
woman (singular)
women (plural)
writer
writing 152
written
yacht
you're (*you are*)

EXERCISE 84

Sentences to be written at dictation: 1. The embarrassed sophomore proceeded with his impromptu speech. 2. The principal danger, he believed, was that his partner would lose his self-possession. 3. He was not surprised; similar incidents had often occurred formerly. 4. The courageous villain proved equal to the occasion. 5. The prisoner,

Dictation exercises in spelling

after bribing the guard, slipped out and disappeared across
the boundary.   6. The officer rapidly pursued him, firing
as he ran.   7. Too much riding and driving had a bad
effect on his studies.   8. Occasionally he committed deceitful and unbecoming acts in the course of his business.
9. The operation of the new rule will affect the legal profession beneficially.   10. The necessity of thorough preparation will incidentally have a good effect on the law
schools.   11. Macaulay is recognized universally as the
equal of any preceding writer of history.   12. An awkward
question of privilege arising, the matter was referred tem-
porarily to a committee.   13. The effect of the young
orator's speech was instantaneous.   14. The village is
laid out symmetrically according to a plan similar to
that already referred to.   15. There are numerous speci-
mens of his writing in the libraries of all the principal
cities.   16. He who relies on the word of a sophomore or
a professor is sure to be disappointed.   17. Don't lose
sight of the principles of grammar.   18. The principal of
the grammar school advised his boys to arrange occasionally for games with teams in neighboring cities.   19. After
conferring with the principal creditors, I was led to believe
that they were planning to bring suit for the payment of
both the interest and the principal of the mortgage.
20. I could not keep any discipline among them, surprised
and terrified as they were. I therefore divided them into
two separate parties and led them to a quiet place where
they might have an opportunity to recover their self
possession.   21. Without stopping to care for their dying
comrades, the forty guardsmen, ill equipped as they were,
went running up the sloping field, hemmed in the sentries,
seized the outposts, and compelled the enemy to sur-
render.   22. Proving utterly unmanageable, he was
whipped and finally expelled.   23. Having examined the
case, I feel hopeful for his life; it must be admitted,
however, that he may lose an arm.   24. The French
messenger hurried on, hoping to outstrip the English
spy; but the horse on which the latter was riding was
comparatively fresh, and soon had disappeared round a
bend in the road.   25. First I tried to advise him, but
he would take no advice. Later, I applied a walking stick.

to his back. This had a more beneficial effect than advice.
26. The priest, placing his hands on the altar, murmured
some mysterious sentences in the Indian language. 27. I
perceived that the road led to a dense forest. 28. The
woman's tears did not affect his decision; he still pursued
his original purpose. 29. If you happen accidentally to
lose a receipt, he denies having received the money and
tries to collect again. I can't conscientiously recommend
him. 30. The rain was beginning to fall, and the lightning flashed continually. 31. The principal street of the
village is parallel to the railroad. 32. There are few
writers who have never committed a misspelling.

**163. The members of each of the following expres-
sions should be written as separate words:**

(margin note: Incorrect uniting of separate words)

all ready	in fact
(already *means* previously)	in order
	in spite
all right	near by
any day	(on the) other hand
any time	per cent (*but* percentage)
by and by	*pro tempore*
by the bye	some day
by the way	some way
each other	any one
every day	every one
en route	some one
every time	no one
ex officio	

NOTE. — The members of the expressions *a while, any
way* and *some time* should be written as separate words
when *while, way,* and *time* are used as nouns; but each
expression should be written as a single undivided word
when it is used as an adverb.

EXERCISE 85

Write the following sentences, filling each blank with
a while or *awhile*. After each sentence state in parenthesis
the construction of the expression supplied. 1. Stay ——
longer. 2. —— ago there were not any houses here.
3. He stood —— in thought. 4. I'll try it for —— and
see how it works. 5. I'll try it ——. 6. You'd better
sleep ——.

(margin note: Awhile and a while)

EXERCISE 86

Sometime and some time

Write the following sentences, filling each bank with *some time or sometime*. After each sentence state in parenthesis the construction of the expression supplied. 1. I'll visit you ——— next summer. 2. There must have been a volcano here ———. 3. He came in last night and stayed ——— with us. 4. Be careful; ——— you'll get caught. 5. He pondered over the matter ———. 6. He pondered over the matter for ———. 7. ——— was spent in the examination of the books.

EXERCISE 87

Anyway and any way

Write the following sentences, filling each blank with *any way* or *anyway*. In parenthesis after each sentence, state the construction of the expression supplied. 1. ——— you arrange it will suit me. 2. I can't explain it in ———. 3. Well, ———, what's the difference? 4. I don't care, ———. 5. They could not find ——— to gain entrance. 6. I'm not anxious; for, ———, he knows how to swim.

164. Each of the following expressions should be written as a single undivided word:

myself	twofold
himself	steadfast
herself	extraordinary
itself	overcome
yourself	together
ourselves	without
yourselves	whenever
themselves	nevertheless
oneself	inasmuch
whatever	likewise
whichever	although
whoever	altogether
anything	throughout
something	somewhat
nothing	sometimes
anybody	somehow
everybody	moreover
somebody	thereupon
nobody	furthermore

upward	indoors
downward	upstairs
upright	beforehand
downright	overhead
beforehand	whereas
nowadays	notwithstanding

LEGIBILITY

165. Leave a liberal space between consecutive lines in a manuscript. Do not let the loops of *f's*, *g's*, *j's*, *q's*, *y's*, and *z's*, in any line descend below the general level of the loops of *b's*, *f's*, *h's*, *k's*, and *l's*, in the line below. (Compare Plates I and II.)

Space between lines

166. Do not crowd consecutive words close together. (Compare Plates I and II.)

Space between words

167. Between a period, a question mark, an exclamation mark, a semicolon, a colon, a word immediately before a direct quotation, the last word of a direct quotation — between any of these and a word following on the same line, leave double the usual space between words. (See Plate II, lines 1, 2, 3, and 9; and compare the corresponding places in Plate I.)

Extra space after period, etc.

167a. In a typewritten theme, leave two spaces between a period, question mark, or exclamation mark at the end of a sentence and the word following on the same line. After a comma, semicolon, or colon, leave one space.

Spaces in typewritten matter

168. Do not crowd marks of punctuation close to one another or to the words next them. (See Plate I, lines 1, 2, and 9, and compare the corresponding places in Plate II.)

Crowding marks of punctuation

1   You may well ask "What are his
2   qualifications?" qualifications indeed!
3   He goes round. He really presents this life in
4   a perpetuity too.
5   Doubtless this one is fine —in fact
6   qualification to grade qualities;
7   but still this ability the was through college
8   represent our of the worth justifies
9   the principle stage of ... to disparage
10   a citizen for no other reason than that he
11   is up going man very eagerly in ...
12   that to fulfil during the functions of our ...
13   mean in this abstract certainly ...
14   certain experience! Calling experience first
15   of the ability ... is intelligent life, and
16   from the study of ... order ... during
17   this knowledge, this experience, this familiarity."

PLATE I

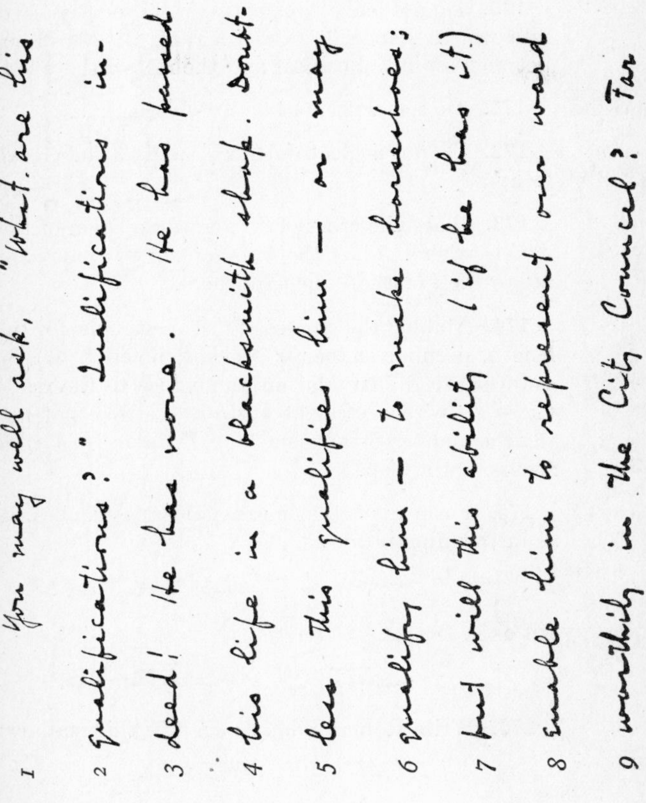

1 You may well ask, "What are his

2 qualifications?" Qualifications in-

3 deed! He has none. He has passed

4 his life in a blacksmith shop. Doubt-

5 less this qualifies him — in many

6 qualify him — to make horseshoes;

7 but will this ability (if he has it)

8 enable him to represent our ward

9 worthily in the City Council? Far

PLATE II

Crowding at bottom of page

169. Do not crowd the writing at the bottom of page; take a new page.

Gaps between letters

170. Do not leave gaps between consecutive letter in a word. Especially avoid leaving a wide interva between an initial capital and the rest of the word.

Oblique *and*

171. Do not write *and* on an oblique line.

Dots and cross-strokes

172. Do not neglect dotting *i*'s and *j*'s and crossin *t*'s and *x*'s.

173. Place the cross of a *t* across the stem of the *t* not elsewhere. Place the dot of an *i* or a *j* immediatel above the *i* or the *j*, not elsewhere.

174. Making the crosses of *t*'s conspicuous for thei length, peculiar shape, or peculiar direction is a hin drance to legibility and an annoyance to the reader Cross a *t* with a straight horizontal stroke not mor than a quarter of an inch long. Make a *t* a close stroke, not a loop.

Shape of quotation marks and apostrophes

175. Form quotation marks and apostrophes, no as in this illustration:

Ann's motto is "What's the use?"

but as in this:

Ann's motto is "What's the use?"

Shape of Roman numbers

176. Write Roman numbers, not in this manner:

II, III, IV, VIII, IX

but in this:

II, III, IV, VIII, IX.

177. In forming a letter do not decorate with flour-
ishes not necessary for identifying it, or with shading.
Avoid especially such forms as the following:

Prefer plain forms like the following:

Conspicu-
ous orna-
ment

ARRANGEMENT OF MANUSCRIPT

The Manuscript as a Whole

178. The paper for composition should be unruled,
unless special circumstances, such as the regulations
of a class, require the contrary. The writing should
be done either with a typewriter or with black, or
blue-black, ink. Only one side of each sheet of paper
should be written on. A manuscript should never be
rolled; it should go to its destination either flat, or
folded as simply as possible.

Writing
materials

Only one
side of
paper to be
used
Rolling not
permissible

Pages

179. The pages of a manuscript should be numbered at the top, in Arabic, not Roman numbers.

Page num-
bers

180. The title should be written at least two inches
from the top of the page. Between the title and the
first line of the composition, at least an inch should
intervene.

Position of
title

181. The first line of each page should stand at
least an inch from the top of the page.

Margin at
the top

182. There should be a blank margin of at least an
inch at the left side of each page.

Margin at
the left

Paragraphs

Mechanical Marks of a Paragraph

Indention:
Of ordinary paragraphs

183. In manuscript the first line of every paragraph should be indented at least an inch. (See Plate II, line 1.)

Of numbered paragraphs

184. No exception to the foregoing rule should be made when paragraphs are numbered.

> Wrong:
> I. What power has Congress to punish crimes?
> II. State in what cases the Supreme Court has original jurisdiction.
> III. How are presidential electors chosen? Would it be constitutional for a State legislature to choose them?

> Right:
> I. What power has Congress to punish crimes?
> II. State in what cases the Supreme Court has original jurisdiction.
> III. How are presidential electors chosen? Would it be constitutional for a State legislature to choose them?

Irregular indention

185. The first lines of all paragraphs should begin at the same distance from the margin; do not indent the beginning of one paragraph an inch, that of another two inches, that of another half an inch, etc.

Incorrect indention

186. Only the first line of a prose paragraph should be indented, except for special reasons as for instance in 212, 213, 214.

Incorrect spacing out

187. After the end of a sentence do not leave the remainder of the line blank unless the sentence ends a paragraph; begin the next sentence on the same line, if there is room. This rule is violated in Plate I, line 4.

Division of a Composition into Paragraphs

Paragraphing as an Aid to Clearness

188. Paragraphing, if properly employed, gives the reader as much assistance in understanding a whole composition as punctuation gives him in understanding a sentence. Parts of a composition that are distinct in topic may by paragraphing be made distinct to the eye also — an effect that decidedly promotes clearness. For instance, suppose an essay on Queen Elizabeth discusses three topics: (1) Elizabeth's personal character, (2) her character as a ruler, and (3) her popularity with her subjects. To embody the three passages corresponding to these three topics in separate paragraphs makes evident at once the beginning and the end of each passage, and thus enables the reader to grasp without effort the structure of the essay. On this consideration are based the following rules (189–193): *The fundamental principle*

189. A passage entirely distinct in topic from what precedes and follows should (except when Rule 207 applies) be written as a separate paragraph. *Applications: (i) Paragraphing of distinct parts*

Thus, suppose an essay on gasoline engines presents —

> (*m*) An explanation of the operation of gasoline engines.
> (*n*) An estimate of gasoline engines as compared with other kinds of engines.

Parts *m* and *n* should be embodied in separate paragraphs. Suppose a story tells —

> (*m*) The hero's visit to the bank and his transactions there.
> (*n*) What was happening meanwhile at the hero's factory.

Parts *m* and *n* should be embodied in separate para graphs.

Paragraphs of introduction and conclusion

190. A passage that serves as an introduction or conclusion to a composition consisting of several paragraphs should be paragraphed separately, even if it consists of only one or two sentences.

Correct paragraphing:
> The large body of recent State legislation compelling railway companies to reduce passenger fares, though it probably sprang from good intentions, is likely to have three unfortunate consequences.
>
> [*The main body of the essay consists of three paragraphs, each discussing one of the three unfortunate consequences.*]
>
> One cannot foretell, of course, how many years will elapse before these three results of the recent railway legislation will work themselves out; it may be five years, or it may be a dozen. But that they will sooner or later work themselves out seems, in the light of history, practically certain.

Paragraphs of transition

191. A passage that serves merely to make a transition from one group of paragraphs to a following group should be paragraphed separately.

Correct paragraphing:
> [*The achievements of Macaulay as a man of letters are discussed for three or four paragraphs.*]
>
> Macaulay's political achievements, though less distinguished than his literary achievements, are worthy of a somewhat detailed notice.
>
> [*Two or three paragraphs follow, dealing with Macaulay's political career.*]

Paragraphing of direct quotations

192. In narratives, as a rule, any direct quotation together with the rest of the sentence of which it is a part, should be paragraphed separately.

Right:

There were no takers. Not a man believed him capable of the feat. Thornton had been hurried into the wager, heavy with doubt; and now that he looked at the sled itself, the concrete fact, with the regular team of ten dogs curled up in the snow before it, the more impossible the task appeared. Mathewson waxed jubilant.

"Three to one," he proclaimed. "I'll lay you another thousand at that figure, Thornton. What d'ye say?"

Thornton's doubt was strong in his face, but his fighting spirit was aroused — the fighting spirit that soars above odds, fails to recognize the impossible, and is deaf to all save the clamor for battle. He called Hans and Pete to him. Their sacks were . . .

193. Rule 192 should be especially observed in the report of a conversation; each speech, regardless of length, should be paragraphed separately.

Dialogue

Wrong:

"When did you arrive?" I asked. "An hour ago," he answered. "Didn't you get my letter?" "No." "Strange," he said.

Right:

"When did you arrive?" I asked.

"An hour ago," he answered. "Didn't you get my letter?"

"No."

"Strange," he said.

194. Observe that in order to paragraph an isolated quotation separately (as is done in the example under Rule 192), the line following the quotation must be indented.

Indention after a quotation

195. A quotation may be detached by paragraphing from the introductory expression (*e.g.*, *he said*) if this expression precedes it.

Indention in the midst of a sentence

Right:
> Mr. Peggotty looked around upon us and nodding
> his head with a lively expression animating his face
> said in a whisper,
> "She's been thinking of the old 'un."

But a quotation should not be so detached from the
introductory expression if the quotation does not close
the sentence.

Wrong:
> Thinking I could stand it if my friend could, I called
> out to him,
> "Come on. Who's afraid?" and started into the
> house.

Wrong:
> Thinking I could stand it if my friend could, I
> called out to him,
> "Come on. Who's afraid?"
> and started into the house.

Right:
> Thinking I could stand it if my friend could, I
> called out to him, "Come on. Who's afraid?" and
> started into the house.

(ii) Grouping of related parts

196. When several consecutive short passages present slightly different topics, yet collectively form a larger division of a composition, the distinctness and unity of the whole division should be made apparent, rather than the individuality of its parts. Hence the following rule:

Improper paragraphing of minute parts

197. Several consecutive short passages composing a larger unit of a composition should not be written each in a separate paragraph, but should be combined into one paragraph.

Thus in an essay on a steel factory, describing —

(*a*) The process of sheet-rolling,
(*b*) The process of rail-rolling,
(*c*) The process of casting,

part *b* should not be written as follows:

Steel ingots six feet long and six inches square were heated to a white heat in a large oven.

When sufficiently hot, an ingot was removed and taken on an endless chain to the first set of rollers.

These rollers were eighteen inches in diameter. When the ingot had been passed through them, it was a bar of steel ten feet long and five inches thick.

Then the bar of steel was put on another endless chain and taken to a second pair of rollers.

This process was continued, the bar being passed successively through five or six pairs of rollers.

It came from the last pair a red-hot rail of standard size.

It was next bent slightly so that the base was convex. This was to allow for unequal contraction in cooling.

The rail was now left to cool.

When cold, it was taken to the cold rollers and rolled perfectly straight.

The foregoing passage should be written as a single paragraph; and so should part *a* and part *c* of the same essay.

198. The beginning of a new paragraph naturally leads the reader to think that the discussion of a new topic is beginning. Therefore, to begin a new paragraph where the discussion of a new topic does not begin misleads the reader. Hence the following rule:

(iii) Paragraphing where there is no change of topic

199. A sentence that does not introduce a new topic but continues the topic of the preceding sentence should not be made to begin a new paragraph.

The paragraphing in the following passage, for example, is illogical and objectionable:

> The beauty of Fra Angelico's character has been the admiration of all who ever studied the life of that devout and gentle artist. He might have lived in ease and comfort, for his art would have made him rich; instead, he chose the cloister life.. Fra Angelico was gentle and kindly to all.
>
> He was never seen to display anger and if he admonished his friends, it was with mildness. . . .

In this passage, the discussion of the gentleness of Fra Angelico begins in the sentence " Fra Angelico was gentle," etc.; the sentence " He was never," etc., continues the discussion of this topic — does not introduce a new topic. Hence, there should be no paragraph division where one now stands; the sentence " He was never," etc., should follow without a break.

(iv) Unity of a paragraph

200. A paragraph, by its visible detachment from what precedes and follows, suggests the unity of the passage it embodies. A passage not having unity should therefore not be put into one paragraph and thus presented under the guise of unity. Hence the following rule:

201. See that every paragraph has one central topic, under which all the statements in the paragraph logically fall.

Paragraphing for Emphasis

Sentences made conspicuous by detachment

202. A sentence or a short passage which the writer wishes to make especially emphatic may be paragraphed separately.

Thus, in the following passage the italicized part does not require to be paragraphed as being distinct from the preceding part; but it may properly be set apart for emphasis.

Indefinite narrative should not be entirely avoided; it is useful, and for some purposes is preferable to concrete narrative. Parts of a story that are not of dramatic interest, speeches that are of no interest or importance, — these may properly be conveyed by indefinite rather than by concrete narrative. But remember this:

Actions occurring at important points of a story should be related by concrete, not indefinite narrative.

Paragraphing for Ease in Reading

203. Reading an extended composition or passage in the text of which there are no breaks to rest the eye is fatiguing. Hence the following rules (204 and 205):

Unbroken text fatiguing

204. A composition more than 300 words long should not be written without paragraphing.

Neglect of paragraphing

205. A passage more than 300 words long, even if it constitutes a single unit of the composition, should usually not be written as a single paragraph, but should be divided into two or three paragraphs of convenient length (*i.e.*, not longer than 200 words).

Paragraphs too long

Thus, an essay on Lincoln, presenting —

1. A narrative of his life (350 words)
2. An estimate of his greatness (100 words)

should not be written as two paragraphs corresponding to the two main divisions of the material, but should be paragraphed in some such way as the following:

¶ Events of life up to 1860 (200 words)
¶ Career as president (150 words)
¶ Estimate of his greatness (100 words)

Over-fre-
quent para-
graphing

206. On the other hand, it should be remembere
that reading a passage not more than about 200 word
long is not fatiguing to the ordinary reader, and tha
over-frequent paragraphing annoys as much as lack o
any paragraphing fatigues.   Hence in the followin
rules (207 and 208):

207. A composition no longer than 150 word
should usually be written without any paragrap
divisions.

208. Do not paragraph with needless frequency an
without good reason.

Writing Verse

Left-over
parts of
lines

209. If an entire line of poetry cannot be writte
on one line of the page, the part left over should b
placed as shown below:

> Right:
> Lombard and Venetian merchants with deep-lade
> argosies;
> Ministers from twenty nations; more than roya
> pomp and ease.
> Wrong:
> Lombard and Venetian merchants with deep-lade
> argosies;
> Ministers from twenty nations; more than roya
> pomp and ease.

Grouping
of verse
into lines

210. A quotation of poetry should be grouped int
lines exactly as the original is grouped.

> Bad:
> Once to every man and nation
> Comes the moment to decide
> In the strife of truth with falsehood for the
> Good or evil side.

Right:

> Once to every man and nation comes the moment
> to decide
> In the strife of truth with falsehood for the good or
> evil side.

211. A quotation of verse occurring in a prose composition should begin on a new line. The prose following such a quotation should also begin on a new line, indented if it begins a new paragraph, flush with the left-hand margin if it continues the paragraph containing the quotation. But a single phrase, a part of a line, may be quoted without beginning a new line.

Verse set apart on the page

Wrong:

> While Tennyson admits that sorrow may be for our ultimate advantage and that, as his great memorial says, "Men may rise on stepping stones
> > Of their dead selves to higher things,"
> > > yet he finds it impossible to get any present consolation from the thought.

Right:

> While Tennyson admits that sorrow may be for our ultimate advantage and that, as his great memorial says,
> > "Men may rise on stepping stones
> > Of their dead selves to higher things,"
> yet he finds it impossible to get any present consolation from the thought.

See also the first *Right* example under Rule 246; and see p. iv.

Extended Quotations of Prose

212. A passage of prose quoted from a written composition or a formal speech, if it is three or four sentences long or longer, should be set apart from the matter preceding and following it, in the same way as a quotation of verse (see Rule 211).

Extended quotations set apart on the page

Right:

The part of the letter of instructions providing for an examination of candidates I quote verbatim. This part is as follows:

"and that, furthermore, all candidates be examined as to their knowledge of constitutional law; that this examination be conducted in writing; and that the following questions, among others, be asked:

"1. What power has Congress to punish crimes?

"2. State in what cases the Supreme Court has original jurisdiction.

"3. How are presidential electors chosen? Would it be constitutional for a state legislature to choose them?"

These instructions, it will be perceived, leave the committee no discretion in regard to waiving the examination.

For other examples see Rules 137, 141, 199, 202.

Tabulated Lists

Indention **213.** In a list of items set down in tabular form, the first line of each item should extend farther to the left than the remaining lines of the item.

Wrong:

The principal powers of the President are —

(*a*) The power to conduct foreign affairs.

(*b*) The power to command the army and navy in time of war.

(*c*) The power to veto bills.

(*d*) The power to appoint officers (subject to the approval of the Senate).

Right:

The principal powers of the President are —

(*a*) The power to conduct foreign affairs.

(*b*) The power to command the army and navy in time of war.

(*c*) The power to veto bills.

(*d*) The power to appoint officers (subject to the approval of the Senate).

214. A list of items in tabular form should be set apart from the matter preceding and following it, in the same manner as a quotation of verse (see Rule 211).

Bad:
> Under this subject there are three important headings:
>> (*a*) Position of pronouns
>> (*b*) Use of connectives
>> (*c*) Position of phrases; all of which are to be carefully studied.

Right:
> Under this subject there are three important headings:
>> (*a*) Position of pronouns
>> (*b*) Use of connectives
>> (*c*) Position of phrases
> all of which are to be carefully studied.

NOTE. — Another way of correcting the errors above shown is to write the passage without tabulating the items; thus:

> Right: Under this subject there are three important headings: (*a*) Position of pronouns; (*b*) Use of connectives; and (*c*) Position of subordinate expressions; all of which are to be carefully studied.

For other illustrations see Rules 140, 189, 197.

ALTERATIONS IN MANUSCRIPT

215. Words to be inserted should be written above the line, and their proper position should be indicated by the sign ∧ (not " v ") placed below the line. Words so inserted should not be enclosed in parentheses or brackets unless these marks would be required were the words written on the line.

NOTE. — Obscurity results from writing an insertion in the manner shown in the *Bad* example below:

Bad: as an agreeable means
Although tennis is at present very popular ∧ it
of exercising the muscles,
probably will never rank with football as a game for
supremacy between colleges.

Right: as an agreeable means of exercising the muscles,
Although tennis is at present very popular ∧ it
probably will never rank with football as a game for
supremacy between colleges.

Right: as an agreeable means
Although tennis is at present very popular ∧ ~~it~~
of exercising the muscles, it probably
∧ ~~probably~~ will never rank with football as a game for
supremacy between colleges.

Erasure

216. Erasures should be made by drawing a line through the words to be canceled. Parentheses or brackets should not be used for this purpose.

Transposition

217. Words written in one place which are to be transposed to another should be canceled (see Rule 216) and inserted in the proper place by the method shown in Rule 215. No other method of transposition should be used.

Indicating a new paragraph

218. When it is desired that a word standing in the midst of a paragraph should begin a new paragraph, the sign ¶ should be placed immediately before that word. The change should not be indicated otherwise.

Canceling a paragraph division

219. A paragraph division should be canceled by writing " No ¶ " in the margin. The change should not be indicated otherwise.

PUNCTUATION

The Period (.)

Close of a sentence

220. Use the period —

(*a*) **After a complete declarative or imperative sentence.**

(*b*) **After an abbreviated word or a single or double**
initial letter representing a word; as *etc., viz., Mrs.,*
i.e., e.g., LL.D., pp.

NOTE. — It is scarcely practical to make a distinction
here between abbreviations and contractions. *Dr.* for
Doctor, Mr. for *Mister, Mrs.* for *Mistress* are usually
called abbreviations although they are shortened by the
omission of letters within the word. There is variation
in the use of the period after them.

EXERCISE 88

Write the following passage, putting a period at the end
of every complete independent predication, and capitalizing the word following every period.

Suddenly he felt his arm grasped a feeling of horror
swept over him some living thing thin rough flat icy and
slimy from the depth of the cavity had twined itself round
his arm its pressure was like that of a strap being drawn
tight in less than a second something had closed round his
wrist he drew back hastily but the power of motion had
almost left him he was nailed to the spot with his left hand
he grasped his knife which he had held between his teeth
and setting his back to the rock made a desperate effort to
withdraw his arm he only succeeded in loosening the
deadly clasp for a moment it immediately tightened again
a second object long and pointed issued from the cavity
it appeared for a moment to lick Gilliatt's naked chest
then it wound itself around him at the same time a terrible
sense of pain compelled every muscle of his body to quiver
a third whip-like shape issued from the rock and lashed his
body suddenly it fixed itself upon him as firmly as the
others had done a fourth object this one with the swiftness
of an arrow darted toward his stomach and clasped it
tightly it was impossible to tear away these four slimy
bands they enlaced his body immovably adhering by a
number of suckers a fifth long slimy object glided from the
cavity it passed by the others and wound itself around
Gilliatt's chest these whip-like ribbons were pointed at the
end they grew broader like the blade of a sword toward
the hilt all five evidently sprang from one center they

crept and glided over Gilliatt he felt their strange pre
sures he seemed to feel the suction of many miniatu
mouths these shifted their positions from time to ti
suddenly a huge slimy mass round and flattened issu
from the cavity it was the center to which these five lim
were attached like spokes of a wheel on the opposite si
of this center Gilliatt saw the commencement of thr
other limbs the ends of these three were concealed b
neath the rock in the middle of the slimy mass were tw
eyes these eyes were fixed on Gilliatt he knew that he w
in the clutches of a devilfish.

The Comma (,)

Direct ad-
dress

221. Use the comma —

(*a*) **To set off a substantive used in direct addres**

Right: Come here, my boy.
Right: For once, Tom, you are correct.
Wrong: For once, Tom you are correct.

Appositives

(*b*) **To set off appositives.**

Right: He introduced his uncle, Mr. Harris.
Right: We motored over to Greenfield, the count
seat, to see the annual fair.
Wrong: We motored over to Greenfield, the count
seat to see the annual fair.

NOTE. — An appositive used to distinguish its princip
from other persons or things called by the same nam
should not usually be separated from its principal b
punctuation.

Right: The poet Masefield. Charles the Bold. M
son Robert. The expression "Over the top."

Absolute
phrases

(*c*) **To set off absolute phrases.**

Right: The brakes being worn, we stopped barely i
time.
Right: I doubt whether they will come, the road
being so bad.
Right: It seems queer, the affair being as you say
that he should be angry.
Wrong: It seems queer, the affair being as you sa
that he should be angry.

(*d*) **To set off words, phrases, or clauses which have a parenthetic function, but for which parenthesis marks or double dashes are not suitable.** Especially to be observed are parenthetic phrases indicating the character or the connection of a statement — for example, *in the second place, of course, to tell the truth, for example, that is, in fact, I think, I believe, he says, I repeat.*

Right: Moreover, his story does not agree with yours.

Right: For example, this morning the toast was burned.

Right: This is very considerate of you, to say the least.

Right: The trip was, to tell the truth, rather a failure.

Right: The house stood, I believe, on this very spot.

Wrong: The house stood, I believe on this very spot.

NOTE 1.—For setting off a parenthetic expression, prefer commas to parenthesis marks where commas will make the sentence clear; but notice that the use of commas for this purpose may cause obscurity in some cases — particularly when the parenthetic expression is a complete sentence.

Obscure: By all appearances, of course this is a secret, he is likely to win.

Clear: By all appearances (of course, this is a secret) he is likely to win; [or] By all appearances — of course, this is a secret — he is likely to win [see Rule 236 *c*].

NOTE 2. — The comma as a rule is not used to set off *also, perhaps, indeed, therefore, of course, at least, in fact, nevertheless, likewise,* and other parenthetical expressions that do not require a pause in reading.

(*e*) **To set off a geographical name explaining a preceding name; to set off the number of a year defining a month or a day named immediately before; and to set off the items of a date or an address.**

Right: He lived in Summit, New Jersey.

Right: I returned on May 14, 1919.

Right: The wreck occurred on Friday, June 13, 1923.

Coördinate clauses joined by a conjunction

(f) Ordinarily to separate coördinate clauses joined by one of the pure conjunctions, *and, but, for, or, neither, nor.* (Cf. Rule 231 *b*.)

> Right: The telephone rang violently, but no one answered.
> Right: The question which lay before them, and which had been argued for weeks, was still unsettled.

Comma before *for*

NOTE 1. — The observance of the foregoing rule is especially important in the case of clauses connected by the coördinating conjunction *for*. Unless a comma is placed between such clauses, the *for* is liable to be mistaken momentarily for a preposition.

> Misleading: She was obliged to give up the dinner for her cook was leaving.
> Clear: She was obliged to give up the dinner, for her cook was leaving.

NOTE 2. — This rule concerns only coördinate *clauses* joined by conjunctions; it does not refer to a clause containing a compound predicate of two verbs.

> Comma unnecessary: He seized the rope, and hauled the boat alongside.
> Right: He seized the rope and hauled the boat alongside.

Dependent clauses

(g) As a rule, to set off a dependent clause preceding its principal clause. When the dependent clause follows the principal clause, a comma is not necessary if the clause is restrictive (see Rule 224), but a comma is usually required if the clause is non-restrictive. (But see Rule *h*, below, and Rule 231 *c*.)

> Right: When the ship is in, the lock is closed.
> Right: If you have time, telephone me from the station.
> Right: Telephone me from the station if you have time.
> Right: He was not in his room, though his light was burning.
> Right: I am very glad to subscribe, especially since Pryor is to contribute.

Right: He told us that the boat was ready.
Right: I do not know how it occurred, and I have no idea whether Harris was mixed up in it.

(*h*) **Usually, to set off an introductory adverbial phrase containing a verb.** One not containing a verb should usually not be followed by any mark of punctuation. (But see Rule *i*, below.) Distinguish between adverbial phrases, that is, phrases modifying a predicate, an adjective, or an adverb; and parenthetic phrases, that is, phrases which modify the whole statement. (See Rule *d*, above.)

Introductory adverbial phrases

Right: In order to live, we must eat.
Right: Despite his efforts to escape, he remained a prisoner.
Right: Upon opening the door, she smelled escaping gas. [Gerund phrase.]
Right: To succeed in your undertaking, you must follow your lawyer's advice. [Infinitive phrase.]
Right: After all the hardships he has suffered, he deserves some repose. [Phrase containing a clause.]
Right: In about an hour our belated friends arrived.

(*i*) **To indicate separation between any sentence-elements that might be improperly joined in reading, were there no comma.**

To prevent mistaken junction

Misleading: Ever since he has devoted himself to athletics.
Clear: Ever since, he has devoted himself to athletics.
Misleading: Inside the fire shone brightly.
Clear: Inside, the fire shone brightly.
Misleading: While we were washing the lieutenant a man for whom we had no affection, suddenly appeared.
Clear: While we were washing, the lieutenant, a man for whom we had no affection, suddenly appeared.
Ambiguous: He would not admit to himself that he loved her because she was wealthy.

Clear: He would not admit to himself that he loved her, because she was wealthy.

[A comma should be used before the adverbial *because* clause if the writer wishes to indicate that the clause does not modify the nearer verb.]

Ambiguous: He stepped up to his opponent shaking his fist under his nose.

Clear: He stepped up to his opponent, shaking his fist under his nose.

[Here the comma is used before the participle phrase to indicate that the phrase does not modify the nearest noun.]

For the comma before *such as,* see Rule 259; after *namely, that is,* etc., see Rule 260.

Consecutive adjectives

222. Two adjectives modifying the same noun should be separated by commas if they are coördinate in thought; but if the first adjective is felt to be superposed on the second, they should not be separated by a comma.

Right: A faithful, sincere friend. [The adjectives are coördinate in thought; both modify "friend."]

Right: A big gray cat. [The adjectives are not coördinate in thought; "gray" modifies "cat," but "big" modifies "gray cat."]

Series of the form *a, b,* and *c*

223. In a series of the form *a, b,* and *c,* a comma should precede the conjunction. The practice of omitting the comma before the conjunction is illogical and is not favored by the best modern usage.

Objectionable: There were blue, green and red flags.

[The punctuation here couples "green" and "red" and makes them appear to be set apart, as a pair, from "blue"; whereas the intention is to make all three adjectives equally distinct.]

Right: There were blue, green, and red flags.

For other examples, see the text of Rules, 3, 15, 31, 47, 122, 144 *b*, 145, 165, 174, 230.

224. (a) **A non-restrictive relative clause should be
set off by the comma; a restrictive relative clause
should not be set off by the comma** A non-restrictive
clause is a clause the omission of which would not
change the meaning of the main clause. (If it can
be *omitted*, it can be *set off by commas*.) A restrictive
clause is a clause the omission of which would change
the meaning of the main clause.

> Right: My old fountain pen, *which never leaked or
> clogged,* is broken. [Non-restrictive clause; can be
> omitted: "My old fountain pen is broken."]
> Right: A fountain pen *which leaks* is worse than none.
> [Restrictive clause; cannot be omitted: "A foun-
> tain pen is worse than none."]
> Right: Foch, whose genius won the war, was a
> theorist and a school-teacher. [Non-restrictive.]
> Right: The general whose genius won the war was a
> theorist and a school-teacher. [Restrictive.]

(b) **A non-restrictive phrase following its principal
should be set off by the comma; a restrictive phrase
following its principal should not be set off by the
comma.**

> Right: The ruined spire, *rising above the deserted
> village,* marked the end of our journey. [Non-
> restrictive.]
> Right: The tree standing in the corner of the garden
> was the favorite haunt of the children. [Restric-
> tive.]

EXERCISE 89

Write the following sentences, designating after each
one whether the relative clause is restrictive or non-restrictive, and omitting or inserting commas accordingly:
1. He committed a serious error in correcting which he
had much trouble. 2. He inquired of the man who had
charge of the gate. 3. The old gentleman across the aisle
who had been getting more and more nervous now stood

up. 4. In my grandfather's day the coach attained a speed of fifteen miles an hour which was the highest speed it ever attained. 5. Some sparks fell among the straw which covered the floor. 6. The days that I spent there were happy ones. 7. Tom Briggs whom I used to know when I was a boy is now a famous engineer. 8. Don't give up the advantages that you have gained. 9. The man who won the race is a junior. 10. The Brooklyn bridge which spans the East River has lately been repaired. 11. Here they found a number of brass cannon which they destroyed. 12. The book which we are reading has more in it than the Ethiopian's book. 13. The Bible which is a collection of books written at different times contains a wide range of literature. 14. Philip spoke of the historical background of the chapter which the man was reading. 15. The Nicene creed is a statement that was drawn up by the Council of Nicæa. 16. The locomotive that was used in 1840 looks ridiculously old-fashioned today. 17. There is no scientific theory which is not open to revision. 18. Not much is expected of those who have recently been initiated. 19. The great philosopher Plato who flourished long before the Christian era anticipated some of the teachings of Christ. 20. He that ruleth his temper is greater than he that taketh a city. 21. I am the Lord thy God that brought thee out of the land of Egypt. 22. Can you name the place where he is hiding and the persons who aided in his escape? 23. I detest a man who is snobbish. 24. A woman who uses rouge is a deceiver. 25. Suggest some book that would be suitable for a birthday present. 26. Those who cannot swim should keep away from the water. 27. A painting that one does not get tired of is extremely rare. 28. One of the most beautiful chapters is the one in which the still, small voice is spoken of. 29. The friends who tell us the truth are not always those we enjoy most. 30. A photographer who delivers his pictures when they are promised is sure to get rich. 31. My early education was given me by my parents who taught me my A B C's and my numbers. 32. The spokes should be made of ash which for this purpose is better than oak. 33. He married Cynthia Neckington who though she was beautiful had a temper that made his life miserable. 34. I resign in favor of Mr. Anselm Gregory for whom I ask your hearty support. 35. The battle was won by Admiral Dewey about whom little had up to that time been generally known.

225. After an interjection which is intended to be only mildly exclamatory, use a comma rather than an exclamation point. *With interjections*

> Right: Oh, come; you'd better.
> Right: But alas, this was not the case.

226. Separate a short direct quotation from the rest of the sentence by a comma. (Cf. Rule 233. For other rules of punctuation with quotation marks, see Rule 261.) *Before quotations*

> Right: He said with a frown, "They are acting sus-
> piciously."
> Right: "You are entirely mistaken," she retorted.

227. Guard against the use of commas where they are not necessary. Especially, do not put a comma between a verb and its subject. As a rule, do not put a comma where no pause is made in reading. *Unnecessary commas*

228. Do not put a comma, or any other mark of punctuation, before the first member of a series of sentence-elements, unless it would be required there if one element, instead of a series, followed. *Misuse before a series*

> Wrong: During my senior year I studied, Latin,
> Greek, and chemistry.
> Right: During my senior year I studied Latin, Greek,
> and chemistry.
> Wrong: It is valuable, (1) to the student, (2) to the
> statesman, and (3) to the merchant.
> Right: It is valuable (1) to the student, (2) to the
> statesman, and (3) to the merchant.
> For other examples, see the text of Rules 42, 43, 96,
> 113, 116, 137.

Misuse be-
fore a sub-
stantive
clause

229. Put no comma before a substantive clause introduced by *that* or *how* when the governing verb (such as *said, thought, supposed*) immediately or very closely precedes the clause.

Wrong: The boatswain said, that the wheel was damaged.

Right: The boatswain said that the wheel was damaged.

Wrong: I always supposed, that the foreman was to blame.

Right: I always supposed that the foreman was to blame.

Wrong: They told us, how they had escaped.

Right: They told us how they had escaped.

EXERCISE 90

GENERAL EXERCISES IN THE USE OF THE COMMA

Punctuate the following sentences correctly. After each sentence put the number of the rule which applies. 1. Ever since I have been a regular attendant at the theater. 2. However capable as he was he failed of his purpose. 3. He should as I said before read Pope's *Atticus*. 4. He is to say the least not trustworthy. 5. He is too weak however to keep any promise at all. 6. They all seemed I thought ashamed of the exhibition. 7. His eyes flashed as he drew his sword and his breath came short and quick. 8. He bought the land with his own money and his bank account was not extremely large either. 9. Mr. Blount was evidently anxious for his eyes kept wandering toward the door. 10. It is a very good story for the author is unusually clever and witty. 11. He is benefited by the new rules but yet he is discontented. 12. Dickens' *David Copperfield* which is my favorite novel is somewhat autobiographical. 13. I do not want books that instruct I want books that amuse. 14. It is strange that a play so tragic as *Lear* should give you pleasure. 15. The door flew open and Ralph Rackstraw covered with mud entered the church. 16. When a shotgun is brought in from the field it is usually dirty. 17. Since I had always before that time been so much alone it was not easy for me to make friends. 18. A few days after they sailed the boat sprang a leak. 19. There also was the village doctor a man of fifty years. 20. Thomas De Quincey author of *Joan of Arc* was an opium-eater. 21. A fine fellow a member of the yacht club was drowned. 22. My dear fellow what made you so careless? 23. The letter was addressed to Syracuse New York and dated May 19 1836. 24. The horse is the most useful of all animals to man. 25. I went away with a good picture of a Chinese laundry in my mind. 26. In the center is a stove around which a number of farmers laborers and boys were gathered. 27. No latest fashions or shimmering silks were displayed in that window. 28. I am glad to see you old man. 29. One day a poor old ragged tramp walked into the yard of a prosperous farm in Dane County and knocked timidly on the door. 30. She felt that she had been slighted. 31. When I used to carry my dinner pail to the little school at Nichol's Corner I felt very self-important. 32. He brought some flowers to Miss Miriam and her sister was jealous. 33. Tomorrow my dear I shall recieve a check. 34. I am not to tell the truth very fond of the game. 35. Indeed I shall take no such answer. 36. Alas it could never be true.

230. Do not use a comma between coördinate independent clauses that are not joined by one of the pure conjunctions, *and, but, for, or, neither, nor,* except when the clauses are short, have no commas within themselves, and are closely parallel in form and substance. Use a semicolon if it is rhetorically desirable to indicate close relationship between the clauses; otherwise use a period. This error is an inexcusable fault in writing, because, like the "period fault" (see Rule 24) it shows inability to recognize what constitutes a sentence. (See Rules 231 *a* and 231 *b*.)

Wrong: He had not the habit of concentration, this was the cause of his failure.

Right: He had not the habit of concentration; thi
was the cause of his failure.

Wrong: He threw the weapon from him, it clattere
noisily on the floor.

Right: He threw the weapon from him; it clattere
noisily on the floor.

Wrong: We have won for two years, if we win today
we retain the trophy.

Right: We have won for two years; if we win today
we retain the trophy.

Right: The curtains fluttered, the windows rattled
the doors slammed.

Exercise 91

The
"comma
fault," and
the con-
founding of
clauses and
sentences

Study Rules 24 and 230. Write the following sentence
and groups of sentences correctly punctuated and capi
talized: 1. Well I must go now good-bye I'll see you later
2. She knew nothing of the world her one duty being th
care of her father's house while her sister knew nothing o
household affairs and cared nothing for the quiet pleasure
of the fireside the opera the ballroom and the promenad
absorbing all her interest. 3. As soon as we had finishe
our lunch we jumped down into the pit this was th
entrance to the cave we had come to explore stooping a
little in order not to strike our heads on the low roof w
entered the cave the boys leading the way with thei
candles. 4. If one says "a black and white dog" on
means one dog the coat of which is partly black and
partly white while if one says "a black and a white dog"
one means two dogs. 5. I suppose I must go if I don'
he'll be anxious. 6. A million dollars would yield ai
income quite sufficient for my needs and a little to spar
thus disposing of the great problem of earning a livin
allowing me also to devote myself to the good of othe
people. 7. The postman then approached he would surel
stop I thought. 8. Since this is the case I intend eithe
to continue my course in engineering or else at the end o
this year to drop this course and begin the study of lav
making a specialty in the latter case of economics an
history. 9. It was delightful to have no classes to atten
nothing to do but rest and read also to meet my ol

friends who had come back as I had to spend the vacation at home.   10. This belt runs very slowly and on it the pressman puts the papers they are then carried to the distributing room.   11. At three o'clock the second edition is printed none of this edition is sold in the city. 12. The first papers of the third edition go to the news-dealers these take from fifty to two thousand copies each next the newsboys get their ten or twenty copies each. 13. Should the railroad cut a man's land the man generally has the company agree to build a pass under the track or a roadway over it thus giving the owner easy access to the two fields separated by the track.   14. If that were my good fortune I should surely go next summer to Eng-land the country in which my father was born and which I have always longed to visit also to Switzerland for I am certain I should excel in mountain climbing.   15. After they have decided upon the route they send out two parties of surveyors the first party takes surface measure-ments and drives stakes with the measurements written on them this party also keeps a careful record of all the measurements marked on the stakes.   16. Grout is next thrown in and tamped and leveled this forms the body of the sidewalk.

The Semicolon (;)

231. Use the semicolon —

(*a*) **Between clauses of a compound sentence that are not joined by a conjunction.**

> Right: He did not go to Canada; he went to Mexico.
> For other examples see the text of Rules 10, 20, 40, 42, 84, 88, 93, 158.

NOTE. — As a means of combining sentences into com-pound sentences, the semicolon may easily be abused. A series of sentences should not be grouped together in this way unless the compound sentence so formed has a dis-tinct and readily-felt unity.

(*b*) **Between clauses of a compound sentence that are joined by one of the conjunctive adverbs *so, there-fore, hence, however, nevertheless, moreover, accord-***

Between clauses of a compound sentence

Caution

Before *so, therefore,* etc.

ingly, besides, also, thus, then, still, otherwise, **and** *in* **fact.**

> Wrong: I saw no reason for moving, therefore I stayed still.
>
> Right: I saw no reason for moving; therefore I stayed still.

> Wrong: He went below and lit the fuse, then he returned to the deck.
>
> Right: He went below and lit the fuse; then he returned to the deck.

Conjunctive adverbs distinguished from simple conjunctions

NOTE. — Good usage makes a clear distinction, as regards punctuation, between conjunctive adverbs and simple coördinating conjunctions (e.g., *and, but, or, for*). A comma is ordinarily used (see Rule 221 *f*) between clauses of a compound sentence that are connected by a simple conjunction; but a comma should emphatically not be used between clauses connected by a conjunctive adverb. Compare the two following sentences:

> Right: The president bowed, and Hughes began to speak.
>
> Right: The president bowed; then Hughes began to speak.

Before *and, but,* **etc. in certain cases**

(*c*) **Ordinarily, between the clauses of a compound sentence that are joined by a simple conjunction when these clauses are somewhat long, or are subdivided by commas.** See, for example, the second sentence of the foregoing note, and also the text of the notes under Rules 14 and 88.

Between involved sentence-members

(*d*) **To separate two or more coördinate members of a simple or complex sentence when those members, or some of them, have commas within themselves.**

> Right: He said that he had lent his neighbor an ax; that on the next day, needing the ax, he had gone to get it; and that his neighbor had denied borrowing it. [The three objects of "said" are separated not by commas, as ordinarily three objects of

verb should be, but by semicolons, because one of the objects has commas within itself.]

For other examples see the text of Rules 134, 135, and 137.

(e) **To separate any two members of a simple or complex sentence when, for any reason, a comma would not make the relation between them immediately clear.**

Instead of a comma, to prevent obscurity

> Misleading: If I were a millionaire, I would have horses, and motors, and yachts, and the whole world should minister to my pleasure.
>
> Clear: If I were a millionaire, I would have horses, and motors, and yachts; and the whole world should minister to my pleasure.
>
> See also the sixth sentence in the text of Rule 140 and the first in the text of Rule 142.

EXERCISE 92

Write the following sentences, properly punctuated: 1. These screws control the reticule hence they are called reticule screws. 2. I objected to the plan however since he was bent on it I yielded. 3. A hot fire is necessary therefore a strong draft must be provided. 4. The wood had been injured by warping moreover the metal parts were badly rusted. 5. Sickness delayed their moving therefore we did not get the house so soon as we had planned. 6. What you say is true nevertheless the thing is impossible. 7. The meerschaum becomes finally saturated with nicotine then there is less danger of its breaking. 8. All the cracks were filled with tow thus the craft was made seaworthy 9. She never laughed nor even smiled moreover her conversation was always of a melancholy tone. 10. She has conversed with Mirabeau hence she must be very old. 11. She wished my father to be informed accordingly I wrote to him that evening. 12. He continually reproached her and she was always offended at his reproaches thus their friendship rapidly grew cold. 13. I saw no reason for declining his invitation besides I enjoyed his society and wished to be with him longer.

Sentences or clauses introduced by so, therefore, etc.

14. He is a graduate of Oxford moreover he has traveled extensively on the continent. 15. She now discovered that she had dropped the letter somewhere in the street hence she felt very anxious lest her destination should be found out. 16. Neither would yield a step accordingly there was nothing to do but draw their swords. 17. He practised assiduously and constantly frequented Vougeot's studio thus he became fairly proficient. 18. I know because I saw him go out besides his room is empty as you see. 19. Chapman wasn't in the mood for a picnic moreover he disapproved of picnics on Sunday. 20. The chevalier has disavowed his claim hence the last difficulty is removed. 21. Alexander was sure he could persuade the old lady accordingly he called on her next day. 22. Adrienne was blonde, fat, and jolly thus she seemed well fitted for her part. 23. The old sergeant had a stock of interesting stories to tell me besides he was a good chess-player. 24. He'll get to the crossroads before I do still he can't do any harm there. 25. I have received no word from him for two weeks however I have no anxiety. 26. He is brave and strong and true nevertheless he cannot win against such a force as he has to contend with. 27. They were not decadent in fact they were eminently robust. 28. It is a most erratic production in fact I believe the author is a little insane.

EXERCISE 93

Semicolons to be inserted

Write the following expressions, placing a semicolon after the first predication in each: 1. You have had a temptation I will do you the justice to suppose it was a strong one. 2. The money drawer was open it suggested a means of escape. 3. John was not interested in this talk he stuck to his work and said nothing. 4. There was much to be done my bag was still to be packed and several good-bye calls must be made. 5. My correspondent happened to know Nicholson he and Nicholson were members of the Cliquot Club. 6. He was at home again presently he would see his father. 7. My master is not in sir he is staying at his house in Murrayfield. 8. He can't be rich no man gets rich at that trade. 9. My visit was unfortunately timed the lady it appeared was undergoing a shampoo.   10. The lodge seemed deserted not a light could be seen in any window.   11. He knocked there was no answer.   12. A lighted candle stood on the gravel walk it threw sparkles on the holly bushes.   13. He rose to go this was evidently no place for him.   14. I have not come to amuse you I have come to tell you some plain facts.   15. The gentleman has spoken of the easy way let us now consider the just way.

232. Do not use a semicolon between two members of a simple or complex sentence except in accordance with Rule 231 *d* or 231 *e*; use a comma if any punctuation is required at such a place.

Improper use in place of a comma

> Wrong: If you get no thanks from a person you have favored; you have no respect for him.
> Right: If you get no thanks from a person you have favored, you have no respect for him.
> Wrong: He was black-eyed; dark-complexioned; and altogether very handsome.
> Right: He was black-eyed, dark-complexioned, and altogether very handsome.

The Colon (:)

233. The colon should be used after a word, phrase, or sentence constituting an introduction to something that follows, such as a list, an extended quotation, or instances of a general statement preceding. It is the proper mark to follow the salutation of a business letter.

A sign of introduction.

> Right: There are three causes: poverty, injustice, and indolence.
> Right: Burke said in 1765: [A long quotation follows].
> Right: The case was this: I wouldn't and he couldn't.
> Right: He did it in the following way: First, he cut an ash bough, which he bent into a hoop. Then . . .
> Right: Dear Sir: Gentlemen: My dear Mr. Harris:

EXERCISE 94

Exercises in the use of the colon

Write the following expressions, correctly punctuating and capitalizing: 1. This is my commandment that ye love one another. 2. Our firm has offices in the following countries Austria, France, Italy, and Japan. 3. Success will be assured if you proceed in the following way first turn the paddle two or three times next pour in a few drops of oil. . . . 4. I should be convinced, but for this damning fact a frog was found in the milk can. 5. Figures of speech are divided into the following classes term figures, modal figures, and sentence and paragraph figures. 6. My statement is proved by this fact that when the door was opened, the odor of gin was perceived. 7. The means employed to move motor cars are these four gasoline, steam, electricity, and plow horses. 8. There be three things which are too wonderful for me — yea, four which I know not the way of an eagle in the air, the way of a serpent upon a rock, the way of a ship in the midst of the sea, and the way of a man with a maid. 9. For three things the earth is disquieted for a servant when he reigneth, for a fool when he is filled with meat, and for an odious woman. 10. Cicero then turned upon the traitor with these words "Quousque tandem, Catalina. . . . " 11. The text of Mr. Dunn's resolution is as follows "Whereas the Supreme Ruler of mankind has seen fit. . . . " 12. I will accept on this one condition that my power shall be absolute. 13. I can say this for him he knows a handsaw from a hawk. 14. The following facts we wish to cite in favor of the plan first the old plan has always proved exceedingly unsatisfactory the experience of President Colburn may serve as an illustration second the new plan is approved by the Reverend Dr. Mannering the most eminent modern authority on juvenile delinquency third . . .

The Question Mark (?)

Direct, not indirect questions

234. Use the question mark after a direct question, but not after an indirect question.

Bad: He asked what caused the accident?
Right: He asked what caused the accident.

Right: He asked, "What caused the accident?"
Right: Will he come? and how long will he stay?

234a. Use the question mark between parentheses to indicate that a statement is conjectural. It should not be used as a notice of humor or irony. (Cf. Rules 252 *e* and 292.)

Right: This event occurred in 411 B.C.(?)
Wrong: After his polite (?) remarks, we have nothing
to say.

Right: After his polite remarks, we have nothing to
say.

The Exclamation Mark (!)

235. Use the exclamation mark after a sentence, a virtual sentence, an exclamation in question form, or an interjection, to indicate strong emotion.

Right: I cannot and will not believe it!
Right: A pretty situation! What! How dare you
say so!

The Dash (—)

236. Use the dash —
(*a*) **When a sentence is abruptly broken off before its completion.**

Interruptions

Right: If the scythe is rusty — by the way, did you
get that scythe at Pumphrey's?

(*b*) **Instead of a comma, in case the comma would have been required had the matter between the dashes, or introduced by the dash, been omitted.**

Comma and dash

Right: Only one thing was wanting — a boat.
Right: If you should see him — you might meet him
on the train — give him my message.

Parenthetic
use

(*c*) **As a substitute for parenthesis marks.**

> Right: I dressed — you may not believe this, but it
> is true — in ten minutes.

With sum-
marizing
words

(*d*) **Before a word summarizing the preceding part
of a sentence.**

> Right: If you go to bed early, get up early, never
> loiter or trifle, always employ periods of enforced
> idleness in serious thought or instructive reading —
> if you do all this, you will be derided by the Omicron
> Pi Chi fraternity.

Before an
expression
having the
effect of an
after-
thought

(*e*) **Before a repetition or modification having the
effect of an afterthought.**

> Right: Oh yes, he was polite — polite as a Chester-
> field — obsequious in fact.

When a
sentence-
member is
set apart
on the page

(*f*) **After the word immediately preceding a sentence-element that is set apart on the page from the
first part of the sentence.** For illustration, see the
text of Rules 221, 231, 236, 240, 247, and 252, and
the *Right* examples under Rule 213.

> NOTE. — If another mark of punctuation precedes the
> sentence-member set apart, the dash may be dispensed
> with. See the *Right* examples under Rules 211 and 212.

Before ap-
positives

(*g*) **Before an appositive that is prepared for by the
preceding words; or before an appositive that is separated by several words from its principal substantive.**

> Right: I wish to ask regarding one particular law —
> the pension law.
> Right: One of my old class-mates hailed me on the
> street — a man named Roberts.

Indiscrimi-
nate use

**237. Do not use dashes indiscriminately, where
commas, periods, or other marks of punctuation belong.** The free use of dashes as substitutes for other

kinds of punctuation is a careless, slipshod, and debilitating practice that should be avoided like any excess.

Exercise 95

General Exercise in Punctuation

Write the following sentences, punctuating them correctly. After each mark of punctuation, write within brackets the number of the rule in accordance with which the mark is used. 1. On the south side for about fifty feet in it is divided into two stories. 2. It will never rank high as an intercollegiate game for the students find greater enjoyment in a contest between teams. 3. First of all let me say do not come here unless you have plenty of money for expenses are high. 4. I advise you however to investigate for yourself. 5. Ruling-pens like any other sharp instrument become dull with use. 6. When the instruments are laid away especially if they are not to be used for some time the compasses should be left open for otherwise they will lose their spring. 7. The better the health of the men is the more they can accomplish. 8. The benefit does not lie only in the development of individual students but it lies also in the good done to the college as a whole. 9. The report will spread to remote villages and people in the backwoods will be induced to seek the college. 10. The yard is bordered on the west side by a row of pine trees and other trees and shrubs are planted about the lawn. 11. Along the east side are a number of plum trees and several flower beds dot the lawn near by. 12. This statement was made to Mr. A. E. Storey chairman of the committee. 13. If our laws are not what they should be it is time they were amended. 14. While we were eating a child the son of one of the natives approached. 15. Some were armed with bolos but an order was given that no one should fire. 16. After the ship is in the upper gate of the lock is closed. 17. Bishop of Beauvais thy victim died in fire. 18. I slept very late slept in fact until noon. 19. The back of the table its square corners its size its heaviness these are features I did not perceive. 20. At the *séance* the following incident occurred a gauze robed figure gliding as it seemed from behind a screen said she was the spirit of my sister and fell on my neck.   21. This phenomenon has received a recognized name among alienists namely *aphasia*. 22. The great difference in fact between the two kinds of thinking is this that empirical thinking is reproductive but reasoning is productive.   23. It shone by its own light a strange thing to see.   24. We think that the premises of both controversialists were unsound that on these premises Addison reasoned well and Steele ill and that consequently Addison brought out a false conclusion while Steele blundered upon the truth.   25. It was due to the great satirist who alone knew how to use ridicule without abusing it who without inflicting a wound effected a great social reform who reconciled wit and virtue after a long and disastrous separation during which wit had been led astray by profligacy and virtue by fanaticism. 26. The pamphlet contains seventy-two pages and much information concerning the work of the past year is furnished within this space much more than was given to the public in the smaller publications of 1921 1922 and 1923.   27. The state's attorney who has been indefatigable in the effort to obtain evidence against Magill the detective on the case and the special grand jurymen are all puzzled.

Parentheses ( )

Relative position of other marks

238. When a sentence contains matter set off by parentheses, a comma, a period, or other mark of punctuation belonging to the part before such matter, should be placed after the second parenthesis mark, not elsewhere.

> Wrong: I will ask him by telephone, (assuming he has a telephone) and I think he will agree (though I may be mistaken.)
> Wrong: I will ask him by telephone (assuming he has a telephone,) and I think he will agree, (though I may be mistaken).

Right: I will ask him by telephone (assuming he has a telephone), and I think he will agree (though I may be mistaken).

239. A comma should not be used with parentheses unless it would be required were there no parenthetic matter.

Incorrect use of commas with parentheses

Wrong: The sheriff gave him (as his oath required), the most effective help. [The sentence "The sheriff gave him the most effective help" requires no comma after "him."]

Right: The sheriff gave him (as his oath required) the most effective help.

240. Do not use parentheses to enclose matter that is not parenthetical. Do not use them —

Misuse in general

(*a*) **To emphasize a word; italicize.** (See Rule 284.)

Misuse for emphasis

Bad: "The man (who) they thought was dead surprised them" is correct.

Right: "The man *who* they thought was dead surprised them" is correct.

(*b*) **To enclose a word about which something is said as a word. Such words should be italicized.** (See Rule 284.)

Misuse with words discussed

Wrong: (Party) is often incorrectly used for (person).

Right: *Party* is often incorrectly used for *person*.

(*c*) **To indicate the title of a book; italicize.** (See Rule 284.)

Misuse with literary titles

Wrong: Garland's story (Among the Corn Rows) is pathetic.

Right: Garland's story *Among the Corn Rows* is pathetic.

(*d*) **To enclose a letter, number, or symbol, unless it is used parenthetically.**

Misuse with letters and symbols

Bad: A (v) shaped plate of steel.
Right: A v-shaped plate of steel.

Bad: It is marked with the figure (2).
Right: It is marked with the figure 2.

Misuse for
canceling

(*e*) **To cancel a word or passage.**   (See Rule 216.)

Brackets [ ]

Words in-
terpolated
in a quo-
tation

**241. Square brackets, [ ], are used to enclose a
word or words interpolated in a quotation by the
person quoting.**   Words enclosed in parentheses, ( ),
occurring in a quotation, are understood to belong to
the quotation; words enclosed in brackets, [ ], are
understood to be interpolated by the writer quoting.

Right: "I would gladly," writes Landor, "see our
language enriched . . .   At present [in the eight-
eenth century] we recur to the Latin and reject
the Saxon . . . "

Quotation Marks (" ")

NOTE. — See Rules 192 and 193 for the paragraphing of
direct quotations and of dialogues.

For direct,
not indirect
quotations

**242. Use quotation marks to enclose a direct quota-
tion, but not to enclose an indirect quotation.**

Wrong: He said "that he was grieved."
Right: He said that he was grieved.
Right: He said, "I am grieved."

Omission

**243. Do not fail to put quotation marks at the be-
ginning and the end of every quotation.**

Misuse
within a
quotation

**244. Do not punctuate sentences of a single speech
as if they were separate speeches.**

Bad: She said, "Is this the truth?"   "Then I must
tell my husband."   "He ought to know."

Right: She said, "Is this the truth? Then I must tell
my husband. He ought to know."

**245. When an expression like *said he* is inter-
polated within a quotation or placed after it,** the following rules apply:

Quotations with said he interpolated:

(*a*) **The expression should not be included within the quotation marks at the beginning and the end
of the quotation.**

Said he excluded

Wrong: "If that is true, he said, I am lost."
Right: "If that is true," he said, "I am lost."

(*b*) **The quoted words preceding the expression
should be followed by a question mark or an exclamation mark if they form a complete interroga-
tory or exclamatory sentence; otherwise by a
comma; never by a period or semicolon.**

Marks after part preceding said he

Wrong: "Will you help," he asked?
Right: "Will you help?" he asked.

Wrong: "I will help." he answered.
Right: "I will help," he answered.

Wrong: "I will help you;" he said, "you deserve it."
Right: "I will help you," he said; "you deserve it."

(*c*) **If the quoted words preceding the expression
form a complete sentence, a period should follow
the expression, even if a question or exclamation
mark follows the words preceding.**

Marks after said he: Period

Wrong: "Won't you come?" she said, "we need you."
Right: "Won't you come?" she said. "We need
you."

(*d*) **If the quoted words preceding the expression
would be followed, but for the expression, by a
semicolon, a semicolon should follow the expression.**

Semicolon

Right: "He didn't go to Canada," the teller informed
me; "he went to Mexico."

(*e*) **In every case in which a period or a semi-colon is not required** (according to Rules *c* and *d*, above) **after the expression, a comma should follow the expression.**

> Right: "I am," growled the assassin, "your dooms-man."

(*f*) **The expression should not be capitalized.**

> Right: "Go to the treasury," said the king, "and help yourself."

(*g*) **The part of the quotation following the expression should not be capitalized unless it is a new sentence.**

> Wrong: "Hammer on the window," advised the policeman, "Until he gets up."
> Right: "Hammer on the window," advised the policeman, "until he gets up."
> See also the *Right* examples under Rules *d, e,* and *f*.

246. Titles of literary, musical, and artistic works, and of periodicals may be inclosed in quotation marks, but the preferred practice is to italicize titles of whole publications or works and to use quotation marks for the titles of chapters, articles, etc. (See Rule 286.)

> Right: The second chapter of Meredith's *Evan Harrington* is entitled "The Heritage of the Son."

247. When a quotation mark and another mark of punctuation both follow the same word —
(*a*) **A question or exclamation mark should stand first if it applies to the quotation and not to the sentence containing the quotation.**

> Wrong: He said, "Are you hurt"?
> Right: He said, "Are you hurt?"

(*b*) **The quotation mark should stand first if the question or exclamation mark applies, not to the quotation, but to the sentence containing the quotation.**

> Wrong: Did the letter say, "Come tonight at ten?"
> Right: Did the letter say, "Come tonight at ten"?

(*c*) **In either case no comma or period should be used in addition to the quotation mark and the question or exclamation mark.**

> Wrong: He cried "Fire!", and began to run.
> Right: He cried "Fire!" and began to run.
> Wrong: Did he say "I object."?
> Right: Did he say, "I object"?

(*d*) **A period or a comma should always precede the quotation mark.**

Period or comma always inside

> Right: "If you have a light," said John, "give it to me."
> Right: He asked if I carried what he called "the makings," but I could not satisfy him.

(*e*) **A semicolon or a colon should always follow the quotation mark.**

Colon or semicolon always outside

> Right: I have seen that "abode of poverty"; and the "poverty" is truly marvelous.
> Right: I have this to say regarding the man's "abject poverty": that it is fictitious.

248. A quotation within a quotation is marked by single quotation marks; one within that by double marks.

Quotation within a quotation

> Wrong: I repeated those lines of Tennyson,
>> "Thou shalt hear the "Never, never," whispered by the phantom years,
>> And a song from out the distance in the ringing of thine ears,"
> until I knew them by heart.

Right: I repeated those lines of Tennyson,
"Thou shalt hear the 'Never, never,' whispered by
the phantom years,
And a song from out the distance in the ringing of
thine ears,"
until I knew them by heart.

Wrong: "Then," continued Brightman, "the captain
shouted, "Cast off!"
Right: "Then," continued Brightman, "the captain
shouted, 'Cast off!'"

Quotations
of several
paragraphs

**249. When a quotation consists of several para-
graphs (see Rule 212), quotation marks should be
placed at the beginning of each paragraph, and at the
end of the quotation; not elsewhere, except in accordance with Rule 245 *a*.** For illustration, see the
example under Rule 212.

With un-
familiar
technical
terms

**250. Quotation marks may sometimes be used to
mark a technical term presumably unfamiliar to the
reader.** (See, for example, the text of Rule 258 and
the *Right* example under *Element* in the Glossary.)
But —

Familiar
technical
terms

NOTE. — No such marking is needed for technical or
quasi-technical terms that are perfectly familiar to the
reader. None is ordinarily needed, for instance, for
*wire-puller, boss, off-year, touch-down, kick-off, haze, corner
the market.*

Slang and
nicknames

**251. Quotation marks may sometimes be used to
indicate apology for slang or nicknames. But note:**

Good Eng-
lish mis-
taken for
slang

(*a*) **No such apology is needed** for *hard hit, brace
up, rough it, to duck, to oust, to loaf, to cut a figure, the
whys and wherefores, the forties, willy nilly, day dreams,
proxy, bugbear, humbug, hoax, tomfoolery, bamboozle,
whoop, ninny, milksop, skinflint, parson,* and other
good English expressions wrongly supposed to be
slang.

(*b*) **In a humorous or colloquial context such** Apology
apology for slang or for nicknames is artistically in- out of place
consistent with the style, and obstructs the legitimate
purpose of the style.

> Inartistic: When radicalism "threw up its hat" for
> "Rob" Rowland, "rough-house," and reform, con-
> servatism "took to the tall timbers." "Rob,"
> though "cock of the walk" in the capital, has been
> "sassed" by his home paper, which attributes his
> influence to hypnotism and "hot air."
>
> Improved in effectiveness: When radicalism threw up
> its hat for Rob Rowland, rough-house, and reform,
> conservatism took to the tall timbers. Rob, though
> cock of the walk in the capital, has been sassed by
> his home paper, which attributes his influence to
> hypnotism and hot air.

(*c*) **The nicknames of persons in real life or in** Nicknames
fiction who are known by nicknames altogether, or that are
virtually
as commonly as by their proper names, should not be proper
enclosed in quotation marks. names

> Wrong: "Cal" Coolidge, "Battling" Nelson, "Al"
> Smith, "Babe" Ruth, and "Bill" Hart were present.
>
> Right: Cal Coolidge, Battling Nelson, Al Smith,
> Babe Ruth, and Bill Hart were present.

> Wrong: Two women, "the Duchess" and "Mother"
> Shipton, and two men, Mr. Oakhurst and "Uncle
> Billy," were ordered to leave town.
>
> Right: Two women, the Duchess and Mother Ship-
> ton, and two men, Mr. Oakhurst and Uncle Billy,
> were ordered to leave town.

> Wrong: As I was "bucking" for "Perky's" "quiz,"
> I was interrupted by "Fatty" Holmes and
> "Smudge" Williams, who refused to "clear out."
> [See Rule *b*, above.]
>
> Right: As I was cramming for Perky's quiz, I was
> interrupted by Fatty Holmes and Smudge Williams,
> who refused to clear out.

252. Do not use quotation marks —

(a) **To enclose the title at the head of a composition, unless the title is a quotation.**

(b) **To enclose proper names, including names of animals.**

> Wrong: I expect to go to "Oberammergau."
> Right: I expect to go to Oberammergau.

> Wrong: "Thomas" and "Rover" were good friends.
> Right: Thomas and Rover were good friends.

(c) **To enclose proverbial expressions that do not constitute grammatically and logically complete statements.**

> Wrong: It was "nipped in the bud."
> Right: It was nipped in the bud.

> Wrong: He seemed to be "as mad as a March hare."
> Right: He seemed to be as mad as a March hare.

(d) **To enclose words coined *extempore*.**

> Wrong: The manning and "womaning" of the enterprise will be difficult.
> Right: The manning and womaning of the enterprise will be difficult.

> Wrong: It is not bronchitis or peritonitis or any of the "itises."
> Right: It is not bronchitis or peritonitis or any of the itises.

(e) **To serve the undignified and inartistic purpose of labeling your own humor or irony.** (Cf. Rules 234*a* and 292.)

> Bad: Such is the ardor of this "pious" Hotspur.
> Right: Such is the ardor of this pious Hotspur.

> Bad: Senator Platt's speech on the bill was a sort of "funeral oration."
> Right: Senator Platt's speech on the bill was a sort of funeral oration.

Sidenotes:

Sundry misuses: With the title of a composition With proper names

With proverbs

With words coined *extempore*

For labeling humor

(f) **For no reason at all.**

Bad: If the Creator in his "power and munificence" is good to me, I shall gain "distinguished success."

Right: If the Creator in his power and munificence is good to me, I shall gain distinguished success.

Use without any reason

Exercise 96

Write the following expressions, punctuating and capitalizing correctly: 1. You are my first patient the doctor said what is your name 2. Do not talk at random said Stevens too much improvisation leaves the mind void 3. Felix is a pretty name said she it is Latin I think 4. This is strange said Josephine the coach never stopped here before 5. Listen to me the mayor continued there is still room for a man to slip under this cart and raise it 6. I will go at once he repeated does the old woman know the facts 7. Do not interrupt me now said the lawyer when my clerk returns you may speak to him 8. Of course I have a mother replied the child hasn't every one a mother 9. I don't understand you said the peasant what underground passage do you mean 10. We must hurry along Charles said the old gentleman are you sure this is the right road 11. A mere spark was all that was needed he said the explosion was not surprising 12. This man has saved my life said Gauvain does any one here know who he is

Said he interpolated and concluding a predication

Exercise 97

Write the following sentences, placing between the two predications in each sentence the words here enclosed in brackets, and supplying the necessary punctuation: 1. Remove this rubbish; I want the room clean [he commanded] 2. Do not stay long; you will be wanted presently [he said] 3. I am sure it will be pretty; his gifts always are [she said] 4. They are very good friends; they might be taken for two sisters [she observed] 5. I have finished; you may go now [said his father] 6. This is my own affair; you must not interfere [said the colonel] 7. I must start at once; the trial will occur tomorrow [the lawyer said] 8. Tell him to wait; I shall come down

Said he with semicolon

presently [she said to the servant] 9. I have men
enough; there is no need of hiring others [said Ryan]
10. I knew nothing of this transaction; George never
mentioned it to me [said I]

EXERCISE 98

Said he interpolated — miscellaneous examples

Write the following expressions, punctuating and capitalizing correctly: 1. Well Cosette the landlady said why
don't you take your doll 2. It is very simple the man
replied she does it because it amuses her 3. I wish to go
to bed now said the traveler where is my room 4. That
sir Thenardier explained is my wife's wedding bonnet
5. By the way his wife continued don't forget that I mean
to turn her out tomorrow 6. And suppose suggested Jean
that you were rid of her 7. Where is Frances Street
asked the old lady isn't it in this neighborhood 8. Sir
he said I need fifty francs 9. Be silent my dear whispered
the husband let's see what he will say 10. You are right
he exclaimed give me my hat and I'll follow him 11. I
ought to have brought my gun he reflected the fellow may
be obstinate 12. Well continued the officer we found the
door bolted 13. What of that I answered does that prove
any bad intention 14. I beg your pardon said Javert the
offense was accidental 15. Who is he every one asked
16. The nun is dead remarked Fauchelevent that is her
knell we hear 17. Is she your daughter asked Henry if
so of course she is welcome 18. That is the doctor going
away the porter said to me he has probably not been
able to relieve the patient 19. I don't understand you
said Mrs. Bethune of whom are you speaking 20. I will
do it Reverend Mother said Fauvent solemnly I will do it
just as you direct 21. You have a gimlet remarked Jean
Valjean make a few holes in the cover 22. If the weather
is good I heard him say I will meet you here at ten
23. Father said the child what is in that box that smells
so nice 24. I do my duty said the woman you neglect
yours 25. I prefer answered the soldier not to disobey
orders 26. What are you afraid of interrupted Clancy
speak up and be quick about it 27. I advise you said
Madeleine threateningly not to interrupt me at present
28. Do you wish asked the servant to see my master

29. What did you say asked Bryce   30. Is there any harm in that inquired the girl   31. More often do you say what do you mean by more often   32. Alas cried the woman where are my children   33. Shall I go and find them asked the priest   34. Instead of asking weakly will you please let me pass why didn't you say sternly let me pass   35. Great heavens exclaimed Bangs in a fury was ever a general addressed in such terms   36. Was it not your duty asked my mother to remain at your post   37. He shrunk back toward the wall crying in the extremity of his terror my God my God   38. Do you know who it was who died saying don't give up the ship   39. Come sir brace up what do you mean by that melodramatic expression all is lost   40. She kept repeating how wonderful how wonderful   41. His letter says is the messenger dependable how does he come to use that abominable word dependable.   42. Ah cried the woman in high indignation how heartless how cruel   43. Why kill so many asked Cimourdain when two would suffice   44. Two said Imanus puzzled what two   45. What poem begins with the words this is the forest primeval   46. Have you ever heard the saying the pen is mightier than the sword   47. Do you consent asked Lantenac   48. Why do you come here thundered the old man who asked you to come   49. What is the meaning of the words the wind bloweth where it listeth   50. I asked is there fighting in Dol   He answered yes my ci-devant seigneur is fighting another ci-devant   What do you think he meant by my ci-devant seigneur

The Apostrophe (')

253. In the possessive singular of a noun an apostrophe should precede the inflectional *s;* *e.g.,* " the boy's cap." In the possessive plural of a noun of which the nominative plural ends in *s,* an apostrophe should follow the final *s;* *e.g.,* " the boys' caps." In the possessive plural of other nouns, an apostrophe should precede the final *s;* *e.g., men's, women's, children's, oxen's.*

Nouns ending in s

254. Do not form the possessive singular of a noun ending in *s* by putting an apostrophe before or after the *s;* add *'s* to the complete word. If a word of two or more syllables ends in *s* and is not accented on the last syllable, the possessive may be formed by adding either the apostrophe or *'s.*

Wrong: Dicken's novels. Burn's poems.
Right: Dickens' novels, or Dickens's novels.
(Burns's poems.)
For conscience' sake. For righteousness' sake.

Misuse with *its*, etc.

255. Never use an apostrophe with the possessive adjectives *its, hers, ours, yours, theirs.* The form *it's* is a contraction for *it is.* The possessive singular of *one* should be written *one's* and the possessive plural *ones'.*

With contractions

256. In a contracted word an apostrophe should stand in the place of the omitted letter or letters, not elsewhere.

Wrong: Hav'nt, do'nt, does'nt, ca'nt, is'nt, oclock.
Right: Haven't, don't, doesn't, can't, isn't, o'clock.

In forming plurals

257. The plural of letters of the alphabet and of numerical symbols is formed by adding *'s* to the letter or symbol. The plural of a word considered *as a word* may also be formed in the same way. But the regular plural of a noun should never be formed by adding *'s.* The apostrophe is commonly omitted from the plural of figures referring to interest-bearing bonds.

Right: His *U's* were like *V's* and his *2's* like *Z's.*
Right: In your letter there are too many *I's* and also too many *and's.*
Wrong: The Powers's, the Jones's, the Waters's and the Rogers's sold piano's and folio's.

Right: The Powerses, the Joneses, the Waterses, and the Rogerses sold pianos and folios.

Right: Rock Island 4s.

EXERCISE 99

Write the following, inserting apostrophes wherever they are required: 1. We took a few moments rest. 2. My fathers house is larger than yours. 3. The ten Eastern delegates objection was disregarded. 4. I had two weeks vacation on my aunts farm. 5. Peters wifes mother lay sick. 6. Girls costumes are more elaborate than boys. 7. Millionaires lives are not always happy. 8. A bulls neck is thicker than a giraffes. 9. Glue is made of cows hoofs. 10. A weeks work is better than three months vacation. 11. He went to the farmers house to ask for the ladys hand. 12. An agents error is an employers loss. 13. For your souls good you may have an hour reprieve. 14. The singers voice touched the peoples hearts. 15. Smiths son is attending a boys school. 16. Soldiers lives are less eventful than policemens lives. 17. Our dinner consisted of frogs legs and pheasants wings. 18. Kates example affected Marys character. 19. Hamlets unkindness caused Ophelias madness. 20. Laborers wages depend on capitalists pleasure.

Miscellaneous possessives of nouns

The Hyphen (-)

258. Hyphenate an adjective formed of two or more words when used before the noun. Examples:

Compound words

(*a*) (Noun plus adjective) *dirt-cheap, coal-black, water-tight.*

(*b*) (Adjective plus noun or noun plus noun, plus d or ed) *bright-eyed, strong-minded, silver-tongued, bull-necked, eagle-eyed.*

(*c*) (Adverb plus participle, or numeral plus noun) *far-reaching, well-meaning, well-educated, worn-out, three-inch.*

(*d*) (Participle preceded by a substantive denoting means or agency) *self-possessed, iron-clad, tear-stained.*

(*e*) (Noun, adjective, participle or gerund preceded by the name of an object acted upon or concerned) *tax-collector, dog-catcher, self-control, labor-saving.*

(*f*) (Groups of words which are to be read as a single part of speech, when the omission of the hyphen might obscure the sense) *A matter-of-fact statement, my right-hand man, a high-school graduate, a month-old baby, an all-round man.*

NOTE. — *To-day, to-night, to-morrow, good-bye* are sometimes written with a hyphen.

No simple rule can be given for determining whether a compound word should be hyphenated or written " solid." One must simply learn, from observation and from dictionaries, what is the correct practice in each case. Note that the following words should not be hyphenated: *together, without, nevertheless, moreover, inasmuch, instead, childhood, farewell, wardrobe, chipmunk, nickname, surname, midnight, railroad, misprint, pronoun, semicolon, withstand, outstretch, rewrite.*

258*a*. Do not join an adjective in *ly* to an adjective or participle; *e.g., carefully laid plans.*

258*b*. Use a hyphen between the numerator and the denominator of a fraction written in words unless either part is written with a hyphen: *three-fourths, three twenty-fourths, nineteenths, thirty-one fortieths.* Do not hyphenate *one half* in " He gave me one half and kept the other half."

258*c*. Usually hyphenate compounds of *fellow, father, mother, brother, sister, daughter, great, life, world, ex, pan, ultra,* and of a noun derived from a transitive verb.

Examples: *fellow-beings, father-in-law, mother-tongue, great-grandmother, life-interest, world-power, ex-President Taft, pan-American, ultra-violet, story-teller.*

259. In dividing a word at the end of a line (see Rules 263–266, below), place a hyphen after the first element of the word, and there only; never put a hyphen at the beginning of a line.

At the beginning of a line

EXERCISE 100

A passage to be written at dictation. Officer Callahan, a man of oxlike intellect (indeed, he is very ill educated and stupid, although well-meaning, perhaps), arrested my well-beloved bulldog, Touch-and-go, today, and gave him into the hands of Jensen the dog-catcher, who in turn passed him on to the pound master. My iron-jawed, short-haired favorite, dressed up as usual in his silver-studded collar, but wearing no muzzle, was according to his daily custom walking statelily down Hill Street. There in her flower garden Miss Josephine Jones, neat looking and daintily dressed, was tending her rosebushes; with her was her silky-haired, chicken-hearted setter, following her with its dovelike eyes or sometimes, in its scatter-brained fashion, chasing a butterfly. As Touch-and-go passed by the yard, this empty-headed butterfly-chaser danced up to him, leaping over the two-foot wall that borders the yard, and noisily yelping, setter-like, to attract the newcomer's attention. This is a well-established fact; several passers-by saw and have testified that the setter was the aggressor. Miss Josephine, terror-stricken, raised an outcry, but it was too late; the setter was already fast in the vice-like grip of the bulldog. Now, the last-mentioned performer in this little comedy was only trying to teach the over-familiar puppy dog a much-needed lesson in good manners; but the tender-hearted mistress thought that the light-weight was about to be murdered by the heavy-weight. She therefore wrung her lily-white hands and shouted for the police. Police Officer Callahan, that bull-necked, round-bellied, heavy-footed peace-preserver, was about half a mile up the street,

Dictation exercises in hyphening (See Rules 102–124)

eating unpaid-for peanuts and conversing with a white-aproned nursemaid. With the speed of a steam roller and the self-important air of a general-in-chief, Callahan drew near and arrested Touch-and-go. The setter and his mistress comforted each other for a few minutes, and then the first-mentioned resumed his insect-chasing, and the second-mentioned her rosebush-tending. But, as above stated, Touch-and-go wore no muzzle, therein violating our strictly enforced city laws; so he was turned over to the above-mentioned dog-catcher, who, bidding a polite good-bye to Miss Josephine, took him to the pound. I paid a twenty-dollar fine this afternoon and recovered my bow-legged hero. Tomorrow he will wear that much-detested muzzle.

Miscellaneous Rules

Punctuation with *such as*

260. When *such as* is used to introduce an example or several examples, it should be preceded by a comma (see Rule 221 *h*), a dash (see Rule 236 *b*), or a semicolon (see Rule 231 *e*), and should be followed by no mark of punctuation, unless a parenthetical expression is inserted between the *such as* and the word that it introduces.

> Right: I read many historical novels, such as *Romola, Rienzi,* and *Quo Vadis.*
> See also the text of Rules 18, 144 *b*, 145, 146, 223.

Punctuation with *namely, viz.,* etc.

261. In introducing an example or an explanation with one of the expressions *namely, viz., e.g., that is,* and *i.e.,* apply the following rules:

(a) **The expression should always be followed by a comma.**

> Wrong: I selected it for two reasons namely: because it was well made, and because it was inexpensive.
> Right: I selected it for two reasons: namely, because it was well made, and because it was inexpensive.

See also the text of Rules 16 *a*, 106, and 136, and the note to Rule 3.

(*b*) **When the expression introduces a sentence or a principal clause, the expression should be preceded by a period or a semicolon** (see Rules 230, 231 *a*).

> Right: There is a vital difference between them; *i.e.*, the Greek is an artist, and the Roman is a statesman.

See also the text of Rules 111, 90 *g*.

(*c*) **When the expression introduces a merely appositive member, or several such, the expression should be preceded by a semicolon** (see Rule 231 *e*), **by a dash** (see Rule 236 *b*), **or by a colon** (see Rule 233).

> Right: They arrested the man who was really responsible — namely, the cashier.
> Right: There are three parties: namely, Tories, Whigs, and Radicals.

See also the text of Rules 2*d*, 106, 123, 124, 269.

NOTE. — When the expression and the words it introduces are enclosed in parentheses, the foregoing Rules *b* and *c* do not apply. See the text of Rules 99, 121, 136.

EXERCISE 101

Write the following, punctuating correctly: 1. I demand only one thing namely justice. 2. Only two dances are used namely the waltz and the highland fling. 3. Two words I fear I habitually misspell namely *athlete* and *disappoint*. 4. You will find there a person whom I wish you to know namely Madeline Mooney. 5. Remember particularly the books I mentioned first namely *Middlemarch, Kenilworth,* and *Hard Cash*. 6. It is attractive but for a serious drawback namely the interminable piano strumming above. 7. She bade me admire what she called her chief treasures namely an intaglio of Sophocles, a Della Robbia replica, and a bronze bulldog. 8. Surety bonds are required of three officers *viz.* the president, the treasurer, and the janitor. 9. He has disregarded an

Namely

important requirement *viz.* the requirement made in article
VI.   10. They should appear at those times when they
have promised to appear *viz.* whenever the choir master
shall request it.   11. On that corner you will find three
interesting buildings *viz.* the subtreasury, the cathedral,
and a saloon.   12. We shall study the three principal
varieties *viz.* tropes, miracles, and moralities.   13. He was
found waiting at his post namely the cottage which he
had been ordered to guard.   14. One characteristic of his
I must commend namely the fact that he steadfastly
discountenances stained glass.

Marks of punctuation at the beginning of lines

**262. Never put a period, a comma, a semicolon, a
colon, an exclamation point, or a question mark at
the beginning of a line; put it instead at the end of
the preceeding line.**

EXERCISE 102

General exercise in spelling, punctuating, capitalizing, italicizing, and paragraphing

Write the following passage, correctly punctuating,
capitalizing, and paragraphing it: The principal peculiarity of professor collins was absent-mindedness this
often led him to mislay or lose articles necessary to his
business such as books lecture notes etc one day as he and
another professor were walking down a street in the village
in which the college was situated professor collins suddenly
stopped looked perplexed and said why my notes for
today's lecture have disappeared oh that's all right said
his friend smiling give an impromptu lecture the subject
is too complicated for that answered professor collins
truly this is serious if I don't find those notes soon I must
disappoint my class of forty law students what is that in
your hand asked his friend a package I intended to mail
at that last post-box was the answer it contains some
copies of the law review my notes were in a separate
envelope of about the same size wait for me a minute said
the other professor with a knowing look he went to the
post-box which they had passed a minute before and took
from the top of it a large envelope this he brought to professor collins saying don't lose these necessary things
again professor collins delighted at being relieved from

the anxiety which he had been suffering seized the package and said gratefully as Longfellow puts it thanks thanks
to thee my worthy friend oh never fear I'll not lose them
again at least not today.

SYLLABICATION

**263. In dividing a word at the end of a line, make
the separation between syllables, not elsewhere.** (See
also Rule 259.)

There is no uniform principle for determining just
what are the several syllables of any given word; one
must rely largely on learning, by observation and by
reference to dictionaries, what is the correct syllabication in individual cases. Nevertheless, a good many
errors may be avoided by observing the following
simple rules:

Rules for syllabica-tion:

(*a*) Do not set apart from each other combinations
of letters the separate pronunciation of which is impossible or unnatural.

Follow pronuncia-tion

A. Wrong: Exc-ursion; go-ndola; illustr-ate; instruction; pun-ctuation.
  Right: Ex-cursion; gon-dola; illus-trate; in-struc-
tion; punc-tuation.

B. Wrong: Prostr-ate; pri-nciple; abs-urd; fini-shing;
sugge-stion.
  Right: Pros-trate; prin-ciple; ab-surd; finish-ing;
sug-ges-tion.

C. Wrong: Nat-ion; conclus-ion; invent-ion; introd-
uct-ion; abbr-eviat-ion.
  Right: Na-tion; conclu-sion; inven-tion; intro-duc-
tion; abbre-via-tion.

D. Wrong: Diffic-ult; tob-acco; exc-ept; univ-ersity;
dislo-dgment.
  Right: Diffi-cult; to-bacco; ex-cept; uni-versity;
dis-lodg-ment.

Prefixes

(*b*) As a rule, divide between a prefix and the letter following it.

> Wrong: Bet-ween; pref-ix; antec-edent; conf-ine; del-ight.
> Right: Be-tween; pre-fix; ante-cedent; con-fine; de-light.

Suffixes

(*c*) As a rule, divide between a suffix and the letter preceding it. Divide, *e.g.*, before -*ing*, -*ly*, -*ment*, -*ed* (when it is pronounced as a separate syllable, as in *delight-ed*), -*ish*, -*able*, -*er*, -*est*.

> Right: Lov-ing; love-ly; judg-ment; invit-ed; Jew-ish; punish-able; strong-er; strong-est.

Doubled consonants

(*d*) As a rule, when a consonant is doubled, divide between the two letters. This rule often takes precedence of Rule *c* above.

> Right: Rub-ber; ab-breviation; oc-casion; ad-dition; af-finity; Rus-sian; expres-sion; omis-sion; com-mit-tee; ex-cel-lent; stop-ping; drop-ping; ship-ping; equip-ping.

The digraphs *th*, *ch*, etc., not to be divided

(*e*) Never divide in the midst of *th* pronounced as in *the* or *thin*; *sh* as in *push*; *ph* as in *phonograph*; *ng* as in *sing*; *gn* as in *sign*; *tch* as in *fetch*; and *gh* pronounced as in *rough*, or silent. Never divide *ck* except in accordance with Rule *f*, below. Do not divide vowel digraphs.

> Wrong: Cat-holic; ras-hness; disc-harge; diap-hragm; gin-gham.
> Right: Cath-olic; rash-ness; dis-charge; dia-phragm; ging-ham.

> Wrong: Consig-nment; wat-ching; doug-hty.
> Right: consign-ment; watch-ing; dough-ty.

> Wrong: Bo-at, sa-il, Spa-in.
> Right: Boat, sail, Spain.

The divisions *post-humous* (see page 326), *dis-habille*
(see page 326), *Lap-ham*, *nightin-gale*, *distin-guish*,
sin-gle, *sig-nature*, and *Leg-horn*, form no exceptions to
the foregoing rule, for in them *th*, *sh*, etc., are pronounced each as two distinct sounds.

(*f*) In dividing words like *edible*, *possible*, *bridle*, **Final *le***
trifle, *beagle*, *crackle*, *twinkle*, *staple*, *entitle* do not **not to be**
set *le* apart by itself; always place with it the preced- **set apart**
ing consonant. (But see Rule 266.)

> Right: Edi-ble; possi-ble; bri-dle; tri-fle; bea-gle;
> crac-kle; etc.

NOTE. — To Rules *b*, *c*, and *d*, above, there are exceptions. For a statement of these, and for a comprehensive
treatment of syllabication, the reader is referred to the
Introduction of Webster's International Dictionary.

264. Never divide a monosyllable.

**Monosylla-
bles**

> Wrong: Tho-ugh, stre-ngth.

265. Do not divide a syllable of one letter from the rest of the word.

**A syllable
of one let-
ter**

> Wrong: Man-y, a-gainst, a-long, ston-y.

266. Dividing words at the end of lines should be avoided as much as possible. And such awkward divisions as the following should never be made:

**Awkward
and too
frequent
division**

> Bad: eve-ry, ev-en, on-ly, eight-een.

EXERCISE 103

Write each of the following words on two lines, showing **Syllabica-**
how it may be correctly divided at the end of a line. For **tion:**
example:

re-	remem-
member	ber
in-	incom-
complete	plete

Miscellaneous

A. *gradual, genuine, signal, crimson, ridiculous, cholera, popular, optimist, emphasis, comparison, account, quarrel, censure, recognize, depression, melancholy, deduction, inference, gorgeous, purple, frivolous, summon, energetic, scientific, engineering, geniality, artificiality, hypocrite, condemnation, automatic, unconscious, prominence, happiness, justifiable, innumerable, intelligent, comparatively, contemporary, elaborate, hostility, suspicion, manufacture, civilization, unfriendliness, conjunction, contradiction, vulgarity, attempt, revenge, weakness, philosophy, immeasurable.*

Prefixes

B. *depict, entire, expend, admire, convene, detest, inspire, intervene, obscure, postpone, submit, superstitious, expound, beguile, forlorn, address, endure, conscript, catalogue, epitaph, detail, infuse, intersperse, oblige, postscript, object, prevail, subject, anagram, explain, becoming, epigram, advert, confuse, devotion, increase, interesting, oblique, provoke, prescribe, substitute, explicit, behave, programme, forgive, impossible, adduce, impose, undutiful, unnatural, infrequent, unnecessary, existence, behind, exquisite, untamed, inaccessible.*

Suffixes

C. *kindly, shaving, peaceable, preferment, healthful, sweeter, pianist, heartless, payable, heaviest, goodness, wholesome, wholly, bowing, serviceable, winsome, instrument, mournful, commitment, weaker, thoughtless, organist, wearisome, perishable, wretched, blackest, delightful, brightness, preference, homeless, cruelly, actually, tuneful, blooming, convertible, blithesome, unnamable, discernment, harmful, sacrament, colder, friendless, warmest, daintiness, darkness, violinist, fearless.*

Doubled consonants

D. *sinner, flannel, cellar, robber, saddest, goddess, ripple, giggle, trammel, carriage, assist, rattan, accede, aggravate, session, possession, passion, jabber, accident, affable, traffic, allude, illusion, glimmer, runner, slippery, terror, assist, pressure, intermittent, commit, battalion, dazzling, gibber, flaccid, reddish, stiffen, braggart, distillery, mummery, nunnery, horrible, borrow, barrel, fissure, aggressive, lissom, Prussian, passive, fitting, flutter.*

Digraphs

E. *Catherine, strengthen, splashing, hydrophobia, singing, alignment, switchboard, doughnut, roughness, bother,*

ruthless,   fisherman,   cashier,   Berkshire,   telephone,
diaphanous, antithesis, Shoshone, clangor, danger, signpost,
Litchfield, neighbor, coughing, nothing, smother, gathering,
finishing,   paraphrase,   wrongful,   latchet,   ploughman,
laughter.

ABBREVIATIONS

267. Abbreviations are in bad taste in literary compositions of any kind, including letters. A few abbreviations, — such as *i.e., e.g., q.v., viz., etc., A.D., B.C., a.m., p.m.,* — are excepted from the rule, being commonly used in good literature. Use no abbreviations except those which you know are employed, not by the newspapers or the writers of commonplace business letters, but by recognized masters of English prose.

Generally objectionable

Bad: Last summer I worked for the Chandler Mfg. Co. in Casey, Ill. Casey is on the C. and E. I. R.R.

Right: Last summer I worked for the Chandler Manufacturing Company in Casey, Illinois. Casey is on the Chicago and Eastern Illinois Railroad.

NOTE. — Spell in full the names of streets, including those designated by numerals less than one hundred (see Rules 272 *b* and 308), and the names of months and states. The abbreviations St., Ave., and Ct. are sometimes employed in addresses in business correspondence but should not be used in literary discourse or in the addresses of letters of friendship and formal notes.

268. Observe that many abbreviations that are proper when combined with other expressions are improper when standing alone. Thus:

Abbreviations right in some places; wrong elsewhere

Right: I came at ten p.m.
Vulgar: I came this p.m.

Right: He lives in room No. 12.
Bad: Let me know the No. of your room.

Right: My dear Dr. Hart.
Vulgar: My dear Dr.

Observe also that many abbreviations (such as *vol.*, *ch.*, *p.*, *Co.*, *ed.*) that are permissible in footnotes, parenthetic citations, and similar places, are not permissible in formally constructed sentences. In writing the name of a company, use & only with the abbreviation *Co.* unless the company uses the symbol in its letterhead.

Abbreviation of titles

269. Abbreviation of titles is, in general, inelegant and objectionable. Spell out *Professor, President, Captain, General, Colonel,* etc. Some abbreviations are, however, always proper; *viz.*, (1) *Mr., Mrs., Messrs.,* and *Dr.,* when prefixed to names; (2) *Esq.,* and the initial abbreviations *D.D., Ph.D., Jr., Sr.,* etc., when suffixed to names. (See Rule 268.) *Reverend* and *Honorable* are usually abbreviated.

EXERCISE 104

Abbreviations to be eliminated

Rewrite the following sentences, substituting complete words for the improper abbreviations: 1. Walking north on Hamilton St., one sees the Schoolcraft Bldg. 2. On Aug. 15 I took the boat for South Haven, Mich. 3. I was employed as a shipping clerk by the Arbuckle Coffee Co. in Boston. 4. He got employment on the ranch of Witting Bros. in the southern part of Neb. 5. For four years I was employed by the Modern Steel Structural Co. in Waukesha, Wis. This co. secured the contract for the Majestic Bldg. in Milwaukee. 6. At Redwing, Minn., I rec'd my early education. 7. In the spring of 1905 I obtained a position with the Sunset Telephone Co. and held it until Sept. of that year, working chiefly in northern Cal. Then I went to Portland, Ore., and took in the Fair. 8. Among the charms of Hancock Co., Col., is a sublime view of the distant, snowy peaks of the Rocky Mts. 9. In Aug., 1907, I attended a co. fair in Pekin, Ill., and saw Dan Patch win a race. 10. The mfg. co. in our town paid a dividend of 6% this month.

THE REPRESENTATION OF NUMBERS

270. Do not spell out dates, street numbers, page numbers, or numbers of divisions (parts, chapters, paragraphs, sections, rules, etc.) of a book or a document. — *Dates, folios, etc., and house numbers*

> Wrong: On October thirteen, eighteen hundred and eighty-one, I was born at three hundred and sixty-two Adams Street. See page nine hundred and sixteen of our family Bible.
>
> Right: On October 13, 1881, I was born at 362 Adams Street. See page 916 of our family Bible.

NOTE. — Ordinal numbers designating days of a month may be either spelled out or represented by figures.

> Right: The thirteenth of May fell on Friday.
> Right: The 13th of May fell on Friday.

Ordinal numbers designating pages or divisions of a book or document are governed by Rule 272.

271. In designating a sum of money in connected discourse, apply the following rules: — *Sums of money*

(*a*) Do not use the sign $ for sums less than one dollar. — *The sign $ improper for sums less than a dollar*

> Wrong: It costs $0.20.
> Right: It costs twenty cents.

(*b*) Do not write .00. — *The expression .00 never to be used*

> Wrong: He subscribed $342.00 to the fund.
> Right: He subscribed $342 to the fund.

(*c*) For a sum amounting to a number of dollars and a number of cents, always use the sign $ and figures. — *Fractional sums*

> Right: It costs $3.18.

Even sums:
Frequent

(*d*) If several sums are mentioned within a short space, use figures for all, putting the sign $ before all numbers representing dollars.

> Right: My room costs $5 a week and my board $6.50; my contribution to the church is 30 cents; my incidental expenses range from $9.35 to $22.50 a month.

Isolated:
A sum in
cents

(*e*) In case of an isolated mention of a sum in cents, spell out the number.

> Right: The price is ninety cents.

A sum in
dollars

(*f*) In case of an isolated mention of a sum in dollars without a fraction, spell out a number expressed in one or two words, such as *three, sixteen, two hundred, six thousand, one million;* for other numbers, such as 102, 350, 1130, 1,500,000, use the sign $ and figures.

> Right: He contributed twenty thousand dollars.
> Right: It sold for eighteen hundred dollars.
> Right: His fortune amounts to $72,500.

Numbers
not
treated in
Rules 270,
271
Frequent
numbers
— figures

272. In representing, in connected discourse, numbers other than those treated in Rules 270 and 271, apply the following rules:

(*a*) In case several numbers are mentioned in a short space, use figures for all. See for example the text of Rules 203–208, where numbers occur frequently and representation of them by words would inconvenience the reader.

Numbers
not fre-
quent

(*b*) If the numbers to be represented are not frequent, spell out numbers that may be expressed in one or two words, such as *eighteen, ninety-seven, two hundred, eighteen hundred, twenty thousand, one million, fifty million;* use figures for those that require three or more words, such as 108, 233, 1,250, 18,231, 1,500,230.

> Wrong: The college is 25 miles from Columbus and has 900 students.
> Right: The college is twenty-five miles from Columbus and has nine hundred students.

> Wrong: In this city there were four hundred and thirty-four saloons to three hundred and eighty-five thousand, one hundred and ninety-two people.
> Right: In this city there were 434 saloons to 385,192 people.

> Wrong: He lives on 72d street.
> Right: He lives on Seventy-second Street. [See Rules 277 and 308.]

(c) Do not use numerals at the beginning of a sentence. Spell the numbers out or recast the sentence so as to begin it with another word.

> Wrong: 1914 was a momentous year.
> Right: The year 1914 was momentous.
> Right: Nineteen hundred fourteen was a momentous year.

273. From Rule 272 *b* it follows that a number representing a person's age or one designating an hour of the day should nearly always (see Rule 272 *a*) be spelled out. *Ages, and hours of the day*

> Right: At twelve o'clock all the children below eight years of age are sent home.

274. A sum of money or a number that is spelled out should not be repeated in parenthesized figures, except in legal or commercial letters and instruments. When such repetition is made, (*a*) a parenthesized sum should stand at the end of the expression that it repeats, not elsewhere; and (*b*) a parenthesized number *Parenthetic repetition of numbers*

220 CAPITALS

should stand immediately after the number that it repeats, not elsewhere.

> Wrong: I enclose ($10) ten dollars. [a]
> Wrong: I enclose ten ($10) dollars. [b]
> Right: I enclose ten dollars ($10). [a]
> Right: I enclose ten (10) dollars. [b]

EXERCISE 105

Figures or words to be determined

Sentences to be written at dictation. 1. There are 72,563 grammar schools in the United States. 2. He walked a mile and one eighth in twenty-six minutes. 3. The thirty-fourth name happened to be Smith. 4. It is two hundred miles away. 5. The two-hundred-and-seventh day of this year will be Friday. 6. The veto was overruled by a three-fourths majority. 7. Three fourths of the people there are Italians. 8. The three-mile march was too much for Abner. 9. The proportions are as follows: Jews, 20 per cent; Greeks, 10 per cent; Portuguese, 5 per cent; Italians, 25 per cent; Germans, 40 per cent. 10. From June 17, 1906, to May 6, 1908, I lived at 23 Covington Place. 11. On the seventh page I found a reference to page 72 of volume 3. 12. At nine o'clock on next Friday night, August 23, I shall be twenty-one years old. I shall then be in possession of sixty thousand dollars, of which I will give fifteen cents to charity. 13. Thirty-four thousand, six hundred and eighty-one dollars and twenty cents is the sum he spent during the Christmas vacation. 14. Fourteen thousand, five hundred and one men are employed here.

CAPITALS

Proper names

Days and months

275. Capitalize proper nouns in general, including the names of the days of the week, the names of the months, the names of political parties, historical events, periods, documents, geographical names, names of buildings, titles of organizations and institutions, names of governmental bodies and depart-

ments, names of the Deity and pronouns used instead
of those names, names for the Bible, and divisions of
a book. Thus: The Socialist Party, the Fall of
Rome, the Middle Ages, the Declaration of Inde-
pendence, the Azores, the Woolworth Building, the
Red Cross Society, the Home for the Friendless, the
Senate, the Department of Labor, God the Father,
Jehovah, Chapter III. But note:

(a) The words *spring, summer, midsummer, autumn,* Not seasons
fall, winter, and *midwinter* should not be capitalized.

(b) *North, south, east, west,* and their compounds *North,*
(*north-west,* etc.) and derivatives (*northern,* etc.) *south,* etc.
should not be capitalized except when they designate
divisions of the country.

> Right: As we sailed north we saw a ship going west.
> Right: The West is prosperous. — The people of the
> South are migrating westward. — The Northern
> delegates clashed with the Southern.

**275a. Capitalize words denoting family relation-
ship, such as *father, mother, sister,* only when they
are used with the name of a person or as a substitute
for it.**

> Right: I heard that Uncle John had written to
> Mother.
> Right: She accompanied her brother.

276. Titles of persons should be capitalized when Titles of
they are used in connection with proper names. When persons
used otherwise than in connection with proper names,
titles of governmental officers of high rank should be
capitalized; other titles should not.

> Right: There go Professor Cox and Colonel Henry. —
> A certain professor became a colonel in the volunteer
> army. — The President and the Postmaster-General

sent for the postmaster of our town and the secretary of our society.

Common-noun elements of proper names

277. **Capitalize** *club, company, society, college, high school, railroad, county, river, lake, park, street,* or any other common noun, when it is made a component part of a proper name; not otherwise.

> Wrong: I went to that College one year.
> Right: I went to that college one year.

> Wrong: Do you mean Hamilton college?
> Right: Do you mean Hamilton College?

NOTE. — Many writers consistently go contrary to this rule. Thus: Bleeker street, Portland county, Pennsylvania railroad, the Saturday club, Wilson school.

Words of race and language

278. **Capitalize nouns and adjectives of language or race,** such as *German, Latin, Indian, Negro,* etc.

Words in literary titles

279. **Capitalize only the important words of literary titles.**

> Right: I read *The Light that Failed* and *A Tale of Two Cities.*

At the beginning of a sentence or quotation

280. **Capitalize the first word of a sentence.** This rule applies in general to quoted sentences; but not to a quoted sentence from which words are omitted at the beginning, nor to a quoted sentence-element incorporated in an original sentence.

> Wrong: The conductor cried, "hands off!"
> Right: The conductor cried, "Hands off!"

> Wrong: It seemed to be "Without form and void."
> Right: It seemed to be "without form and void."

> See also Rule 38, note, and the last sentence in the note to Rule 88.

281. Capitalize the first word of every line of poetry. See the *Right* examples under Rules 209–211.

At the beginning of lines of poetry

282. Do not capitalize a clause following a semicolon.

Misuse after a semicolon

Wrong: Send him to the library; His father wants to speak to him.

Right: Send him to the library; his father wants to speak to him.

283. Do not capitalize words which there is no reason for capitalizing, such as *locomotive, forest, organ, rhetoric, mathematics, history, whooping cough, landlady, bulldog, electricity, citizen, flour mill, profession, gold mine, teachers' convention, high school.*

Use without reason

EXERCISE 106

Write the following sentences, filling the blanks with *English, French, German, Latin, Greek, Dutch, Indian,* or *Spanish:* 1. In the battle the —— captain met a —— corporal. 2. Some —— and —— books entertained him, while he drank —— wine and smoked a —— pipe. 3. The —— ships were destroyed by the ——, assisted by their —— allies.

Capitals

EXERCISE 107

An exercise to be written at dictation. My friend Professor Cincinnatus Jones gives instruction in oratory, history, algebra, and swimming in the Kansas City College of Agriculture. Many young men from the West and the South come under his enlightening influence every year. The president of the agricultural college just referred to secured Professor Jones when the latter was employed by the Department of Agriculture in Washington. The Secretary of Agriculture, by the way, was a Democrat, as was the patriotic President in whose Cabinet he had the honor of sitting; the professor also happened to belong to the Democratic Party. Now, the president

Dictation exercise in capitalization

of the college — President Francis X. Fitzgibbons, Ph.D.,
LL.D. — went up to Jefferson City, the capital of the
state, to consult with the governor. That staunch old
Republican, Governor Mannington, was in office at that
time. He was visiting ex-Governor Hemstead on Clinton
Avenue when President Fitzgibbons arrived. The president took a street car and went straight to the house
where the governor was. Now, the mayor of the city,
a Socialist, several members of the state senate and house,
most of them Prohibitionists, the chief of police, a Populist,
and seven aldermen of various political faiths happened to
be calling on the ex-governor at the same time. In walks
President Fitz and says,

"Governor, will you help me get Jones for a professor-
ship in my faculty?"

"Jones?" says the governor. "Major General Jones,
formerly pastor of the First Baptist Church?"

"No. I mean C. Jones, assistant clerk in the Department of Agriculture, author of *How to Make Corn Grow* and
also of *Why I Am a Bee-keeper*."

"Oh yes, that clever Scotchman. His grandfather was
a colonel in the Mexican War, wasn't he?"

"Yes, and beloved by all his regiment — privates,
corporals, sergeants, lieutenants, captains, and majors
alike. And his grandson is worthy of him. But Governor,
I don't want to conceal the fact that he is a Democrat."

"I swear by the Book, Doctor," said the governor,
"I don't care if he is the chief doorkeeper of Tammany
Hall, on Fourteenth Street, New York City; I will get
him for you."

At that, all the assembled men clapped their hands,
and a German politician, a member of the city council
and the proprietor of a vaudeville theater on East Twenty-
ninth Street, remarked that this was a second Missouri
Compromise.

Next day — it was Friday — Governor Mannington
went east to Washington and lifted Jones bodily from the
government service. He came west again in no time, bringing the new professor with him, on the Santa Fé Railroad.
Jones spent the summer in preparing his first lectures, and
began his professional duties in the following autumn.

Italics

284. To italicize a word in a manuscript, draw one straight line below it. Representation in MS.

285. Italicize titles of literary, musical, and artistic works, and of periodicals. Do not italicize the author's name. Italics with titles of books, etc.

> Right: Walter Scott's *The Talisman*, Rider Haggard's *King Solomon's Mines*, Talfourd's *Ion*, and the *Atlantic Monthly* furnished his principal amusement.

NOTE. — It is permissible to enclose titles in quotation marks instead of italicizing them; but the simpler and better approved practice is to italicize.

286. If the title of a single literary, musical, or artistic work begins with *the*, this word should not be omitted in writing the title, and it should be capitalized and italicized. Titles beginning with *the:* Single works

> Wrong: Do you like Kipling's *Man Who Was* and Chaminade's *Silver Ring?*
> Right: Do you like Kipling's *The Man Who Was* and Chaminade's *The Silver Ring?*
> Wrong: I felt depressed after reading the *House of Mirth*.
> Right: I felt depressed after reading *The House of Mirth*.

287. In writing the name of a newspaper or other periodical, however, a *the* limiting the noun of the title should not be capitalized or italicized even if it is part of the title; and the name of a city modifying adjectively the noun of the title should not be italicized. Periodicals

> Right: She found there some copies of the *Pall Mall Gazette*, the *Evening Telegraph*, the *Century Magazine*, the New York *Evening Post*, and the Madison (Wisconsin) *Democrat*.

Names of
ships

288. Italicize names of ships.

Right: I cut the *Hispaniola* from her anchor.

Italics
with words
discussed

289. When a word is spoken of *as a word* — not used to represent the thing or idea that it ordinarily represents, and not quoted — it should be italicized. When a word is spoken of as a quoted word, it should usually be inclosed in quotation marks and not italicized.

Right: The misuse of *grand, awful,* and *nice* is a common fault.
Right: In the expression "we, the people," "people" is in apposition with "we."

Note. — With words discussed, it is permissible to use quotation marks instead of italics, even when the words are not quoted; and it is sometimes necessary and advisable to do so. In this book, for example, quotation marks are used with incorrect expressions discussed, because this practice helps, in some cases, to distinguish the wrong phraseology from the right. But the better practice in general is to italicize.

With for-
eign words

290. Italicize unnaturalized foreign words introduced into an English context.

Right: He is a *bona fide* purchaser.

For em-
phasis

291. Avoid the habit of frequently italicizing words for emphasis; do not emphasize a word in this way unless there is some especially good reason — as, for instance, the fact that obscurity would result from lack of emphasis.

Bad: The curse of this age is *commercialism* coupled with *hypocrisy.*
Right: The curse of this age is commercialism coupled with hypocrisy.
For examples of necessary emphasis by italics, see Rules 2 *e* and 289.

292. Do not italicize for the purpose of calling attention to your humor or irony; this practice is undignified and inartistic. (Cf. Rules 235 and 250 *e.*)

> Bad: The villain in the play was *charming*.
> Right: The villain in the play was charming.

EXERCISE 108

Write the following passage, capitalizing and italicizing correctly:

Dickens's a tale of two cities is to me more interesting than Hugo's the toilers of the sea. But Scott's the talisman is better than either. The New York sun and the journal of psychology are less interesting than the damnation of Theron Ware by Harold Frederick. As for Burns's the cotter's Saturday night — well, Dombey and son is far superior. But I fear that, like the porter in Macbeth, I am rambling.

III. ANALYTICAL OUTLINES

Outlines

293. An outline is an orderly plan of the material to be used in a composition. The material is condensed into topics, sentences, or paragraphs, so numbered and indented as to show their logical relationship. There are, therefore, three kinds of outlines: topic, sentence, and paragraph outlines. (Throughout an outline, the writer must adhere to one type consistently.) The topic and the sentence outlines are more commonly used. Of these two the sentence outline is to be preferred, for it states more explicitly the writer's thought. (Compare the two outlines in Section 294.)

Nouns, not verbs, in topic outline

In a topic outline, make all the titles, as far as possible, in the form of nouns, with or without modifiers. *E.g.*, write " Rapidity of Movement " rather than " Moves Rapidly."

Sentence outline

If, on the other hand, a sentence outline is desired instead of a topic outline, write each division in the form of a sentence which expresses the central idea of the division. Subheads may be expressed as subordinate members of this sentence, or as separate sentences.

Numbering and Arrangement of Titles

294. Number and indent the titles of an outline according to the following method:

THE GOVERNMENT OF SWITZERLAND

Topic Outline

Specimen topic outline

I. Value to Americans of a knowledge of Swiss institutions.

II. The legislative department.
    A. The National Council.
        1. Apportionment.
        2. Elections.
    B. The Council of States
        1. Apportionment.
        2. Elections.
    C. Powers of the legislature.

III. The executive department.
    A. Organization.
    B. Executive powers. — Comparison of Swiss and American executives.

IV. The judicial department: the constitutional court.
    A. Organization.
    B. Judicial powers. — Comparison of Swiss and American judiciaries.

THE GOVERNMENT OF SWITZERLAND

Sentence Outline

I. Knowledge of Swiss institutions is of value to Americans.

II. The legislative department consists of a bicameral legislature, called the Federal Assembly, composed of the National Council and the Council of States.
    A. The National Council, the more numerous branch, represents the people.
        1. It consists of one member for each 20,000 persons, with at least one member from each canton or half-canton.
        2. Members are elected for three years, by popular vote.
    B. The Council of States, the less numerous branch, represents the cantons.
        1. It consists of two members from each canton, and one from each half-canton.

Specimen sentence outline

2. The method of election, term, and
qualification are prescribed by
each canton itself.

C. The legislature is the supreme authority in
the state, and has all powers not re-
served to the people or to the cantons,
and not granted to any other body.

III. The executive department consists of a Federal
Council of seven members, elected by the
Federal Assembly for three years.

A. One member of the Federal Council is
designated by the Federal Assembly to
act as Federal President for one year;
each of the seven members acts as head
of an executive department.

B. The Federal Council is subordinate to the
Federal Assembly, and its powers are
not comparable to those of the American
executive; the Federal President is
merely a presiding officer with no independent powers of importance.

IV. The judicial department consists of a Federal
Court of twenty-four judges, elected by the
Federal Assembly for six years.

A. For ordinary purposes the court sits in
small divisions.

B. Its jurisdiction is largely constitutional,
though in this respect it is not so powerful as the American Supreme Court.

Irregular
alignment

295. Place coördinate titles at the same distance
from the left-hand margin.

*The Terms " Introduction," " Conclusion," and
" Body "*

Misuse of
*Introduc-
tion* and
Conclusion

296. Do not entitle the first division *Introduction*
nor the last *Conclusion* unless their material is distinct
from the body.

Wrong outline for an account of a sleigh-ride:

I. Introduction: the start.
II. The journey out.
III. Conclusion: the return.

Right:

I. Introduction: winter in Dakota.
II. The start.
III. The journey out.
IV. The return.
V. Conclusion: comparison of sleighing and other sports.

297. Do not use the title *Body* or *Discussion;* place the titles belonging to the body, or discussion, of an essay flush with the left-hand margin, as in the topic outline under section 294.

Body or Discussion not to be used

Over-minute Subdivision

298. Do not indicate minute and unimportant divisions.

Over-minuteness

Bad:

1. Situation of building.
   a. In Ames County.
   b. On a hill.
   c. Facing east.

Right:

1. Situation of building.

Certain Illogical Practices

299. Do not write as a subtitle what is logically a part of the governing title; join it to the governing title or omit it.

Part of a title written like a subtitle

Bad:

I. Founding of the city.
   1. By Dionysius Jones.

II. Its principal industry.
    1. Piano manufacturing.

Right:
I. Founding of the city.
II. Principal industry, piano manufacturing.

Bad:
I. Ancestors.
    1. Scotch.
II. Birthplace.
    1. Farm in Indiana.

Right:
I. Scotch ancestors.
II. Birthplace: description of the Indiana farm.

See also titles I and IV in the topic outline in section 294.

Second or third subtitle written like first

300. Do not write as the first subtitle what is logically the second or third; write it as a memorandum after the governing title, or else insert the subtitles that should logically precede it.

Bad:
I. Situation.
    1. Advantages.

Right:
I. Situation: its advantages.

Also right:
I. Situation.
    1. Geographical location.
    2. Advantages.

Bad:
II. Attempts to destroy it.
    1. Why they failed.

Right:
II. Attempts to destroy it.
    1. The first attempt.
    2. The attempt of 1901.
    3. Reason for the failure of all attempts.

See also title III, B, of the topic outline on page 229.

301. Do not write as a subtitle what is logically co-ordinate with the preceding title.

Bad [The rule is violated in titles II, 1, and II, 1, *a*]:

    I. The departure.
    II. The arrival in the city.
          1. Journey to the store.
             a. Purchases.
  III. Return home.

Right:

    I. Departure.
    II. Arrival in the city.
  III. Journey to the store.
  IV. Purchases.
    V. Return.

Also right:

    I. Departure.
    II. Experiences in the city.
          1. Arrival.
          2. Journey to the store.
          3. Purchases.
  III. Return.

302. Do not place a subtitle coördinate with its governing title.

Bad [The rule is violated in title II]:

    I. Disadvantages of football.
          1. Physical harm.
          2. Distraction from studies.
    II. Encouragement of gambling.

Right:

    I. Disadvantages of football.
          1. Physical harm.
          2. Distraction from studies.
          3. Encouragement of gambling.

303. Do not write the title of the composition like the title of a division.

Bad:

   I. Shipbuilding in Maine.
         1. Introduction.
         2. Principal seats.
         3. Methods.
            etc.

Right:

          SHIPBUILDING IN MAINE

   I. Introduction.
  II. Principal seats.
 III. Methods.
       etc.

IV. LETTER WRITING

LETTERS IN THE FIRST PERSON

The Heading

304. The first member of a correct letter written in the first person is the heading — *i.e.*, a statement of the address of the writer and the date of writing. The address should precede the date. Address before date

Right: Groveport, Ohio, June 4, 1926

Right: Groveport, Ohio,
                               June 4, 1926.

Right: Groveport, Ohio
                     June 4, 1926

305. The address in the heading should be such as would be sufficient for a postal direction. The address: Insufficient address

Right: 212 State Street,
                     Chicago, Illinois.

Right: Route 3, La Salle, Illinois.

Right: Route 3, La Salle, Illinois

306. If the address contains a street direction, this should precede the name of the city. Street direction before city

Right: 28 High Street,
                   Columbus, Ohio.

Right: 28 High Street
                   Columbus, Ohio

307. A house number should be written in Arabic figures and should be preceded by no word or sign. House numbers

Right: 15 H Street; not #15 H Street, or Fifteen H Street.

Numbers of streets

307a. Street numbers less than one hundred are usually spelled out. (See Rule 272 *b*.)

> Right: 285 Forty-second Street.   [See Rule 277.]
> Permissible: 285 42nd Street.

Omission of *Street*

308. In writing a street direction do not omit *Street*.

> Wrong: 17 Main.
> Right: 17 Main Street.

The date: Complete-ness

309. The date should consist of the name (not the number) of the month, the number of the day of the month, and the complete number of the year.

> Inelegant: 3/21/'26.
> Right: March 21, 1926.
> Right: 21 March, 1926.

Figures, not words

310. All the numbers in the date should be written in Arabic figures, not represented by words. (See Rule 270. But cf. Rule 338.)

> Wrong: March the twenty-first, nineteen hundred and twenty-four.
> Right: March 21, 1924.

***St, nd*, etc., not to be used**

311. The number of the day should not be followed by *st, nd, rd, d,* or *th*.

> Undesirable: March 21st, 1926.
> Right: March 21, 1926.

Abbreviations not to be used

312. Do not use any abbreviations in the heading. It is permissible to waive this rule in business letters, but it is more dignified to observe it invariably. The name of the month should not be abbreviated.

> Undesirable: Norton, Mass., Jan. 3, 1926.
> Right: Norton, Massachusetts,
>   January 3, 1926.

313. The entire heading, if short, may be written on one line. If two lines are necessary, the date should be written alone on a separate line. If three are necessary, the street direction should stand on the first line, the name of the city and state on the second, and the date on the third.

Right: Fayette, Ohio, May 21, 1926.

Wrong: 21 North Street,
                             Lima, Ohio, June 1, 1926

Right: 21 North Street, Lima, Ohio,
                             June 1, 1926.

Right: 5051 Madison Avenue,
                                Chicago, Illinois,
                                   August 27, 1926.

313a. The lines of the heading may have the same indention, or each line may be indented about one fourth of an inch more than the preceding line.

Right: 5743 Dorchester Avenue,
                                Chicago, Illinois.
                                   June 18, 1926.

Right: 5743 Dorchester Avenue,
                                Chicago, Illinois.
                                June 18, 1926.

Right: Alfred A. Black
                             730 Fifth Avenue, New York
                                June 18, 1926

314. The heading should be written at the beginning of the letter at the right side of the page. (See the letters on page 249.)

314a. In printed, lithographed, or engraved letterheads, the name of the writer or of the firm, and the address are usually placed in the middle of the page; the date may be written at the right of the page or in the center under the address.

315. Do not write a part of the heading (see Rule 304) at the beginning of the letter and a part at the close; and do not repeat the heading or a part of it at the close when it has been written at the beginning.

Bad:

York, Ia., May 1, 1927.

Dear John,

* * *

Yours sincerely,
Robert Graves,
20 Charlotte St.

Bad:

York, Ia., May 1, 1927.

Dear John,

* * *

Yours sincerely,
Robert Graves.

20 Charlotte St.,
York, Ia.

Right:

20 Charlotte Street,
York, Iowa,
May 1, 1927.

Dear John,

* * *

Yours sincerely,
Robert Graves.

Note. — In informal social letters the address of the writer and the date of the writing may be placed on the last page of the letter on a space lower than the signature and at the left-hand margin.

316. Punctuation may be used or may be omitted at the end of the lines of the heading, but care should be taken to follow a consistent practice. (See also 322.) If end-punctuation is used, there should be a comma after *Street*, *Avenue*, etc.; a comma or a

period after the state; and a period after the year.
There should be punctuation within the lines; a
comma should be used after the city and after the
day of the month, but not between the month and
the day. All abbreviations should be followed by
periods. (See the letters on page 249.)

The Inside Address

317. The inside address — a statement of the name
and address of the person written to — is an essential
part of a complete business letter.

Essential to a complete letter

317a. The inside address, which may be written in
two or three lines, should in commercial letters be
placed at the left-hand side of the page one or two
spaces below the last line of the heading. The first
line should be flush with the left-hand margin; the
rest of the address may also be placed at the margin-
line or indented, each line about one-fourth of an inch
more than the preceding.

Position in commercial letters

Right: Henry White and Company,
      19 West Forty-fourth Street,
      New York City.
Right: Henry White and Company,
      19 West Forty-fourth Street,
      New York City.

317b. In letters of friendship, in business letters
not dealing with mercantile transactions, and in professional letters, the inside address may stand either
above the salutation or at the bottom of the letter at
the left-hand side of the page. Placing the inside
address at the end is a little more elegant than placing
it at the beginning. In letters of friendship the in-

side address may be omitted unless the one written to is almost a stranger or occupies a position of honor.

Letter to an individual in a firm

318. If, in the case of a letter to a firm, the particular attention of a member of the firm is desired, the following forms may be used:

>Right: Messrs. Meade, Brown, and Harrison,
>   19 Wabash Avenue,
>   Chicago, Illinois.
>
>   Attention of Mr. M. L. Brown.
>   Gentlemen:
>
>Right: Messrs. Meade, Brown, and Harrison
>   19 Wabash Avenue
>   Chicago, Illinois
>
>   Attention: Mr. M. L. Brown
>   Gentlemen:
>
>Or: Gentlemen: Attention of Mr. M. L. Brown

Omission of street direction permissible

319. The street direction may be omitted from the inside address. In a letter of which a copy is kept the street direction in the copy is often found convenient.

>Right:
>   The Tiffany Company,
>   New York City.
>   Gentlemen:

Name without address

320. Do not write a name alone above the salutation.

>Wrong:
>   Mr. Harvey Myers.
>   My dear Sir:
>Right:
>   Mr. Harvey Myers,
>   Seattle, Washington.
>   My dear Sir:

321. In the inside address do not omit *Mr.* or whatever other title is proper, before the name of an individual. Before a firm name composed of individual names, it is correct to write *Messrs.* or to omit the title. *Messrs.* is improper before a name not composed of individual names. Use no abbreviations of titles except *Mr., Esq., Messrs., Mrs., Dr., Rev.* and *Hon.*, and suffixed initial titles, like *Ph.D.* (See Rule 269.)

Abbreviations not to be used

> Right: Messrs. Hoyt and Marsh,
> Chicago, Illinois.
> Hoyt and Marsh,
> Chicago, Illinois.
>
> Lacking in courtesy and propriety:
> J. H. Woolson,
> Morristown.
> Heath Pub. Co.,
> N. Y. City.
>
> Right:
> Mr. J. H. Woolson,
> Morristown, New Jersey.
> D. C. Heath and Company,
> New York City.

Note 1. — By way of exception, the long names *United States of America* and *District of Columbia* may be abbreviated respectively to *U. S. A.* and *D. C.* It is permissible in business letters to abbreviate the names of States also; but the better practice is to spell out those names. Abbreviation of the short names *Maine, Ohio,* and *Iowa* is objectionable in any letter.

Permissible exceptions

Note 2. — The title *Esq.* is a proper substitute for *Mr.* When *Esq.* follows a name, no title should precede the name.

Use of the title Esq.

> Wrong: Mr. Ralph Williams Esq.
> Right: Ralph Williams, Esq.

322. Punctuation marks may be used or may be omitted at the end of the lines of the inside address;

Punctuation of the address

but care should be taken to follow a consistent practice. If marks are used at the end of the lines, a
period should be placed after the last line and commas
after the others. Punctuation marks may be necessary within the line; for example, a comma should
be placed between the city and the state. Periods
should be used after all abbreviations.

Open Punctuation

Right: Marshall Field and Company
State and Madison Streets
Chicago, Illinois

Close Punctuation

Right: Marshall Field and Company,
State and Madison Streets,
Chicago, Illinois.

The Salutation

Business letters

323. The following are proper salutations for business letters:

Dear Sir: Dear Madam:
Gentlemen: Ladies:
My dear Sir: My dear Madam:
My dear Mr. Park:

Note 1. — The first word of the salutation and all
nouns are capitalized.

Note 2. — There is no hard and fast line drawn
between business letters and letters of friendship, and the
usages of the latter may be employed in the former when
the degree of acquaintance allows. *Dear Mr. Park* is more
intimate than *My dear Mr. Park.* *Dear Sir* is more common that *My dear Sir* in business letters, the omission of
the *my* in this case not implying any greater degree of
intimacy.

Letters of friendship

324. The following are proper salutations for letters
of friendship:

Dear Susan,   Dear old Dad,
My dear Mr. Smith,   My dear Miss Jones,
Dear John,   Dearest Mother,
Dear Mrs. Jackson,   Dear Aunt Edith,

NOTE — Salutations without *My* are more intimate than those with *My*.

325. The salutations " Dear Friend," " My dear Friend," and " Friend John " are not in reputable use; avoid them. *Improper salutations*

326. Never use a name alone as a salutation. *A name for a salutation*

Bad:
                Melmore, O., Sept. 3, '27.
Mr. Percy Clapp: —
    Please inform me . . .
Right:
                Melmore, Ohio, September 3, 1927.
My dear Mr. Clapp,
    Will you please inform me . . .

327. In the salutation never use any abbreviation, except *Mr.*, *Mrs.*, and *Dr.* (See Rule 269.) *Abbreviations not to be used*

Bad: My dear Prof. Walker,
Right: My dear Professor Walker,
Bad: Dear Capt. Ayer,
Right: Dear Captain Ayer,

328. The salutation of a business letter should be followed by a colon. The comma is customarily used after the salutation of an informal letter of friendship, but a colon is allowed. See the two letters on page 249. *Punctuation*

329. The salutation should be written flush with the left-hand margin. The body of a pen-written letter should begin on the line below; of a typewritten *Position of the salutation* letter, two spaces below. All paragraphs should receive the same indention, one inch; the first should not be indented farther than the others.

If a single-spaced typewritten letter has double spacing between the paragraphs and if the block style is used in the heading and the address, it is allowable to write all paragraphs flush with the left margin, without indention.

The Complimentary Close

Business letters

330. The following are proper complimentary closes for business letters:

> Yours truly,
> Yours very truly,
> Very truly yours,

Respectfully yours and *Yours respectfully* are used in writing to school, college, and government officials.

Letters of friendship

331. The following are proper complimentary closes for letters of friendship, or for business letters in which there is an intimate relation between the writer and the person addressed:

> Yours very truly,   Cordially yours,
> Yours sincerely,   Faithfully yours,

Vulgar closes

332. Do not use any abbreviation, such as " yrs " or " resp'y " in the complimentary close; nor write " respectively " for *respectfully;* nor write " and oblige " in the place of the complimentary close. Do not omit the word *yours.*

Position and punctuation

333. The complimentary close should be written on a separate line, about two spaces below the last line of the body of the letter (in typewritten letters), should stand near the middle of the line, should have only the first word capitalized, and should be followed by a comma.

334. Expressions introducing the complimentary close, such as " I am," " believe me," " good-bye," now rarely used, should occupy their regular positions in the body of the letter. *Position of preceding words*

> Right:
> Accept my congratulations upon your new appoint-
>   ment; and believe me
>   Yours sincerely,
>   Henry Cobb.

The Signature

335. The signature should be placed about two spaces below the complimentary close, and near the right-hand margin of the letter. *Position of the signature*

335a. The signature should always be written by hand. In a typewritten letter in which the name of the writer does not appear on the letterhead, the name may be typewritten beneath the written signature or at the left-hand side of the page with the initials of the stenographer. Letters from firms should be signed with the name of the firm, typewritten, and directly beneath that, in handwriting, the name of the person who is responsible for the letter. Sometimes in the signature of a letter from a firm the name of the firm is omitted; sometimes the writer's official capacity is indicated. *Signatures in business letters*

> Right: D. C. Heath and Company
>   Albert Grant Odell
> Right. John R. Clark
>   Business Manager

In business letters a woman should sign her full name and add below in parenthesis her title (*Mrs.*) and her husband's name. If she is a widow, she should sign her own name, preceded by *Mrs.* in parenthesis. An unmarried woman should sign her name preceded by *Miss* in parenthesis.

Right: Mary Osborn Williams.
      (Mrs. John R. Williams.)
Right: (Mrs.) Mary Osborn Williams.
Right: (Miss) Elizabeth Elliot.

Signatures in social notes

335b. In informal social notes, the name should never be preceded by the title (*Mrs.*, *Miss*). A married woman should sign her given name, her maiden name, if she chooses, and her surname.

Wrong: Mrs. John R. Williams.
Right: Mary Osborn Williams.

Literary Style

Certain vulgarisms:

336. The following faults, characteristic of ill-educated writers and of writers without good taste, are to be especially avoided in letters:

Ellipsis

(a) The omissions of pronouns, articles, and prepositions.

Bad: Received your letter of the 6th ult. While very doubtful of the result, will try to carry out your instructions.
Right: I have received your letter of August 6. [See Rule 337, below.] Though I am very doubtful about the result, I will try to carry out your instructions.

Bad: We enclose check for three dollars.
Right: We enclose a check for three dollars.

Bad: Direct letter care Thomas Cook.
Right: Direct the letter in care of Thomas Cook.

Bad: Mr. H. P. Thurston, editor *Jenksville Patriot.*
Right: Mr. H. P. Thurston, editor of the Jenksville *Patriot.*

NOTE. — The omission of *I* is proper in diaries and in letters written in the style of a diary — *i.e.*, intended to present mere hasty memoranda jotted down without any attempt at completeness of form. Thus, Tennyson to his wife: "Slept at Spedding's where I found they expected me. Started this morning 11 a.m. Hay fever atrocious with irritation of railway, nearly drove me crazed, but could not complain, the only other occupant having a curiously split shoe for his better ease . . ." In such letters, clipped expressions harmonize with the context. In a letter, however, that is intended to be complete and regular in form, the omission of *I* and of other grammatically essential words is incongruous and in bad taste. (See Rule 337, below.)

(*b*) Writing " yours," " your favor," or " your esteemed favor " for *your letter.* (See Rule 17, note.) — "Yours," "your favor"

(*c*) The use of the formula " yours of the 17th received," or " yours of the 17th at hand." Write a grammatically complete expression, such as " I have your letter of June 17." — "Yours received"

(*d*) The use of the formula " in reply would say " or " will say." Write a grammatically complete expression, such as " In reply allow me to say." — "In reply would say"

(*e*) The use of the formula " I would say," " I will say," or " I can say." Write " Allow me to say " or " I desire to say," or else omit any such introduction. — "I would, will, or can say"

(*f*) The use of the expression " same " or " the same." Use *it* or *they.* (See *Same* in the Glossary.) — "Same"

Bad: Yours of the 3rd at hand, and in reply would say we are at present out of lamps desired but will send same as soon as possible.

Right: Thank you for your order of March 3. The lamps you wish are out of stock at present, but we will send them as soon as possible.

"Please"

(g) The use of the expression " please " alone. Rather write " Will you please."

"Please find enclosed" "($10) ten dollars"

(h) The use of the formula " Please find enclosed." Write " I enclose."

(i) The use of the formula "($10) ten dollars " or " ten ($10) dollars." (See Rule 274.)

Name of city abbreviated

(j) The abbreviation of the name of a city; e.g., of *Cincinnati* to " Cin.," of *Philadelphia* to " Phil.," or of *New York City* to " N. Y. City."

Participial close

"and oblige"

(k) Monotonously closing all letters with a sentence introduced by a participle, as " Hoping to hear soon . . ." " Thanking you again . . ."; or monotonously closing all letters of request with " and oblige." These old-fashioned endings lack force.

The use of *I*

337. The rule often taught, that it is improper to begin the body of a letter with *I*, is nonsense; beginning with *I* is always permissible and often desirable.

Not to be avoided by mere ellipsis

337a. The monotonously frequent use of *I* in letters is a common fault which it is well to guard against. But one should not, in order to avoid this fault, commit the worse fault of simply omitting *I*; as " Have not heard from you for a long time. Should think you ought to have written before this." The noticeably frequent use of *I* is nothing worse than an awkwardness; the ellipsis of *I* is a vulgarism. (See Rule 336 *a*, above.) As between the two, the awkwardness is preferable. To avoid the repetition of *I*, practise variety of sentence structure, not ellipsis.

A Correctly Written Business Letter

Specimen
letters

17 Lumber Exchange
Minneapolis, Minnesota
January 2, 1927

Mr. Henry Coleman
  Chicago, Illinois
My dear Sir:

I have your letter of December 29. The house about which you inquire is still for sale.

Yours truly
Frank Shaw

A Correctly Written Letter of Friendship

Murray Hill Hotel,
New York City,
September 20, 1927.

My dear Mr. Crawford,

The composition you inquire about is L. Pabst's *Aria con Variazioni* in D flat major. I forget who publishes it; but you can get it by sending to Schirmer's New York house.

Yours sincerely,
Edith Morris.

Mr. George Crawford,
  1301 Beacon Street,
    Boston, Massachusetts.

FORMAL NOTES IN THE THIRD PERSON

338. Formal notes written in the third person should have no heading, no salutation, no complimentary close, no inside address, and no signature. They should be written consistently and solely in the third person; the writer should not refer to himself as *I* or to the addressee as *you*. Except *Mr., Mrs., Messrs.,* and *Dr.,* no abbreviations whatever should be used; and numbers occurring in dates should — unlike those in ordinary letters — be spelled out. For information

Solely in
third per-
son

No abbre-
viations

Numbers
spelled out

about other matters, the following examples will
suffice:

> Mrs. Burton requests the pleasure of Miss Irwin's
> company at dinner on Friday, May the second, at
> seven o'clock.
>
> 935 Webster Street,
>   April the twenty-third.

> Miss Irwin accepts with pleasure Mrs. Burton's
> invitation to dinner on May the second.
>
> 1720 Princeton Avenue,
>   April the twenty-fourth.

> Mr. Matthews regrets that, on account of illness
> he is unable to accept Mr. and Mrs. Eliot's invita-
> tion for January the fifteenth.
>
> 500 Anderson Street,
>   January the tenth.

Use present tense   NOTE. — Use the present tense in letters of regret or acceptance.

> Wrong: Mr. Smith will be pleased to accept . .
>   [The being pleased to accept is present, not future.]
> Right: Mr. Smith accepts; [or] Mr. Smith is pleased
> to accept.

> Wrong: . . . regrets that he will be unable to accept
>   . . . [The inability to accept is present, not
> future.]
> Right: . . . regrets that he is unable to accept . .

SUNDRY MECHANICAL DIRECTIONS

Ink, paper, envelopes   **339.** Use black or blue-black ink in letter writing. Envelopes should always match the paper in color and quality, and envelopes should be of a size to receive the paper when it is properly folded.

NOTE. — Commercial letters are sometimes type-written in brown or other color to harmonize with the tint of the stationery used. The use of ink in violet, green, or other striking color for social correspondence is a fad of questionable taste.

340. Letter-paper consisting of sheets so folded that each sheet is like a little book of four pages, is suitable for all letters — commercial, professional, or social; and for the letters of private individuals, as distinguished from those of public officials and those of business firms. The use of flat sheets is best confined to business or professional correspondence. Writing-paper that is ruled, or limp and flimsy in texture, or conspicuous because of unusual color, should be used for no letters whatever — except in case of emergency.

Writing-paper:

Four-page sheets

Flat sheets

341. The writing should begin an inch or two below the top of any page. It is best to keep a blank margin at least half an inch wide at the left side of every page. Rules 165–177 and 183–187 should be observed in letters as well as in other manuscripts. In typewritten letters a double space should be left between paragraphs.

Margin at top

Margin at left

Legibility

342. When flat sheets of paper are used, it is best that only one side of each sheet be written on.

Flat sheets

343. When four-page sheets are used, all four pages may be written on. The letter should be so written that a person reading the first page has at his left the fold, and at his right the coinciding edges opposite the fold. If the letter occupies more than one but not more than two pages of the sheet, the first and third pages may be written on and the second be left blank. If the letter occupies more than two pages, it is best that the pages be written on in their natural order — *viz.*, 1, 2, 3, 4; not in the order 1, 3, 2, 4 or 1, 4, 2, 3. The lines of writing on all the pages should be at right angles to the fold, not parallel with the fold.

Four-page sheets

Order of pages

344. A letter on a four-page sheet should be enclosed in an envelope in which it will fit when folded with one horizontal crease through the center. The letter should be so folded that the upper and the lower

halves of page 1 face each other; or, in other words, so that the horizontal crease will appear as a groove on pages 1 and 3, and as a ridge on pages 2 and 4. The letter should be so placed in the envelope that the horizontal crease is at the bottom of the envelope.

345. A letter written on flat sheets of paper of note size (approximately 6×8 inches) may be enclosed —

(*a*) In an envelope into which it will fit when folded with one crease running through the center. In this

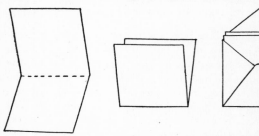

case, the two halves of page 1 should be made to face each other; or, in other words, the crease should appear, to a person reading page 1, as a groove, not as a ridge. Place the letter in the envelope with the crease at the bottom, and with the half containing the heading next to the face, not the sealed side, of the envelope.

(b) In an envelope of commercial size (approximately $3\frac{1}{2} \times 6\frac{1}{2}$ inches). In this case, fold the letter into three sections — a central section and two flaps. As the letter lies right side up on the table, fold up from the bottom about one-third and then from the top fold down over the lower third about one-fourth. The letter so folded should be placed in the envelope

Commercial envelope

Writing parallel with short sides

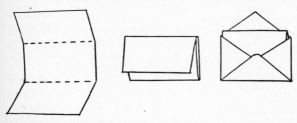

with the two flaps next to the back, not the face, of the envelope; with the top edge of the letter at the bottom of the envelope. The foregoing directions apply to letters in which the lines of writing run parallel to the short sides of the paper. Letters in which the lines run parallel to the long sides should be folded into the same shape; but the right third should be folded first, and the left part folded over it. Such a letter should be placed in the envelope with the flaps next to the back, with the left third flap on top of the right one, and with the outward edge of the left flap pointing upward.

Writing parallel with long sides

346. A letter written on flat sheets of paper of full commercial size (approximately $8\frac{1}{2} \times 11$ inches) may be enclosed —

Flat sheets of full commercial size

Commercial envelope

(*a*) In an envelope of commercial size (approximately $3\frac{1}{2} \times 6\frac{1}{2}$ inches). As the letter lies face up on the table, raise the lower part and fold it upward over the upper part with a horizontal crease running slightly below the center. Keeping the upper part lying next the table, and keeping the horizontal crease toward you, raise the right-hand part and fold it toward the left, making a vertical crease about one third of the distance from right to left. Finally, raise the left-hand part and fold it toward the right, making

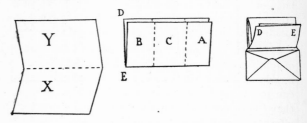

a vertical crease about one fourth of the distance from left to right. When page 1 is read, the horizontal crease and the two vertical creases that divide the upper half of the page should appear as grooves, and the two vertical creases that divide the lower half should appear as ridges. The letter, as folded, consists of a central section and two flaps. Place it in the envelope with the two flaps next to the sealed side, not next to the face, of the envelope; with the smaller flap on top of the larger one; and with the outward edge of the smaller flap pointing upward.

Official envelope

(*b*) In an envelope of official size (approximately 10×4 inches). In this case, it should be folded and enclosed according to the method shown in Rule 345 *b*.

(*c*) In an approximately square envelope, into which it will fit when folded with one horizontal and one vertical crease, both running through the center. In this case, make the horizontal fold first, laying the upper and the lower halves of page 1 face to face — or, in other words, making a crease that will appear as a groove in page 1; then fold with a vertical crease that will appear as a groove in the upper half of page 1, and as a ridge in the lower half. Place the letter in the envelope with the vertical crease at the bottom and the two coinciding halves of the horizontal crease at the right hand, with respect to a person looking at the sealed side of the envelope.

Square envelope

347. The foregoing rules in regard to the manner of folding letters and inserting them in envelopes are merely detailed applications of the simple rule of courtesy: Fold and enclose the letter in such a way that the receiver will be able, with the least possible effort, to get it right side up in his hand, ready to read. A few experiments will show that if any of the directions in Rules 344–346, above, are disregarded in the folding and enclosing of a letter, the addressee, on taking the letter from the envelope and unfolding it in the natural way, will find it with the first page turned from him or with the writing upside down.

The fundamental principle underlying Rules 344–346

The Envelope

348. In writing the address on an envelope, apply Rules 307, 307 *a*, 308, 320, and 336 *a*.

The superscription

Examples:

Mr. Thomas Howe
In care of Captain William Fisk
Wabasha
Minnesota

Abbreviations not to be used

Street
numbers

> The Reverend Charles Wentworth,
> 463 Ninth Street,
> Bridgeport,
> Connecticut.

Bad:

Street not
to be
omitted

> Editor Centerville Ledger,
> # 65 North Liberty,
> Centerville,
> O.

Right:

Ellipsis not
to be used

> For the Editor of the Centerville *Ledger*
> 65 North Liberty Street
> Centerville
> Ohio

Margin and
punctuation

349. The margin, straight or diagonal, and the punctuation, open or close, should correspond with those of the letter.

Right:

> Professor Henry D. Lennington
> 1436 Putnam Avenue
> Woonsocket
> Rhode Island

Right:

> Colonel Charles Kent,
> The Southwick Hotel,
> Kansas City,
> Missouri.

The post-
age stamp

350. The postage stamp should be attached in the upper right-hand corner. It should be right side up, and its edges should be parallel to the edges of the envelope. A postage stamp upside down or affixed in a haphazard fashion raises against the sender of the letter a suspicion of slovenliness.

V. BIBLIOGRAPHY AND FOOTNOTES

Bibliographies

Frequently students will find it necessary to cite references to sources from which they have taken material. Such a list of books relating to a given subject or author is called a bibliography. Although there may be no arbitrary ruling regarding the style followed by authors and publishers in the citation of authority, yet there is a form generally used. First the surname of the author or editor is given, then his initials or given name, next the exact title of the book, the place of publication, the name of the publisher, and the date of publication, all of which information is usually found on the title page of the book. The following examples are punctuated according to the usual form: *(Form used for bibliography of books)*

> Gosse, Edmund W. *Inter Arma.* London, W. Heinemann, 1916.
> Gosse, Edmund W. and Wise, Thomas J. (Editors). *The Posthumous Poems of Algernon Charles Swinburne.* London, W. Heinemann, 1917.

Note—The name of the publisher is frequently omitted. In case no date is given on the title page of the book, the abbreviations n.d. are somtimes used.

The bibliographical form for magazine reference should contain the following information: the name of the author; his initials or given name; the name of the article; the publication in which it appears; the volume and page or pages inclusive, the month, and the year of the issue. (See Rule 246.) *(Form used for bibliography of magazine articles)*

Adams, James T.   "History and Lower Criticism."
  Atlantic Monthly, Vol. 132, No. 3, p. 308, September, 1923.

NOTE. — Frequently the abbreviations for volume and
page are omitted and a colon is used between the volume
and page numbers, as in the following:

Brown, Rollo W.   "The Creative Spirit and the
  American Public."   *Harper's Magazine*, 150:491,
  March, 1925.

The volume number may be written in Roman
numerals as in the following:

Wharton, Edith.   "The Writing of Fiction."   *Scrib-
  ner's Magazine*, LXXVII, 344, April, 1925.

Sometimes either the volume number or the month
and the year are omitted, as in the following:

Webb, Waldron.   "Stars on a Mountain."   *Century
  Magazine*, Vol. 109. p. 786.

Consistency in the form of a bibliography   Even though the writer may vary somewhat from
the usual bibliographical form, yet he should use the
same style consistently.   There should be no variations within the bibliography itself.

Arrangement of the bibliography   The bibliographical list is usually arranged alphabetically according to authors.   If the author's name
is not given, the book or article is generally placed
alphabetically according to the title.

Footnotes

Purpose of footnotes   A footnote may be used for various purposes: it
may contain additional explanatory material or may
give the source of the information contained in the
text.   In a manuscript it is usually inserted on the
page immediately below the word or passage to which
it refers, and it is separated by lines from the body

of the text. The index number should be placed at the end of the passage to which the footnote refers and at the beginning of the footnote. In typewriting, single spacing may be used for footnotes.

> Example: They were to regain youth as had old Aeson.[1]

---

[1] Allusion to the myth of Medea and Aeson in which Medea through her sorceries restores Aeson's youth.

> Example: As far removed from God and the light of Heaven
> As from the centre thrice to the utmost pole.[1]

---

[1] Milton, *Paradise Lost*, Book I, 1. 73.

The information given in the footnote varies. If the book contains a bibliography, it is not always necessary to give more than the name of the author, the title, and the page. If the author's name is mentioned in the text, then it will only be necessary to name the book or the article. In case the author and the book are well known, it is sufficient to give merely the author's surname, usually in the possessive case. Information given in footnote

> Example: Spenser's *Faerie Queene*, Canto V, Stanza 1.

If the reference is made to a work which has appeared in more than one edition, it is often necessary to note the edition.

> Example: Spenser's *Faerie Queene*, London, Macmillan, 1920. Canto V, Stanza 1.

Footnotes should be in as brief a form as clearness will permit. Abbreviations of titles, publishers' names, places of publications, and all words used in Abbreviations in footnotes giving reference are frequently desirable. The following abbreviations commonly appear in footnotes:

	Singular	*Plural*
volume	vol.	vols.
number	no.	nos.
psalm	ps.	pss.
chapter	chap.	chaps.
article	art.	arts.
section	sec.	secs.
page	p.	pp.
verse	vs.	vss.
line	l.	ll.
following pages		ff.

If two references to the same book immediately follow one another, the abbreviation *ibid.* (in the same place) is used.

Example: Dickens' *David Copperfield.* Thos. Nelson and Sons, London, p. 101.
Ibid., p. 34.

If, however, another title intervenes, *ibid.* cannot be used, since it means the reference immediately preceding.

When the author and title of a book have already been given, repetition of the title may be avoided by using *op. cit.* (work cited) with the author's name and the page.

Example: Borrow's *Lavengro*, London, 1914, p. 42.
Borrow, *op. cit.*, p. 61.

When an article or periodical has already been cited in full, repetition may be avoided by the use of *loc. cit.* (place cited).

Example: *New Republic*, XL, 40.
Loc. cit., p. 82.

VI. A GLOSSARY

OF MISCELLANEOUS FAULTY EXPRESSIONS

A.D. Means *in the year of the Lord.* Should not, therefore, be appended to the name of a *century.* Should not be appended to a date self-evidently modern. When used, should precede the date and should not be preceded by a preposition.

> Wrong: The sixth century A.D.
> Right: The sixth century after Christ.
> Right: Arminius died A.D. 21.

About. See **At about.**

Above. When used as an adjective (*e.g.,* The *above* statement) while not incorrect, is less desirable than *the foregoing, the preceding.*

Accept. See **Except.**

Ad. Slang abbreviation for *advertisement.* Write the word in full.

Addicted to, subject to *Addicted to* means *devoted to persistently,* as to a habit or indulgence. Do not confuse with *subject to,* which means *exposed to some agency.* A man may be *addicted to* opium, but *subject to* attacks of rheumatism.

Affect. Means *to influence;* as " War is almost sure to affect trade seriously." Is never used as a noun — always as a verb. Often confused with *effect. Effect* (verb) means *to bring to pass;* as " He will effect a reconciliation." *Effect* (noun) means *result;* as " The drug had a fatal effect."

After. Inaccurate: After having written.
> Right: After writing.

Aggravate. Means *to make worse;* as, " The shock aggravated his misery." Means also to exasperate, embitter (a person). In the sense of *provoke, arouse the evil feelings of,* it is familiar, not literary usage.

All right. There is no such word as *alright.*

All-round. There is no such word as *all-around* recognized by good usage.

All the. " All the farther," " all the higher," " all the faster," or a similar expression should not be used mistakenly for *as far as,* etc. *All the* with an adverb means *by that amount, just so much.*

> Wrong: That was all the farther we went that day.
> Right: That was all the distance we went that day; or, That was as far as we went that day.
> Right: We shall go all the faster for our rest.

Allude. Means *to refer indirectly.* *Refer* means an open, direct mention. " When he *alluded* to profiteers, we knew whom he meant."

Already, all ready. Distinguish *already*, meaning *beforehand*, or *by this time*, from *all ready*, which means *completely ready.* " The hotel was already full." " They were all ready to go."

Alternative. Strictly, means *choice between two things*, or *one of two things between which choice is possible;* as " The alternative is difficult." " One alternative was to jump from the window; the other was to be burned to death." Expanded in familiar usage to mean a choice between more than two things.

Altogether, all together. " The story is altogether false " [*i.e.,* completely false]. " We were all together in the room."

And etc. Never put *and* before *etc.*

> Wrong: Pillows, flags, posters, and etc.
> Right: Pillows, flags, posters, etc.

Anent. The use of this synonym of *about* or *concerning* suggests affectation.

Any place, every place, no place, some place. Vulgarisms for *anywhere, everywhere, nowhere, somewhere.* (See Rule 4.)

Anywheres and nowheres. Vulgarism for *anywhere* and *nowhere.*

Appreciate. Means *to esteem adequately* or *to value highly;* as " I appreciate the service." Should not be modified by *greatly* or *very much.*

As (1). Should not be used too frequently in the sense of *because.* The conjunctions *for* or *since* may often be advantageously substituted. Where *as* occurs in this sense there should often be no conjunction.

> Bad: I want you to come home now as it is time for supper.
> Better: I want you to come home now; it is time for supper.

As (2). In negative statements and in questions implying a negative answer, good usage requires the correlatives *so . . . as* rather than the correlatives *as . . . as.*

> Doubtful: The modern nations are not as artistic as the ancient nations were.
> Preferable: The modern nations are not so artistic as the ancient nations were.

As (3). Not to be used in place of *that* or *whether.* " I don't know *that* [not *as*] we can go."

Asset. *Asset* means *property applicable in the payment of debts.* Should not be loosely used in the sense of *anything valuable or useful;* as, " Smith is an asset to the team."

At about. Prefer *about.*

> Inferior: He came at about three o'clock.
> Right: He came about three o'clock.

Aught. Means *anything*. The name of the symbol 0 is *naught*, not *aught*.

Auto. A colloquialism for *automobile*. Not yet proper in formal writing.

Avail. *Of no avail* is properly used only with some form of *be;* elsewhere use *to no purpose.*

> Wrong: He tried, but of no avail.
> Right: He tried, but to no purpose.
> Right: His attempt was of no avail.

Awful. Means *inspiring with awe;* as " The awful presence of the king." Colloquial or slang as epithet of disapproval. Say not " an awful mistake," but " a serious or disastrous mistake "; not " an awful blunder," but " a ludicrous blunder."

Badly. Colloquially used for *a great deal* or *very much.*

> Wrong: I want badly to see you.
> Right: I want very much to see you.

Balance. Bad English when used in the sense of *remainder*, except as a balance at the bank. (Cf. **Bank on, Take stock in.**)

> Bad: One was an Italian; the balance were Greeks.
> Right: One was an Italian; the rest (or the others) were Greeks.

Bank on, take stock in. Slang in the sense of *rely on, trust in, receive as trustworthy, confidently expect.* (Cf. **Balance.**)

Barbarous, barbaric. *Barbarous* means, in its restricted sense, *cruel; barbaric* is especially related to the barbarian love of noise or show, as, *barbaric* music.

Barn. Means *a farm building used for storing grain or hay.* Should not be used for *stable.*

Beg. When used in asking permission to do a thing, *beg* should govern a noun — *permission, leave,* or some synonym of these words.

> Elliptical: I beg to state. — I beg to differ. — I beg to be absent.
> Better: I beg leave to state. — I beg leave to differ. — I beg permission to be absent.

Besides. Means *additionally,* or *in addition to.* Not to be confused with *beside,* which is always a preposition, meaning " by the side of "; as, *beside* the house.

Between. Usually applies to only two persons or objects. For three or more, use *among.* But: " A railroad between Chicago, Philadelphia, and New York."

Blame . . . on. Crudely used instead of *blame.*

> Wrong: You needn't blame it on me.
> Right: You needn't blame me for it.

Borrow. Not to be confused with *lend*.

> Vulgar: He refused to borrow me his knife.
> Right: He refused to lend me his knife.
> Right: I wanted to borrow his knife from him.

Bunch. Slang for *group* or *party*.

But that, or but what. After *doubt*, *that* is considered more logical than *but that*. *But what* is incorrect.

> Wrong: I had no doubt but what he would bite.
> Right: I had no doubt that he would bite.

Calculate. A provincialism for *think, suppose, expect,* or *intend*.

Can. Denotes power or ability. Should not be used to denote permission.

> Wrong: Can students hand in their theses in manuscript?
> Right: May students [or, are students allowed to, or permitted to] hand in their theses in manuscript?

Can't seem. See **Seem**.

Cause. Complete such an expression as *the cause was* with a predicate noun or a noun clause. (See Rule 117.)

> Wrong: The cause of his failure was on account of his imprudence.
> Right: The cause of his failure was his imprudence; [or] . . . was that he was imprudent.

Certainly. The use of the word *certainly*, as a means of emphasis in relation to matters on which no doubt has been cast, is a colloquialism, and its over-use is monotonous, as in the expressions, " We certainly had a good time "; " That certainly was a hard examination "; " I certainly wonder where she bought that hat."

Characteristic. Means *a distinguishing quality;* as " His chief characteristic is absent-mindedness." Should not be used without intelligent regard to its meaning.

> Bad: One characteristic of my daily life is climbing College Hill.
> Right: One incident of my daily life is climbing College Hill.

Charge. Should be combined, when it means *accuse*, not with *of*, but with *with*.

> Wrong: They charged him of many crimes.
> Right: They charged him with many crimes.

Claim. Means *to demand as due;* as " I claim the reward." Colloquial for *assert* or *maintain*, when there is no question of right, title, or advantage.

> Wrong: He claimed that the William Tell story was only a legend.
> Right: He asserted that the William Tell story was only a legend.

Coincidence. Means *the occurrence of two events at the same time or in remarkable connection with each other;* as " My forgetting my ticket and Bob's appearance just then with a ticket he didn't need, made a lucky coincidence." Should not be used to designate a single event.

Company. A vulgarism for *companion, guest, escort,* or the plurals of these words.

Complected. Not to be used for *complexioned.*

> Wrong: A light-complected girl.
> Right: A light-complexioned girl.

Conscience, consciousness, conscious, conscientiousness. *Conscience* is *the power of making moral distinctions;* not to be confused with *consciousness,* which is simply *the power of being aware of anything. Conscience* is *moral consciousness.* Similarly, distinguish *conscious,* an adjective meaning *aware* or *mentally alert,* and *conscientiousness,* a noun meaning *loyalty to conscience.*

Considerable. A colloquialism when used as a noun.

> Wrong: He lost considerable in the fire.
> Right: He lost considerable property [or, a good deal of property] in the fire.

Contemplate. Should not be combined with a preposition.

> Wrong: He contemplated on [or over] a trip to Alaska.
> Right: He contemplated a trip to Alaska.

Contemptible. Means *worthy of being despised;* as " He is a contemptible sneak." Not to be confused with *contemptuous,* which means *showing scorn;* as " He made a contemptuous answer."

Contemptuous. See **Contemptible.**

Continual. Not synonymous with *continuous,* according to modern usage. *Continual* means *occurring in close succession, frequently repeated;* as " Continual hindrances discouraged us," " He coughs continually." *Continuous* means *without cessation, continuing uninterrupted;* as " Continuous opposition discouraged us," " He slept continuously for ten hours."

Continuous. See **Continual.**

Could of. See **Of.**

Couldn't seem. See **Seem.**

Credible, credulous, creditable. Credible means *believable.* Distinguish from *credulous,* meaning *easily imposed on, believing too easily,* and from *creditable,* which means *praiseworthy.*

Criticize. May mean *to censure,* but may mean merely *to pass judgment on,* whether favorable or adverse.

Crowd. Not to be used for *party* or *company.*

Cunning. Means *artful, ingenious,* or *giving evidence of art or ingenuity;* as " a cunning intriguer," " cunning workmanship." As *pretty* or *amusing* it is a colloquial Americanism.

Cute. Slang. Use *pretty, vivacious, lively, amusing, dainty, piquant, engaging,* or some other word in reputable use and of definite meaning.

Data, phenomena, strata. Plural, not singular forms. The singular forms are *datum* (rarely used), *phenomenon,* and *stratum.*

Date. Inelegant for *engagement* or *appointment.*

Deal (1). Should be combined with *with,* not with *on* or *of,* when the intended meaning is *discuss.*

> Wrong: He deals on three subjects.
> Wrong: He deals of three subjects.
> Right: He deals with three subjects.

Deal (2). Colloquialism for *transaction, agreement,* or *arrangement.*

Demand. Means *to claim or call for peremptorily.* The object of this verb should be the thing claimed, never the person from whom the thing is claimed.

> Wrong: Japan demanded Russia to leave Manchuria.
> Right: Japan demanded that Russia leave Manchuria. [The object of "demanded" is the substantive clause "that . . . Manchuria."]

Demean. *To demean oneself* is merely *to conduct oneself;* as " He demeaned himself as a gentleman." Colloquial in the sense of *to lower or degrade oneself.*

Depot. Best applied to a building for the deposit of merchandise. To designate a building for the accommodation of passengers, it is better to say *station.*

Different. Should not be completed by a *than* clause, but always by a *from* clause. British usage differs in this from American usage.

> Wrong: The method is different than the one that formerly prevailed.
> Right: The method is different from the one that formerly prevailed.

Diner, sleeper, smoker. Colloquial in the United States for *dining car, sleeping car,* and *smoking car.* Not vulgarisms.

Disinterested. Means *without self-interest, unselfish;* as " the judge's disinterested performance of his duty." Not to be confounded with *uninterested.*

Done. An ungrammatical error when used as the past tense of *do,* or as an additional auxiliary indicating past time. Typical illiterate sentences are " He done fine," " He done real good," for " He did well," (see **fine** (1), **real,** and **good**); and " I done lost it," for " I lost it " or " I have lost it."

Don't. A contraction of *do not.* Therefore ungrammatical when used with a subject in the third person singular. (See Rule 29.)

> Wrong: He don't know.
> Right: He doesn't know.
> Right: I don't know, we don't know, you don't know, and they don't know.

Dove. Should not be used as the past tense of *dive*. Say "dived."

Due to. Should not be used unless the *due* modifies some noun.

> Wrong: The forces were divided, due to a misunderstanding.
> Right: The forces were divided through [or because of] a misunderstanding.
> Right: The division of the forces was due to a misunderstanding.

Each other. Properly used as referring to only two. To be distinguished from *one another*, which refers to more than two.

Effect. See **Affect.**

Either, neither. Preferably used to designate one of two persons or things; less commonly, one of three or more.

> Less common: I asked Leahy, Mahoney, and McGinty, but neither of them was willing.
> Preferable: I asked Leahy, Mahoney, and McGinty, but none of them was willing; [or] . . . no one of them was willing.

Elegant. Means *excelling in the power to discriminate properly and select properly,* or *giving evidence of such excellence;* as " an elegant gentleman," " elegant ornamentation." Should not be used loosely. Say not " an elegant view," but a " beautiful view "; not " an elegant game of football," but " an excellent or a masterly game "; not " an elegant march," but " a spirited or rousing march "; not " an elegant pie," but " a delicious pie." Choose an adjective that expresses your meaning definitely.

Element. Means a *component part;* as " The elements of training are exercise, diet, and regularity." Should not be used without intelligent regard to its meaning.

> Bad: Next, the logs are "driven" down stream. Great danger besets the lumbermen in this element.
> Right: Next, the logs are "driven" down stream. Great danger besets the lumbermen in this process.

Else. To be followed by *but*, not by *than*. Often used redundantly, as " no one else but him " for " no one but him."

> Redundant: It is nothing else but selfishness.
> Right: It is nothing but selfishness.

Both expressions, *somebody else's* and *somebody's else* are right, but the former is preferred.

Enormity, enormousness. *Enormity* ordinarily means *outrageous wickedness.* *Enormousness* means *of abnormal size.*

Enough. A result complement limiting *enough* should have the form of an infinitive, not of a clause introduced by *that* or *so that.*

> Wrong: It was near enough that I could touch it.
> Right: It was near enough for me to touch it.
> Wrong: There is humor enough so that the story isn't dull.
> Right: There is humor enough to keep the story from being dull.

Enthuse. The word is unknown to good usage. (See Rule 5.)

> Vulgar: He doesn't enthuse me.
> Right: He doesn't rouse any enthusiasm in me.
> Vulgar: She never enthuses.
> Right: She never becomes enthusiastic.

Etc. The use of *etc.* is incongruous in a context intended to be artistic. Use a definite term in place of *etc.* or simply omit *etc.*

> Wrong: She was more beautiful, witty, virtuous, etc., than any other lady.
> Right: She was more beautiful, witty, virtuous, and loyal than any other lady.
> Right: She was more beautiful, witty, and virtuous than any other lady.

In any context, avoid the vague use of *etc.*; use it only to dispense with useless repetition or to represent terms that are entirely obvious.

Every place. See **Any place.**

Every so often. A colloquial espression for *at regular periods or intervals.*

Except (verb) means to *exclude;* as " He alone was excepted from the amnesty." *Except* (preposition) means *with the exception (i.e., exclusion) of;* as " All's lost except honor." *Except* is not to be confused with *accept,* which means *to receive.*

Exceptional, exceptionable. *Exceptional,* which means *unusual,* is to be distinguished from *exceptionable,* which means *objectionable.* " It was an exceptional offer." " Your language is exceptionable."

Expect. Should not be used for *suppose.*

> Wrong: I expect it's time for us to go.
> Right: I suppose it's time for us to go.

Extra. Not to be used in the sense of *unusually,* as " an extra fine day."

Factor. Means *a force or agent coöperating with other forces or agents to produce a certain result;* as " The factors of success are industry and perseverance." Should not be used without intelligent regard to its meaning.

> Bad: Being ducked in the lake is an inevitable factor in the freshman's experience.
> Right: Being ducked in the lake is an inevitable part of the freshman's experience.

Falls, ways, woods. Plurals, not singulars.

> Wrong: Go a little ways down stream till you come to a falls. Beside it is a woods.
> Right: Go a little way down stream till you come to a fall. Beside it is a wood.
> Right: The falls of the river; the woods and the fields; the ways of men.

Fine (1).   Means *refined, delicate, free from impurity, of excellent quality:* " fine cutlery," " fine dust," " fine sense of honor," " fine gold." Loosely used it is a general epithet of approval: " a fine fellow," " a fine day," " a fine ship."

Fine (2).   The use of this adjective as an adverb is a gross error; as " You look fine " for " You look finely."

First-rate.   May be used as an adjective but never as an adverb.

> Right: It is a first-rate building.
> Wrong: He plays tennis first-rate.
> Right: He plays tennis very well; [or] He plays a first-rate game of tennis.

Firstly.   Most writers prefer *first*, even when followed by *secondly, thirdly,* etc.

Fix (1).   Slang for *plight, situation,* or *condition.*

Fix (2).   Colloquial in the United States for *repair* or *arrange.* The expression " fix up " used in one of these senses is likewise a colloquialism.

Former, latter.   Properly used to designate one of two persons or things, not one of three or more. (Cf. **Either, neither.**) For designating one of three or more, say " first," " first-named," " first-mentioned," or " last," " last-named," " last-mentioned."

Frighten, scare.   Provincialisms when used intransitively.

> Wrong: Does the horse frighten easily?
> Right: Is the horse frightened easily?

Genial, congenial.   *Genial* means *cordial and pleasant in manner.* Do not confuse it with *congenial*, which means *suited to one's disposition;* as " a congenial friend," " a congenial occupation."

Gent.   A vulgarism for *gentleman.*

Gentleman, lady.   Terms properly used to designate persons of refined speech and manners, as distinguished from ill-bred or uncultivated people; the use of them to designate mere sex is incorrect.

> Wrong: Saleslady, business gentleman, lady stenographer. — There are lady cab-drivers in Paris. — There are more ladies than gentlemen who play the piano. — Cornell admits ladies, but Williams admits only gentlemen. — Ladies' cloak room.
> Right: Saleswoman, business man, woman stenographer. — There are woman cab-drivers in Paris. — There are more women than men who play the piano. — Cornell admits women, but Williams admits only men. — Women's cloak room.

The use of *man* and *woman* need never be shunned; even where *lady* or *gentleman* may be used correctly, *man* or *woman* is equally polite, and is often preferable.

> Right: Is your wife a Massachusetts woman? — You are the only woman I know who drives a motor. — Are you the man I met last spring in Denver?

Gentleman friend, lady friend. These terms, not in themselves objectionable, have, through the use that has been made of them, become objectionable. Prefer *man friend* (plural: *man friends*) or *gentleman of one's acquaintance, woman friend* (plural: *woman friends*) or *lady of one's acquaintance.*

Get. " I didn't *get to go* " is a provincialism for " was not able to go." " She *got around* the old lady " is colloquial for " persuaded," " coaxed." *Get on to, get next to, get away with, get across, get left,* are slang

Get up. A colloquialism for *organize, institute, compose, prepare, arrange, print, bind, dress, decorate,* or *ornament.* " A get-up " is a colloquialism for *a dress, a costume.*

Going on.

> Tautological and provincial: How old is he? Sixteen, going on seventeen.
> Right: How old is he? Sixteen.

Good. An adjective; must not be used as an adverb.

> Wrong: Do it good this time.
> Right: Do it well this time.

Got. The perfect tense is colloquial in the sense of *possess.*

> Colloquial: Have you got a knife with you?
> Preferable: Have you a knife with you?

Got up, gotten up. See **Get up.**

Gotten. Often used still, but " got " is the accepted modern form.

> Undesirable: He has gotten his reward at last.
> Right: He has got his reward at last.

Grand. Means *on a large scale, imposing;* as " a grand mountain range." Should not be used loosely. Say not " a grand day," but " a beautiful or brilliant day."

Grip. Colloquial in the United States for *valise* or *bag.* *Gripsack* is likewise a colloquialism.

Guess. Colloquial in the United States to express supposition, expectation, or intention. Say " think," " suppose," " except," " mean," or " intend."

Had better, had best, had rather. Entirely grammatical and fully approved by good usage. *Would better, would best,* and *would rather* are not preferable. *Had better* is preferable to *would better; had best* and *would best, had rather* and *would rather* are equally good.

> Correct but undesirable: You would better not stay long.
> Right: You had better not stay long.
> Right: They had best attempt no violence.
> Right: I had rather go than stay.

Had have or **had of.**   Often incorrectly used for *had*.

> Bad: If we had have [or had of] tried, he would have suc-
> ceeded.
> Right: If he had tried, he would have succeeded.

Had ought.   See **Ought**.
Have got.   See **Got**.
Heap, heaps.   Vulgarisms for *very much, a great deal, a great many*.
Hear to it.   A vulgarism.   Say " consent to it," or " allow it."
Help (1).   Colloquial in the United States for *a servant, servants*, or
> *employees*.
Help (2).   Should not be followed by *but* when used in the sense of
> *avoid;* should be followed by a gerund.

> Wrong: I can't help but regret.
> Right: I can't help regretting.

Hired girl.   Colloquial for *maid* or *servant*.
Home.   Properly used as an adverb expressing motion, as " He went
> home."   " He is home " is wrong when it means " He is at
> home," but right when it means " He has come home."   (See
> Rule 92, note.)
Honorable.   See **Reverend**.
Hung.   Improper when used in reference to an execution.   Say
> " hanged."

> Wrong: He was found guilty and hung.
> Right: He was found guilty and hanged.
> Right: We hung the flag on the balcony.

Hustle.   Colloquial in the United States when used intransitively to
> mean *hasten, hurry*, or *be energetic or industrious*.   Correctly
> used with a direct object.

> Colloquial: People were hustling about in confusion.
> Right: People were hurrying about in confusion.
> Right: The police hustled the loiterers from the hall.

Hustler.   A colloquialism for *an energetic or capable person*.
i.e.   Means *that is;* denotes, therefore, that what follows is equivalent
> to what precedes.   Should not be used when what follows is not
> equivalent to what precedes, or when *that is* will not fit gram-
> matically into the place of *i.e.*

> Right: The act is treated as a capital crime — *i.e.*, a crime
> punishable by death.   [" A crime punishable by death"
> is equivalent to "a capital crime"; and *that is* may be
> grammatically substituted for "*i.e.*"]
> Wrong: I like to read the Bible, *i.e.*, some of the stories in
> the Old Testament.   ["Some of the stories in the Old
> Testament" is not equivalent to "the Bible."]
> Wrong: I like some parts of the Bible, *i.e.*, the stories in the

Old Testament. [*That is* cannot be grammatically substituted for "*i.e.*"]

Right: I like some parts of the Bible — namely, [or *viz.*,] the stories in the Old Testament.

Right: He had committed lese-majesty — *i.e.*, had given an affront to the Emperor. ["Had . . . Emperor" is equivalent to "had . . . majesty" and *that is* may properly be substituted for "*i.e.*"]

If. A colloquialism used as a synonym of *whether* after *see, ask, learn, know, doubt,* and the like.

Inadvisable: I don't know if I can.
Right: I don't know whether I can.

Ilk. An archaic adjective meaning *same.* In the expression *of that ilk,* as correctly used, *ilk* is an adjective modifying *estate* understood; "Sir George Urquhart of that ilk" means *Sir George Urquhart of that same (estate) — i.e., Sir George Urquhart of Urquhart.* The use of *ilk* as a noun meaning *kind* is a blunder.

Wrong: I'm not of her ilk, I'm glad to say.
Right: I'm not of her sort, I'm glad to say.

In. Generally incorrect when used to express motion. Say "into."

Wrong: He went in the bank.
Right: He went into the bank.

In back of. *In front of* is correct; "in back of" is a vulgarism. Say "behind."

In our midst. See **Midst.**

Incredible, incredulous. The former means *unbelievable;* the latter, *disinclined to believe.* "He had caught an incredible number of fish, and I was incredulous when he told me."

Individual. Should not be used indiscriminately for *person.* Properly used to mean *individual person.*

Right: He made a general address to the class, and also gave special advice to the individuals in the class.
Wrong: He is a tall, gaunt individual.
Right: He is a tall, gaunt fellow [or person, or man].

Indulge. Means (*a*) *to treat with forbearance;* as "Will you indulge me for a moment?" or (*b*) *to put no restraint upon oneself;* as "He indulges in [*i.e.*, puts no restraint upon himself in regard to] gambling." *Indulge in* is often misused for *practice* or *engage in.*

Bad: Practice in surveying is indulged in in the autumn.
Right: Practice in surveying is engaged in [or taken] in the autumn.

Inferior. See **Superior.**

Ingenious, ingenuous. An inventor is *ingenious;* a person of a frank, trusting nature is *ingenuous.*

Inside.   Does not require *of* following.   Say simply " inside."

> Right: They were trapped inside the walls.

Inside of.   A colloquial Americanism for *within*, in time expressions.

> Bad: It will disappear inside of a week.
> Right: It will disappear within a week.

Instance, instant, incident.   *Instance* means *a single occurrence, an example;* as " I will give you an instance of this habit."   *Incidents* are *happenings*.

Kind, sort.

> Crude and incorrect: I don't like those kind [or those sort] of photographs.
> Right: I don't like that kind [or that sort] of photographs.

Kind of, sort of (1).   A low colloquialism when used to modify verbs or adjectives.   Say " somewhat," " somehow," " for some reason," " rather," or " after a fashion."

> Bad: People who kind of chill you . . .
> Right: People who somehow chill you . . .
> Bad: The man who does nothing but study, gets sort of dull.
> Right: The man who does nothing but study, gets rather dull.
> Bad: I kind of felt my way at first.
> Right: I felt my way, after a fashion, at first.

Kind of, sort of (2).   Should not be followed by *a* or *an*.

> Inelegant: What kind of a house is it?
> Right: What kind of house is it?
> Inelegant: It is a sort of a castle.
> Right: It is a sort of castle.

Lady, lady friend.   See **Gentleman** and **Gentleman friend.**

Latter.   See **Former.**

Lay.   Often confounded with *lie*.   Remember that *lay* is the causative of *lie; i.e., to lay* means *to cause to lie*.   Remember the principal parts of each verb:

> I lie   I lay   I have lain.
> I lay   I laid   I have laid.

Learn.   A provincialism when used in the sense of *teach;* as " He learned us our lessons."

Leave go of.   A colloquialism.   Say " leave hold of " or " let go."

> Wrong: He left go of the rope.
> Right: He left hold of the rope; [or] He let go the rope.

Less.   Should not be used in place of *fewer*.

> Wrong: Less men were hurt this year than last.
> Right: Fewer men were hurt this year than last.

Liable. Means (a) *easily susceptible;* as " It is liable to injury "; or
(b) *likely;* as " It is liable to be misunderstood." But NOTE:
Liable is not properly used in the sense of *likely* except in designating an injurious or undesirable event which may befall a
person or thing.

> Wrong: We are liable to have a clear day tomorrow.
> Right: We are likely, etc.

Like. Incorrect when used to introduce a subject with a verb. Say
" as " or " as if." *Like* is correct when followed by a substantive
without a verb.

> Vulgar: He acted like the rest did.
> Right: He acted as the rest did.
> Right: He acted like the rest.
>
> Vulgar: I felt like I had done something generous.
> Right: I felt as if I had done something generous.
> Right: I felt like a philanthropist.

Liked. Should not be compounded with *would* or *should*.

> Bad: He would liked to have gone.
> Right: He would have liked to go. (See Rule 53.)

Likely. Not in good use as an adverb meaning *probably* except after
most or *quite.*

Line. The following uses of *line* are loose and incorrect:
(a) The loose use of *line* in the sense of *kind* or *business*, or in
other senses for which there are precise words.

> Bad: What line of work are you now doing?
> Right: What kind of work are you now doing?
> Bad: I am now engaged in the hardware line.
> Right: I am now engaged in the hardware business.

(b) The use of *line* shown in the following *Bad* examples.

> Bad: I like anything in the card line.
> Right: I like any game of cards.
> Bad: Was there anything in the refreshment line?
> Right: Were there any refreshments?
> Bad: He said a few things in the advice line.
> Right: He gave me a little advice; [or] He said a few things
> by way of advice.
> Bad: I'm not very good in the walking line.
> Right: I'm not very good at walking.

(c) The use of " along the line of " or " in the line of " for *in
connection with, in regard to, about, on the subject of, in the nature of,
by way of, in, of.*

> Bad: He was also famous along the line of literature.
> Right: He was also famous in literature.

Bad: The dean said some things along the line of athletics.
Right: The dean said some things about athletics.
Bad: We are planning something in the line of a surprise.
Right: We are planning something by way of surprise.

(d) The use of " along this or that line " or " in this or that line,"
for *in* or *on* or *in regard to this* or *that subject, in this* or *that respect,
of this* or *that sort.*

Bad: Let me tell you something along that line.
Right: Let me tell you something in connection with that
subject.
Bad: If he is so weak in physics and chemistry, he needs some
tutoring along those lines.
Right: If he is so weak in physics and chemistry, he needs
some tutoring in those subjects.
Bad: I need some tacks. Have you anything along that line?
Right: I need some tacks. Have you anything of that sort?

Lines. A provincialism for *reins.*
Loan. Objectionable as a verb.

Inelegant: He loaned me a book.
Right: He lent me a book.
Right: The loan was a great assistance.

Locate. A colloquialism for *settle.* Correct when used transitively.

Bad: He located in Ohio.
Right: He settled in Ohio.
Right: He located his factory in Lima.

Lose out, win out. Slang, not proper except in connection with sports.
Lovely. Means *lovable* or *inspiring love;* as " a lovely character." A
colloquialism when used loosely. Say not " a lovely time,"
but " a pleasant or delightful time "; not " a lovely drive,"
but " an interesting or pleasant drive "; not " a lovely costume," but " a handsome, or dainty, or rich, or striking, or
elegant costume." Choose the adjective that expresses your
meaning definitely.
Luxuriant. Means *of rank* or *vigorous growth.* Not to be confounded
with *luxurious,* which is related to indulgence in pleasures of the
senses. *A luxurious home,* but *luxuriant vegetation.*
Mad. Means *insane.* Colloquial for *angry.*
May of. See *Of.*
Mean. Means *lowly* or *base.* Colloquial when used to mean *cruel,
vicious, unkind,* or *ill-tempered.*
Messrs. The plural of *Mr.* Like *Mr., Messrs.* should never be used
without a name or names following it. (See Rule 324.)

Vulgar: Messrs., will you come in? [To say this is like saying
" Mister, will you come in?" or " Mrs., I have come."]

> Right: Gentlemen, will you come in?
> Right: Messrs. Zangwill and Barrie met the Messrs. McCarthy.

Midst. The expressions *our midst*, *your midst*, and *their midst* preceded by a preposition have been censured by critics and have gathered many ludicrous associations. Instead of " in our midst," say " in the midst of us " or " among us." Instead of " from our midst," many writers use " from the midst of us " or " from among us," or substitute for *midst* some noun such as *neighborhood, community, fellowship*, etc.

Might of. See **Of.**

Miss. Like *Mr.*, *Mrs.*, and *Messrs.*, *Miss*, when used as a title, must always be followed by a name. (Cf. **Messrs.**)

> Vulgar: My dear Miss.
> Right: My dear Madam; [or] My dear Miss Smith.

Most. Dialectic for *almost*. (See Rule 5.)

Mrs. The combination of *Mrs.* with a husband's title is incorrect. *Mrs.* may be followed only (1) by the woman's surname, (2) by her husband's Christian name (or initials) and surname, or (3) if the woman is a widow, by her own Christian name and surname; the husband's *title*, if stated at all, should be put in another part of the sentence.

> Right: Mrs. Boughton. [1]
> Right: Mrs. John C. Boughton. [2]
> Right (for a widow): Mrs. Mary Dole. [3]
> Wrong: Mrs. Professor Yates, Mrs. Dr. Fairbanks, Mrs. President Hughes, Mrs. Bishop Ross, Mrs. Rev. Fisher, Mrs. Captain Johnson.
> Right: Mrs. Richard E. Yates; Mrs. Fairbanks, wife of Dr. Fairbanks; Mrs. Louisa Hughes, widow of President Hughes; Mrs. Jeremiah Ross; Mrs. Noah Fisher; Mrs. C. V. Johnson.

Much. Not to be used for *very*.

> Wrong: My work is much different this year.
> Right: My work is very different this year.

Must of. See **Of.**

Mutual. Incorrect, according to modern usage, in the sense of *shared in common;* for this meaning the proper adjective is *common*. *Mutual*, properly used, means *reciprocal, interchanged*.

> Wrong: As we conversed, we found that we had several mutual friends in Portland. [The title of Dickens's novel *Our Mutual Friend* is a quotation from some ill-educated persons in the story; it therefore furnishes no good argument for the correctness of the expression "mutual friend."]

> Right: As we conversed, we found that we had several common friends in Portland.
>
> Wrong: The two men had a mutual interest in sculpture.
> Right: . . . a common interest in sculpture.
>
> Right: They practiced mutual forbearance and aid [*i.e.*, each one helped and bore with the other]. — Their faces showed a mutual hatred [*i.e.*, showed that each hated the other]. — Mutual friendship [*i.e.*, friendship interchanged between two persons]. — Common friendship [*i.e.*, friendship shared by two persons for a third].

Near by. A colloquialism when used as an adjective. (See Rule 4.)

> Colloquial: A near-by house.
> Right: A neighboring, or adjacent, house; [or] A house that stood near by.

Nearly. Often misused for *near*.

> Wrong: He came nearly getting hurt.
> Right: He came near getting hurt.

Neither. See **Either.**

Nice. Means *keen and precise in discrimination*, or *delicately or precisely made;* as " nice judge of values," " a nice discrimination." A colloquialism when used to mean *pleasant*. Say not " a nice fellow," but " an agreeable, or admirable, or conscientious, or honorable fellow "; not " a nice time," but " a pleasant time "; not " He is nice to us," but " He is kind or courteous to us." Choose the adjective that expresses your meaning definitely.

No good. A vulgarism when used adjectively. Say " worthless," " of no value."

No place. See **Any place.**

No use. Incorrect when used adjectively. Say " of no use," " of no value," or " unsuccessful."

Notorious. Means *of bad repute;* as " a notorious gambler." Not to be used for *famous* or *celebrated.*

Not to exceed. Should not be used except in giving or quoting orders or directions. Often misused for *not more than.*

> Right: They were authorized to spend any sum, not to exceed $500,000. [See Rule 271 *f.*]
> Wrong: The trains are composed of not to exceed twenty cars.
> Right: The trains are composed of not more than twenty cars.

Nowhere near. A vulgarism for *not nearly.*

Observance. Means *the act of paying respect or obedience.* Not to be confused with *observation*, which means *the act of inspecting, looking at.*

> Right: The observance of Good Friday.
> Right: From his observation of the sky, he judged that a storm was approaching.

Observation. See **Observance.**

Of. *Could of, may of, might of, must of, should of,* and *would of* are illiterate corruptions of *could have, may have, might have, must have, should have,* and *would have.*

Off of. Incorrect for *off.*

> Wrong: Keep off of the grass.
> Right: Keep off the grass.

On the side. Slang for *incidental, collateral, occasional,* or the corresponding adverbs.

Only. Incorrect for *but* or *except that.*

> Wrong: He would have been here, only he had to study.
> Right: He would have been here, but he had to study.

Or. Should not be correlated with *neither;* use *nor.*

> Wrong: Neither the long Arctic night or any other cause . . .
> Right: Neither the long Arctic night nor any other cause . . .

Oral. See **Verbal.**

Other times. *Sometimes* is an adverb; *other times* is not. Say " at other times." (See Rules 4 *b* and 92.)

Ought. The combination of *ought* with *had* is conspicuously bad English.

> Wrong: You hadn't ought to have entered.
> Right: You ought not to have entered.
> Wrong: We ought to send, had we not?
> Right: We ought to send, ought we not?

Ought to of. Vulgarism for *ought to have.*

> Vulgar: You ought to of waited.
> Right: You ought to have waited.
> Right: You should have waited.

Out loud. Not a permissible expression. Say *aloud.*

Outside (1). Does not require *of* following. Say simply " outside."

> Right: Outside the barn the cattle were shivering.

Outside (2). *Outside of* should not be used for *aside from.*

> Wrong: Outside of this mistake, it is very good.
> Right: Aside from this mistake, it is very good.

Over with. *With* is superfluous.

> Wrong: The regatta is over with.
> Right: The regatta is over.

Overly. A vulgarism. Say " over." (See Rule 5.)

> Vulgar: I'm not overly anxious.
> Right: I'm not over-anxious.

Pair, set. Singular, not plural, forms.

> Wrong: Two pair of gloves and three set of chisels.
> Right: Two pairs of gloves and three sets of chisels.

Part. See **Portion.**

Partake of. Means *to take a part (of something) in common with others, to share with others;* as " Good and evil alike partake of the air and the sunshine," " The whole delegation partook of his hospitality." The use of *partake of* as if it were synonymous with *eat* is a blunder and usually an affectation.

Party. Means *a person or group of persons taking part (in some transaction).* Incorrect when used to mean simply *person.*

> Right: The parties to the marriage were both young.
> Wrong: The party who wrote that article must have been a scholar.

Per. Use *per* with Latin words, such as *annum, diem, cent;* not, as a rule, with English words. Avoid the expression *as per;* say *according to.*

> Inelegant: Three dollars per day; one suicide per week; seven robberies per month; $3200 per year; two deaths per thousand; thirteen cents per gallon.
> Right: Three dollars a day [or *per diem*]; one suicide a week; seven robberies a month; $3200 a year [or *per annum*]; two deaths for every thousand; thirteen cents a gallon.

Per cent. It is better to use *per cent* only after a numeral. (See Rule 4.)

> Wrong: A large per cent were Chinese.
> Right: Twenty *per cent* were Chinese. [See Rules 220 *b* and 290.]
> Right: A large percentage were Chinese.

Phase. Means *appearance* or *aspect;* as " That phase of the question I haven't considered." Should not be used without intelligent regard to its meaning.

> Bad: I began to indulge in all the different phases of college pleasure.
> Right: I began to indulge in all the different kinds of college pleasure.

Phenomena. A plural noun. See **Data.**

Phone. A colloquialism. Not yet proper in formal discourse.

Piano. Should not be used to mean *instruction in piano-playing.*

> Wrong: She is taking piano.
> Right: She is taking piano lessons.

Piece. A provincialism when used in the sense of *distance* or *short distance.*

Plan. Should not be combined with *on*. Say simply " plan."

> Wrong: We planned on taking a walk.
> Right: We planned taking a walk; [or] We planned to take a walk.

Plenty (1). A colloquialism when used as an adjective. Say " plentiful." (See Rule 4.)

> Wrong: Wheat is plenty.
> Right: Wheat is plentiful.
> Right: There is plenty of wheat.

Plenty (2). Colloquial when used as an adverb. (See Rule 4.)

> Wrong: It is plenty good enough.
> Right: It is quite good enough.

Portion. Best used in its restricted sense, as *a proportionate* part or share, and distinguished from *part*. " A portion of the inheritance "; " a part of the day."

Postal. An adjective. Inelegant for *postal card*.

Posted. Incorrect for *informed*.

> Wrong: Keep me posted.
> Right: Keep me informed.
>
> Wrong: He is well posted about politics.
> Right: He is well informed about politics.

Practical. Means *related to actual use*, as opposed to theoretical or ideal. Do not confuse with *practicable*, which means *capable of being put into practice*. A *practical* scheme (*i.e.*, valuable or sensible) may not be *practicable* until a better opportunity.

Prefer. The thing about which something is said to be preferred should be made the object of the preposition *to*, never put into a *than* clause.

> Wrong: I should prefer to go there than anywhere else.
> Right: I should prefer going there to going anywhere else.

Propose. Means *to offer*. Should not be used for *to purpose* or *to intend*.

> Wrong: I did not propose to divulge the secret.
> Right: I did not purpose [or intend] to divulge the secret.

Proposition. Means *a thing proposed* or *the act of proposing;* as " He made a proposition to sell." Should not be used without intelligent regard to its meaning. Avoid especially the use of *proposition* for *work* or *task*.

> Slang: To sink that shaft was a hard proposition.
> Right: To sink that shaft was a hard piece of work.

> Bad: The library-buffet car is the most comfortable proposition on wheels.
>
> Right: The library-buffet car is the most comfortable vehicle on wheels.

Proven. An irregular form, and has enemies. Better " proved."

Providing. *Provided* is preferable.

> Right: I will lend it, provided he agrees to take good care of it.

Put in. A colloquialism for *spend* or *occupy*.

> Colloquial: I put in three hours in trying to memorize it.
>
> Right: I spent three hours, etc.

Put in an appearance. A legal phrase. In ordinary writing, say *appear*.

Quality. Means *characteristic* or *trait;* as " The qualities of birch bark are lightness of color, thinness, and smoothness." Should not be used without intelligent regard to its meaning.

> Bad: The social qualities of college life are more in evidence in the winter. (See Rule 14.)
>
> Right: The social activities of college life are more apparent in the winter.
>
> Bad: He gives three qualities of a business man: Have something to say, say it, and stop talking.
>
> Right: He gives three maxims for a business man: Have something to say, say it, and stop talking.

Quite. Means (*a*) *wholly;* as " The stream is now quite dried up "; or (*b*) *greatly, very;* as " We could see it quite distinctly." A colloquialism when used in the sense of *slightly, not very.*

> Wrong: The room is quite large, but not large enough for any one to be comfortable in.
>
> Right: The room is moderately large, but not large enough for any one to be comfortable in.

Quite a few. Colloquial for *a good many* or *a considerable number.*

Quite a little. Colloquial for *a considerable amount* or *a good deal.*

Raise (1). A provincialism when applied to human beings, in the sense of *rear, bring up.*

Raise (2). Often confounded with *rise.* Remember that *raise* is the causative of *rise; i.e., to raise* means *to cause to rise.* Therefore *raise* must always have an object. Remember the principal parts of each verb:

> I rise   I rose   I have risen.
>
> I raise   I raised   I have raised.

Real. Colloquial when used for *very.* (See Rule 4.)

> Colloquial: It is real handsome.
>
> Right: It is very handsome.

Reason. Do not complete such an expression as *the reason is* with (*a*) a *because* clause, (*b*) a *because of* phrase, (*c*) a *due to* phrase, or (*d*) an *on account of* phrase; complete it with a *that* clause. (See Rule 117.)

> Illogical: The reason he was offended was because they were arrogant.
> Illogical: The reason he was offended was because of their arrogance.
> Illogical: The reason he was offended was due to their arrogance.
> Illogical: The reason he was offended was on account of their arrogance.
> Right: The reason he was offended was that they were arrogant.

Refer. See **Allude.**

Remember. The name of the thing remembered should not be preceded by *of*.

> Wrong: I remember of meeting him.
> Right: I remember meeting him.

Respectful, respectable, respective. " He was respectful to his elders "; " a respectable old woman "; " their respective positions " — *i.e.*, the positions belonging to each. " Yours respectfully " (not *respectively*) is proper in the complimentary close of a letter.

Reverend, Honorable. Should be preceded by *the*, and should never be followed immediately by a surname. (See Rules 269 and 276.)

> Vulgar: Rev. Carter.
> Vulgar: The Reverend Carter.
>
> Right: The Reverend Mr. Carter.
> Right: The Reverend Amos Carter.
> Right: The Reverend Dr. Temple.

Rig. A provincialism for *carriage, buggy,* or *wagon.*

Right away, right off. Colloquial. Say " immediately," " at once," or " directly."

Right smart. A colloquial vulgarism.

Run. A colloquial Americanism, in the sense of *manage* or *operate.*

Said. See **Say.**

Same (1). No longer in good use as a pronoun except in legal documents.

> Wrong: We will repair the engine and ship same [or the same] to you next week.
> Right: We will repair the engine and ship it to you next week.
> Inelegant: The principal of the bonds was paid and the same canceled. [See Rule 90 *a.*]
> Right: The principal of the bonds was paid and the bonds were canceled.

Same (2). *The same as* should not be used for *in the same way as* or *just as.*

> Wrong: The draft is treated the same as a check is treated.
> Right: The draft is treated just as a check is treated.

Say. Should not be used to mean *give orders*, with an infinitive as object.

> Crude: The guard said to go back.
> Right: The guard ordered us [or told us] to go back.

Scare. See **Frighten.**
School. Should not be used for *college* or *university.*
Search. The phrase " in search for " is incorrect; say " in search of."

> Right: The lion goes in search of sheep.

Seem. " Can't seem " is illogical and improper. Say " seem unable," or " do not seem able."
Seldom ever. Obsolete. Say " seldom " or " hardly ever."
Seldom or ever. A vulgarism. Say " seldom if ever."
Selection. Means *a thing selected;* as " He played a selection from Wagner." Should not be used where there is no idea of selecting.

> Bad: Our class prophet then read an amusing selection, in which he satirized his classmates.
> Right: Our class prophet then read an amusing composition [or skit, or squib, or piece], in which, etc.

Set (1). Often confounded with *sit*. Remember that *set* is the causative of *sit; i.e., to set* means *to cause to sit*. Remember the principal parts of each verb:

I sit	I sat	I have sat.
I set	I set	I have set.

The use of *set* without an object, as expressing mere rest, is a vulgarism; say " sit," " stand," " lie," " rest," or " is set."

> Wrong: The pole sets firmly in the socket.
> Right: The pole is set [or sits] firmly in the socket.
> Wrong: The vase sets on the mantel.
> Right: The vase stands [or rests] on the mantel.
> Wrong: The boat sets lightly on the water.
> Right: The boat lies [or rests] lightly on the water.

Setting hen is commonly used, but is not approved.

Set (2). *Set* for *sets* (plural). See **Pair.**
Shan't. A colloquialism. A contraction for *shall not.*
Shape. Should not be used loosely to mean *manner* or *condition.*

> Wrong: They executed the maneuvers in good shape.
> Right: They executed the maneuvers in an expert manner.

> Wrong: He is in good shape for the debate.
> Right: He is in good condition [or thoroughly prepared] for the debate.

Should of. See **Of.**

Show (1). Colloquial for *play, opera, concert.*

Show (2). A colloquialism for *chance* or *promise.*

> Colloquial: The freshman team had an excellent show of winning.
> Right: The freshman team had an excellent chance of winning.

Show up. A colloquialism when used intransitively in the sense of *appear, attend, come* or *be present;* and when used transitively in the sense of *show* or *expose.*

Sight of. " A sight of " is a vulgarism for *much, many, a great deal.*

Size. Never use *size* as an adjective; say " sized," or " of size."

> Wrong: The different size dies are sorted.
> Right: The different sized dies are sorted.
>
> Wrong: Any size chain will do.
> Right: A chain of any size will do.

Size up. A vulgarism for *estimate, judge, pass upon.*

Sleeper. See **Diner.**

Smoker. See **Diner.**

Snap. See **Vim.**

So (1). Should not be used for *so that.*

> Wrong: They strapped it so it would hold.
> Right: They strapped it so that it would hold.

So (2). Vague and weak when used alone to modify an adjective. (See Rule 93, note.)

> Weak: During the first semester I was so lonely.
> Right: During the first semester I was very lonely.

So (3). See **Too.**

Some. A provincialism, when used as an adverb. (See Rule 4.)

> Wrong: I worked some last winter.
> Right: I did some work last winter.

Some place. See **Any place.**

Sort. See **Kind.**

Sort of. See **Kind of.**

Specie. Means *gold* or *silver money. Species,* meaning *kind,* has the same form in the singular and the plural.

> Right: The first species is more valuable than the other two species are.

Start. " I started to school in 1908 " is wrong, but " I started to school early that morning " is correct. " I started in school in 1908 " is correct, though less desirable than " I began to attend school." In the expressions, " He started in to quarrel," and " He started up in business," the *in* and the *up* are incorrect, and should be omitted.

Stop. Means *to cease* or *to cease from motion.* A colloquialism when used in the sense of *stay.* Good British usage.

> Right: Are you staying [not *stopping*] with friends?

Strata. A plural noun. See **Data.**

Subject, topic. A subject or a topic is a thing spoken about or thought about; the thing said or thought should not be called a subject or topic. (See Rule 117.)

> Wrong: The topic of the first paragraph tells of the French war.
> Right: The topic of the first paragraph is the French war.
>
> Wrong: The book is composed of many interesting subjects.
> Right: The book deals with many interesting subjects; [or] The book is composed of passages on many interesting subjects.

Such (1). When *such* is completed by a relative clause, the relative pronoun of the clause should not be *who, which,* or *that;* it should be *as* (see *as* in a dictionary).

> Wrong: I will act under such rules that may be fixed.
> Right: I will act under such rules as may be fixed.
>
> Wrong: All such persons present who consent will rise.
> Right: All such persons present as consent will rise.

Such (2). When *such* is completed by a result clause, this clause should be introduced, not by *so that,* but by *that* alone.

> Wrong: There was such a mist so that we couldn't see.
> Right: There was such a mist that we couldn't see.

Such (3). Avoid the vague and weak use of *such* without a result clause. (See Rule 93, note.)

> Weak: We had such a good time.
> Right: We had a very good time.

Superior, inferior. Should never be limited by a *than* clause, but always by a *to* phrase.

> Wrong: It was superior from every point of view than the lathe previously used.
> Right: It was superior from every point of view to the lathe previously used.

Suppose. See **Expect.**

Sure. Incorrect as an adverb.

> Wrong: Will you go? Sure.
> Right: Will you go? Surely [I will go].

Suspicion. Incorrectly used as a verb.

> Wrong: I did not suspicion that he was coming.
> Right: I did not suspect that he was coming.

Swell. A vulgarism when used as an adjective. (See Rule 4.)
Take. A colloquialism when used for *study.*

> Colloquial: I took Spanish and chemistry.
> Right: I studied Spanish and chemistry.

Take in (1). A vulgarism for *attend* or *go to.*
Take in (2). A vulgarism for *cheat* or *deceive.*

Take and. Sometimes used redundantly.

> Wrong: It will stay if you take and put it on right.
> Right: It will stay if you put it on right.

Take it. Should not be used in introducing an example.

> Bad: Take it in Wisconsin, the old-fashioned method of
>   logging is becoming extinct.
> Right: In Wisconsin, for example, the old-fashioned method
>   of logging is becoming extinct.

Take sick. A colloquialism for *become sick.*
Take stock in. See **Bank on.**
Team. Means a couple or group of animals or persons; as " a team of
horses," " a team of athletes." A provincialism when applied
to *one* animal or to a vehicle.

> Wrong: Will you ride in my team?
> Right: Will you ride in my buggy [or carriage, or wagon]?

Than, till, until. Often improperly used for *when,* as in the following
Wrong sentences. (See Rule 117.)

> Wrong: Scarcely had he mounted the wagon than the horse
>   started.
> Right: Scarcely had he mounted the wagon when the horse
>   started.
> Wrong: We had hardly got there and put things in order till
>   Jenks came.
> Right: We had hardly got there and put things in order when
>   Jenks came.

That. Colloquial as an adverb. (Cf. **This,** and see Rule 4.)

> Colloquial: He went only that far.
> Right: He went only so far.

> Colloquial: If it is that bad, we must retreat.
> Right: If it is so bad [or so bad as that], we must retreat.
> Colloquial: He didn't want that much, did he?
> Right: He didn't want so much as that, did he?

That there.   See **This here.**
These here.   See **This here.**
This.   Colloquial as an adverb.   (Cf. **That,** and see Rule 4.)

> Colloquial: This much is certain.
> Right: Thus much is certain.
>
> Colloquial: Having come this far . . .
> Right: Having come thus far [or as far as this] . . .
>
> Colloquial: The water hasn't ever before been this high.
> Right: The water hasn't ever before been so high as this.

This here, these here, that there, those there.   Gross vulgarisms.
   Say " this," " these," " that," or " those."
Those kind, those sort.   See **Kind, sort.**
Those there.   See **This here.**
Through.   Inelegant when used as in the following sentence:

> Wrong: He is through writing.
> Right: He has finished writing; [or] He has done writing.

NOTE. — Never say " *is* finished " or " *is* done " in the sense
above shown.

Till for when.   See **Than.**
Too, so, very.   No one of these words should immediately precede a
   past participle; say " too much," " so much," " very much."

> Wrong: He is too exhausted to speak.
> Right: He is too much exhausted to speak.
>
> Wrong: He felt very insulted.
> Right: He felt very much insulted.

Topic.   See **Subject.**
Transpire.   Means *to become known;* as " In spite of their efforts at
   concealment, the secret transpired."   It is both affected and
   incorrect to use the word in the sense of *occur.*
Treat.   Should be followed, when used to mean *discuss* or *speak of,* by
   of, not by *on* or *with.*

> Wrong: The author treats on two subjects.
> Right: The author treats of two subjects.

Trend.   Means *direction;* as " The rivers of this land have a southern
   trend."   Should not be used without regard to its proper meaning.

> Bad: The egg business is only incidental to the general trend
>   of the store.
> Right: The egg business is only incidental to the general
>   business of the store.

Try and. Colloquial for *try to*. Good British usage.

> Colloquial: I shall try and get a good position.
> Right: I shall try to get a good position.

Ugly. Means *repulsive to the eye*. A provincialism when used to mean *vicious*, *malicious*, or *ill-tempered*.

> Bad: The horse has an ugly temper.
> Right: The horse has a vicious temper.
> Bad: The conductor acted very ugly.
> Right: The conductor acted very discourteously [or un-civilly].

Underhanded. Prefer *underhand*.

> Right: He used underhand methods.

Unique. Means the only one of its kind. Cannot be qualified, as "This is quite unique," or "fairly unique," or "the most unique."

United States. This name should usually be preceded by *the*. Do not write: We live in United States.

Until for *when*. See **Than**.

Up. Should not be appended to the verbs *cripple*, *divide*, *end*, *finish*, *open*, *polish*, *rest*, *scratch*, *settle*.

> Wrong: He opened up the box and divided the money up among the men.
> Right: He opened the box and divided the money among the men.

Up to date. A colloquialism when used as an adjective; better used as an adverbial modifier.

> Colloquial: His house is up to date.
> Preferable: His house is modern.
> Right: He brought the history up to date.

Very with past participles. See **Too**.

Vim, snap. Not in good literary use. Say "vigor," "energy," or "spirit."

Violin. Should not be used to mean *instruction in violin playing*.

> Crude: He has just begun violin.
> Right: He has just begun to take violin lessons.

Vocal, voice. Should not be used to mean *instruction in vocal music*. (See Rule 4.)

> Crude: Are you keeping on with your vocal?
> Right: Are you keeping on with your singing lessons [or vocal practice]?
> Crude: She is taking voice.
> Right: She is taking singing lessons.

Voice.   See **Vocal.**

Wait on.   A vulgarism for *wait for*.

> Wrong: If I'm not there, don't wait on me.
> Right: If I'm not there, don't wait for me.

Want (1).   Should not be limited by a clause as in the following sentence:

> Wrong: I want you should be happy.
> Right: I want you to be happy.

Want (2).   " Want in," " want out," " want through," etc., are unauthorized localisms.

> Vulgar: Do you want in?
> Right: Do you want to come in?

Want (3).   " I want for you to get some water " is a provincialism for " I want you to get some water."

Way (1).   Unlicensed abbreviation for *away*.

> Wrong: Way up the hill I saw a deer.
> Right: Away [or *far*] up the hill I saw a deer.

Way (2).   Should not be used adverbially without a preposition governing it.

> Wrong: When he acts that way . . .
> Right: When he acts in that way . . .
>
> Wrong: How could a sane man act the way Beals did?
> Right: How could a sane man act in the way in which Beals
> acted? [or, better] . . . act as Beals did?

Ways for *way*.   See **Falls.**

Well.   This word when used merely to mark a transition (*e.g.*, " You know MacDonald, of course. Well, last night as he stepped into his motor . . .") is a colloquialism, not proper in a formal context.

Where (1).   Often misused for *that* as in the following sentence.

> Wrong: I see in this morning's paper where Cronin has been
> caught.
> Right: I see in this morning's paper that Cronin has been
> caught.

Where (2).   Do not use " where to " in the sense of *whither;* omit the *to.*

> Wrong: Where are you going to?
> Right: Where are you going?

Which.   Should not be used as a relative pronoun in referring to a person.

> Wrong: The people which do that are rascals.
> Right: The people that do that are rascals.

While.   Means (*a*) *during the time in which*, (*b*) *though*, or (*c*) *whereas;* as (*a*) " I played while he sang "; (*b*) " While this may be true, it does not content me "; (*c*) " Yours is in good condition, while mine is quite worn out." Should not be used loosely without regard to its meaning.

> Wrong: One one side was a grove, while on the other was a river.
> Right: On one side was a grove, on the other a river.

Who.   Should not, as a rule, be used in referring to animals; use *which*.
Whose.   In modern usage, the possessive case of *who* only, though originally also of *which*, and sometimes so used.

> Doubtful: Soon we came to a swamp, on whose bank stood a hunter's cabin.
> Preferable: Soon we came to a swamp, on the bank of which stood a hunter's cabin.

Win out.   See **Lose out.**
Wire.   A colloquialism for *telegraph* or *telegram*.   (See Rule 4.)
With.   Often vaguely used in place of more exact connectives.

> Vague: With the men he has helping him, Parker seems certain to win.
> Better: Taking into consideration the men he has helping him, Parker seems certain to win.

Woods for *wood*. See **Falls.**
Would better, would best, would rather.   Correct, but often used under a misapprehension.   See **Had better.**
Would have.   Often incorrectly used in *if* clauses instead of *had*.

> Wrong: If he would have stood by us, we might have won.
> Right: If he had stood by us, we might have won.

Would of.   See **Of.**
Write-up.   Newspaper word for *a report, a description, an account*.
You was.   A vulgarism.   *You*, though it may designate one person, is grammatically plural, and its verb must always be plural.   Say " you were."
Without.   Should not be used as a conjunction for except or unless.

> Wrong: He will not do it without he has a good opportunity.
> Right: He will not do it unless he has a good opportunity.

GENERAL EXERCISES ON THE GLOSSARY

I. See *Except* in the Glossary. Write the following *Accept* sentences, filling the blanks with *accept* or *except:* 1. I *and except* would —— the offer, —— for my religious scruples. 2. He is the best pianist in Europe; I do not —— even Liszt. 3. Most of the rebels were offered pardon and ——ed it; but the leaders were ——ed from the offer. 4. He burned all the household goods, not ——ing even the heirlooms. 5. Why did you —— Charles from your invitation? He wouldn't have ——ed anyway.

II. See *Affect* in the Glossary. Write the following *Affect* and sentences, filling the blanks with *affect* or *effect:* 1. That *effect* statement is true, but it does not —— the case. 2. The failure of the bank did not —— his equanimity. 3. The admonition of the dean had a good ——. 4. The generals ——ed a junction, but this action had no —— on the enemy. 5. His brooding ——ed his health. 6. The utmost efforts of his physician could not —— a cure.

III. See *Like* in the Glossary. Complete the following *Like* sentences: 1. I wish I could run like ——. 2. If you find him engaged at his gymnastics, like ——. 3. She sat for a long time deep in thought, like ——.
Copy the following sentences, filling the blanks with *as, as if,* or *like:* 4. Don't act —— a baby. 5. —— all his predecessors, he was despotic. 6. We never quarrel now —— we did when we were boys. 7. He was hanged, just —— a common spy. 8. He was hanged, just —— he had been a common spy. 9. He votes —— his father did. 10. She sings —— she had a cold. 11. He can run —— a race-horse. 12. He can run —— a race-horse runs. 13. He takes severe training —— a man usually does when he is preparing for a prize fight. 14. He takes very severe training —— a prize fighter. 15. She stood —— a statue. 16. She stood —— a statue might have stood. 17. He whimpered, —— a spoiled child, about every little inconvenience. 18. He whined, —— a spoiled child does, at every inconvenience. 19. —— all his predecessors, he was despotic. 20. —— all his predecessors had been, Henry VIII was despotic. 21. We do not quarrel now —— we did when we were boys. 22. They quarrel constantly, —— boys usually do. 23. They quarrel —— cats and dogs. 24. He was

hanged, —— many another spy caught in such an enterprise. 25. He was hanged —— many another spy has been. 26. I vote, —— my father, for the Conservative party. 27. I vote, —— my father did, for the Conservatives. 28. She sings —— a person afflicted with goitre. 29. She sings —— a person with goitre might sing.

IV. The following sentences are ungrammatical. Rewrite them, correcting the errors. 1. She sings like she had a cold. 2. They executed him like he had been a common spy. 3. The sky looks like we should have rain. 4. He acts like he was the master of ceremonies. 5. The game isn't played like we used to play it. 6. He counted out the money dexterously, like a bank teller does. 7. These waves roar just like the ocean-waves do. 8. She walks clumsily, like a duck waddles. 9. He turns his toes in, like an Indian does. 10. He grew white like he feared the boat would capsize. 11. I felt like I must scream. 12. It seemed like I was in a nightmare. 13. She cried out, like she had been struck. 14. Move your hand just like I move mine. 15. It stretches like a rubber band does.

Real

V. See *Real* in the Glossary. Correct the following sentences: 1. You are real generous. 2. The room is real comfortable. 3. It was a real hard storm. 4. She writes a real pretty hand. 5. I felt real lonesome. 6. She told us a real sad story. 7. Hanksburg is a real pleasant town.

Due to

VI. Study *Due to* in the Glossary. Correct and rewrite the following sentences: 1. Hamlet treated her rudely due to his mental distraction. 2. Shop work is easy for me due to a natural talent for manual work. 3. Due to some one's carelessness the valve had been left open. 4. Due to bad weather the game is postponed. 5. He refused to buy due to the high price asked. 6. Due to his ignorance of French he misunderstood the letter. 7. I was put in the bow due to my light weight. 8. He had to sell his house due to need of ready money. 9. Due to his long exposure he became sick. 10. I kept warm and comfortable due to my fur coat.

Falls, ways and woods

VII. Study *Falls, Ways, Woods* in the Glossary. Correct and rewrite the following incorrect sentences: 1. It is a long ways from here. 2. We carried our boat around a falls. 3. Is there a woods on your farm? 4. This falls is not very high. 5. Walk a little ways with us.

6. He lost himself in a woods.   7. The woods is on fire.
Write three sentences using the expression *a little way*,
three using *a long way*, three using *a wood*, three using *the
woods are*, three using *the falls were*.

VIII. Study *Whose* in the Glossary. Rewrite the fol-   *Whose*
lowing sentences: 1. I sat on the roof, whose slope was
not very steep. 2. I selected a cloth whose texture was
woven loosely. 3. I perceived a steeple on whose top
revolved a gilded vane. 4. It was an antique table,
whose legs bore the pineapple decoration. 5. He ex-
hibited a painting in whose execution he had evidently
expended much labor. 6. Get some of those matches
whose ends are tipped with red. 7. A verb whose subject is a collective noun may properly be in the plural.
8. He lit a fire, whose heat was very comfortable. 9. A
chain any of whose links are weak is a weak chain.
10. You sold me a book whose type is too small.

IX. Study *Could of, Should of, Would of, May of, Must of*   "Could
Might of in the Glossary. Correct the following sentences: of," "may
1. You should of seen me. 2. I would of come if I   of," etc.
could of spared the time. 3. He may of lost his way.
4. I might of lost mine, and then I should of lost this
pleasure. 5. If I could of seen him, I would of told him.
6. She must of suspected treachery, or she would not of
stayed away. 7. If he could of known, the outcome might
of been different. 8. I would not of accepted the offer
even if I could of named my own price.

X. Study *Had have* and *Would have* in the Glossary.   "Would
Correct the following sentences: 1. If we would have   have"
started back fifteen minutes later, we should probably   and "had
have perished in the blizzard. 2. If he would have   have" for
found the way, he would have gone. 3. If I would have   *had* in
known how it would end, I never would have begun.   past per-
4. If he would have been at his post, the accident would   fect
not have occurred. 5. If the weather would have been
colder, the ice would now be safe. 6. If the boat
would have tipped only a little more, it would have been
swamped. 7. If she would have been a second later,
she would have missed the train. 8. If the wind would
have been north, the barn would certainly have caught
fire. 9. If the bridge would have been properly built,
it would not vibrate as it does. 10. If the old gentleman
would have caught the boys, they would have repented
sorely. 11. If the alarm clock would have been set, you
would have waked in time.

"You was" **XI.** Study *You was* in the Glossary. Also write the following sentences, filling each blank with a word to indicate past tense: 1. —— you satisfied? 2. You —— generous. 3. You —— content, ——n't you? 4. You —— mistaken. 5. —— you happy, or ——n't you? 6. You —— never pleased. 7. —— you sure? 8. —— you as severe as you —— justified in being? 9. ——n't you sterner than you —— authorized to be? 10. You —— treacherous, you —— deceitful; therefore you —— punished.

Different **XII.** Study *Different* in the Glossary. Correct and rewrite the following sentences: 1. They speak very differently than you speak. 2. Plumbing is entirely different than steam-fitting. 3. This machine is somewhat different than the one I bought. 4. To sail a brig is widely different than to sail a schooner. 5. He is a different man today than he was when you knew him. 6. His purpose is different than I thought it was. 7. My reward was very different than what I deserved. 8. They did it differently then than they do now. 9. Your machinery is different than what I use. 10. Conditions were radically different than what I expected. 11. His character was different, as a matter of fact, than what the historian says it was. 12. You need a different sort of manager than you now have. 13. The state of affairs in Nicaragua is no different than in Bolivia. 14. *The Witching Hour* deals with a different subject than Mr. Thomas, the author, has used hitherto.

Such . . . as **XIII.** Study *Such* (1) in the Glossary. Write ten sentences containing severally the following expressions: *all such men as hold this belief, such tools as are necessary, such books as I find interesting, such men as seem to be in earnest, such members as desire to dance, all such citizens as love their country, such as are in need of money, for such as keep His covenant, with such fruits as the season afforded, such as prefer horses to motors, such influence as he may have.*

Such . . . that **XIV.** Study *Such* (2) in the Glossary. Complete each of the following sentences with a *that* clause: 1. He is such a coward . . . 2. There was such a drought . . . 3. He has such skill . . . 4. There is such a crowd . . . 5. We made such a protest . . . 6. Such a tempest arose . . . 7. He came with such an army . . . 8. She exercised such tact . . . 9. The lawyer displayed such eloquence . . .

XV. Study *Superior, Inferior* in the Glossary. Complete the following sentences, beginning each added member with a *to* phrase: 1. This method is superior, in the opinion of all who have used it, . . . 2. His style is inferior, so the critics all agree, . . . 3. The team was inferior, both in weight and in experience, . . . 5. This year's class play will be inferior, unless I am much mistaken, . . . 6. The street-car service here is inferior, however you may regard it, . . . 7. The present system is superior, so far as one can judge, . . . 8. His present situation is superior, so far as salary is concerned, . . . *Superior and inferior*

XVI. Study *Prefer* in the Glossary. The " prefer . . . than " fault can be corrected by the substitution of *prefer . . . to* or by the substitution of *prefer . . . rather than.* *Prefer and preferable*

> Right: I prefer building to leasing.
> Right: I prefer to build rather than to lease.

Rewrite each of the following sentences twice, correcting in the two ways shown above: 1. I prefer to miss the train than to run for it. 2. Do you prefer to be expelled than to apologize? 3. He preferred to write a letter than to explain in person. 4. I prefer to enter business at once than to go to college. 5. I should much prefer to pay the money than to dispute with you. 6. They prefer to take their ease than to work. 7. She prefers to go to a party than to study her lessons. 8. I preferred to freeze my nose than to be suffocated by the bad air. 9. I prefer to risk the journey alone than to have your company. 10. He preferred to kill the horse than to let it suffer.

XVII. Study *Than, Till, Until* in the Glossary. Also notice this: " No sooner . . . when " is bad English; say *no sooner . . . than.* *No sooner . . . than*

Wrong: No sooner had we arrived when the play began.
Right: No sooner had we arrived than the play began.
[That is, We had arrived *no sooner than* the play began.]
But note:
Right: Hardly had we arrived when the play began.

Complete the following sentences, using a *when* clause or a *than* clause as the sense requires: 1. No sooner did the boat touch the wharf . . . 2. The clock had scarcely *Hardly . . . when*

finished striking . . . 3. Hardly had I seated myself . . .
4. No sooner had Bassanio departed . . . 5. The policeman had no sooner turned his back . . . 6. Our hero
had hardly opened his eyes . . . 7. She no sooner
reached the bridge . . . 8. Scarcely had the buck
emerged from the brush . . . 9. I had hardly laid down
the pen . . . 10. No sooner did the King show signs of
yielding . . . 11. I no sooner overcome one obstacle . . .

Too and
very with
participles

XVIII. Study *Too*, *Very* in the Glossary. The following
sentences are unidiomatic. Rewrite them, correcting each
by inserting an adverb (*much, greatly, seriously, gravely,
sadly, happily, deeply,* or any other appropriate adverb)
after the " too " or the " very." 1. He seemed very moved
by the appeal. 2. I am very delighted to hear it.
3. They are too offended to forgive us. 4. He is too injured to walk. 5. I am very grieved by this news. 6. She
lay down again, feeling very relieved. 7. We are too
involved in this affair to withdraw. 8. You need not feel
too discouraged. 9. I don't feel very elated. 10. He
can't judge fairly; he is too misled by his prejudices.

APPENDIX A

A Grammatical Vocabulary explaining Grammatical and Other Technical Terms used in this Book

Absolute. A substantive with a modifier (usually a participle) attached to a predication but having no syntactic relation to any noun or verb in the predication is called an **absolute substantive.** An absolute substantive and its modifier are together called an **absolute phrase.** The italicized part of the following sentence is an absolute phrase: " *The wind being favorable,* they embarked." For other examples see Rules 132 *a* and 132 *b*.

Active voice. See **Voice.**

Adjective. A word used to modify or limit the meaning of a substantive; *e.g., black, human, old, beautiful, metallic, dry.*

Adjective clause. A clause used to modify a substantive in the manner of an adjective; *e.g.,* " The rain *that fell yesterday* was a blessing " (the italicized clause modifies the noun " rain "); " The house *where he used to live* is vacant " (the italicized clause modifies the noun " house "); " There was once a city *on the outskirts of which lay a pestilential morass* " (the italicized clause modifies the noun " city "). Adjective clauses are often called **relative clauses.**

Adjunct. Modifiers and predicate substantives or predicate adjectives have the general name of adjuncts. A modifier is said to be an adjunct of the sentence-member it modifies; a predicate substantive or adjective is said to be an adjunct of the verb it completes.

Adverb. A word used to modify verbs, adjectives, and other adverbs; *e.g., slowly, politely, accurately, very, too, then, up, down, out.*

Adverbial clause. A clause used to modify an adjective, an adverb, or a verb; *e.g.,* "He is greater *than his father was* " (the italicized clause modifies the adjective " greater "); " He walked faster *than I did* " (the italicized clause modifies the adverb " faster "); " I will come if my salary is paid when it is due " (the clause " if . . . paid " modifies the verb " will come "; the clause " when . . . due " modifies the verb " is paid ").

Adverbial objective. A substantive used to limit adverbially an adjective, an adverb, or a verb; *e.g.,* " It is worth *ten cents* " (" ten

297

cents " limits the adjective " worth "); " He walked *two miles* farther " (" two miles " limits the adverb " farther "); " He walked *two miles* (" two miles " limits " walked " adverbially).

Antecedent. The word, as used in this book, means the substantive to which any pronoun refers. In the sentence, " He who runs may read," " he " is the antecedent of " who." In the sentence " He picked up a stone and threw it," " stone " is the antecedent of " it."

Anticlimax. See **Climax.**

Appositive. A substantive attached to another substantive and denoting the same person or thing by a different name is called an appositive, or is said to be **in apposition** with the substantive modified. In the sentence " George the king is enjoying his favorite sport, — yachting," " king " is in apposition with " George," and " yachting " is in apposition with " sport."

Article. The word *the* is called the **definite article;** the word *a* or *an* is called the **indefinite article.**

Auxiliary. The verbs *be, have, do, shall, will, may, can, must,* and *ought,* with their inflectional forms (*e.g., was, am, did, should, might, could,* etc.) when they assist in forming the voices, modes, and tenses of other verbs, are called auxiliaries. The italicized words following are auxiliaries: " *Have* you gone? " " I *did* not see," " He *has* not *been* heard," " I *should be* grieved if it *was* broken."

Cardinal number. The words *one, two, three,* and the corresponding words for other numbers are **cardinal numbers;** the words *first, second, third,* etc., are **ordinal numbers.**

Case. The different forms that a substantive takes when it stands in different syntactic relations are called cases. The subject of a finite verb is in the **nominative case.** A substantive that modifies another substantive by indicating a possessor is in the **possessive (genitive) case.** The object of a verb or a preposition is in the **objective (accusative) case.** The three cases of typical nouns and of the principal pronouns that are inflected are shown in the tables of declension under **Substantive.** It will be observed that in the nouns the nominative and objective (accusative) cases are identical, but that in the pronouns they are (with the exception of the nominative and objective (accusative) singular of *it*) distinct.

Causal conjunction. A conjunction that introduces a statement of cause or reason; *e.g., for* (coördinating); *because* and *since* (subordinating).

Clause. A clause is a group of words that is part of a sentence and contains a subject and a predicate. In the sentence (a) " When I awake, I am still with thee," the two groups of words separated by the comma are clauses. A subordinate clause is used like a noun, an adjective, or an adverb. All other clauses, which make independent assertions, are **principal clauses.** The italicized groups of words in the following sentences are principal clauses: (b) " If the rope breaks, *he is lost.*" (c) "*The bell sounded,* and *every one rose.*" Clauses that play the same part in a sentence, whether they are alike principal or alike dependent, are called **coördinate clauses.** See, *e.g.,* the two principal clauses in sentence *c,* above; and the two dependent clauses in the following sentence: (d) "*Though I am tired,* and *though my shoes pinch,* I am going on."

Climax. A series of assertions or coördinate sentence-elements so arranged that each one is stronger or more impressive than the preceding one. See, *e.g.,* the sentences marked *Improved* under Rule 89. A series of assertions or sentence-elements decreasing in strength or impressiveness is an **anticlimax.** See, *e.g.,* the sentences marked *Weak* under Rule 89.

Common noun. A noun used to designate any member of a class; *e.g., man, ruler, country, city, street, building.* A noun used to distinguish an individual member of a class from other members is a **proper noun;** *e.g., John, Anderson, Caesar, Germany, Boston, Broadway, Acropolis.* A **proper name** is an appellation of any kind (including proper nouns) used to distinguish an individual person or thing; *e.g., Henry the Second* (or *Henry II.*), *Revolutionary War, First National Bank, Democratic Party, Second Presbyterian Church, Domesday Book, Forty-first Street, Ohio River, Niagara Falls, Edgar County, Calegonian Literary Society, Sumner High School, Columbia College, Morningside Park.*

Comparative. See **Comparison.**

Comparison. An adjective or an adverb is in the positive degree when it simply designates a quality or manner without indicating the degree in which that quality or manner is present; this form is, with a few exceptions, the shortest form the word can have, — *e.g., sweet, strong, fast, hard.* An adjective or an adverb is in the **comparative degree** (1) when it is in the form which indicates that the quality or manner is present in a greater measure relatively to some standard. It is commonly formed by adding *er* to the positive or combining it with *more.* The **superlative degree** is regularly formed by adding *est* to the positive or combining it with *most.* The formation of the three degrees of an adjective or an adverb is called **comparison.**

Complex sentence. A sentence that contains a dependent clause. See, *e.g.*, sentences *a*, *b*, and *d* under **Clause.**

Compound sentence. Two or more principal clauses connected by coördinating conjunctions; or two or more principal clauses not connected by conjunctions, but written with such punctuation and capitalization, or spoken with such slight pauses between them, as will indicate that they are combined. See, *e.g.*, sentence *c* under **Clause,** and the following sentences: (*a*) " I came, I saw, I conquered." (*b*) " Must I obey you? must I crouch before you? "

Conditional. See **Mode.**

Conjunction. A word used to connect one word with another or one group with another; *e.g.*, *and, if, for.* Conjunctions may be distinguished from prepositions (*q.v.*) by the following fact: Any conjunction can be used to connect one predication with another (*e.g.*, " I opened the door when *he rapped* ") — an office which a preposition cannot perform; one of the two elements connected by a preposition must always be a substantive (*e.g.*, " He fell into *the cold water* "). — **Coördinating conjunctions** are those which, when they join two predications, make those predications of equal rank — neither dependent on the other; *e.g.*, " I called and *they came*." The principal coördinating conjunctions are the **simple conjunctions,** *and, but, or, nor, neither,* and *for;* the correlative conjunctions, *both . . . and, either . . . or, neither . . . nor;* and the **conjunctive adverbs,** *so, also, therefore, hence, however, nevertheless, moreover, accordingly, besides, thus, then, still,* and *yet.* — **Subordinating conjunctions** are those which, when they join two predications, make one of those predications subordinate to the other; *e.g.*, " *They came* when *I called*." The principal subordinating conjunctions are *if, though, whether, lest, unless, than, as, that because, since, when, while, after, whereas, provided.*

Conjunctive adverbs. Words that are used sometimes as adverbs and sometimes as conjunctives. See **Conjunction.**

Consonant. See **Vowel.**

Construction. The grammatical office performed by any word in a given sentence is called the construction of that word. For example, in the sentence " He walks fast," the construction of " he " is that of subject of " walks "; the construction of " walks " is that of predicate of " he "; the construction of " fast " is that of adverbial modifier of " walks."

Coördinate. Sentence-elements that are in the same construction within a sentence are coördinate. In the sentence " He and she talked long and earnestly and at last agreed," " he " and " she," " talked " and " agreed," " long " and " earnestly " are coördinate.

Coördinate clause. See **Clause.**

Coördinating conjunction. See **Conjunction.**

Copula. The verb *to be,* or any of its forms.

Correlative conjunctions. Conjunctions that are used in pairs; *e.g., both . . . and, either . . . or, neither . . . nor, whether . . . or.*

Declension. See **Inflection.**

Demonstrative adjectives. The words *this* and *these, that* and *those,* when they are used as adjectives; *e.g.,* " this man," " those men."

Demonstrative pronouns. The words *this* and *these, that* and *those* when they are used as substantives; *e.g.,* " That is not true," " What is this? "

Dependent clause. See **Clause.**

Direct address. Discourse in the second person (see **Person**); *e.g.,* " Sir, I salute you." The expression **a substantive used in direct address** means a substantive that indicates to whom the discourse is addressed; *e.g.,* " Sir " in the foregoing example.

Direct question. See **Direct quotation.**

Direct quotation (often called direct discourse). Quotation of discourse exactly as it was spoken or written; *e.g., He said, " I will help."* Statement of the substance of quoted discourse without the use of the exact words in **indirect quotation** (or indirect discourse), *e.g., He said that he would help.* A question indirectly quoted is called an **indirect question**; *e.g., He asked whether I would help.* A question directly quoted, or not quoted but directly asked, is a **direct question**; *e.g., Will you help?*

Factitive adjective. An adjective, when it denotes a quality or state produced by the action of a verb, is called a factitive adjective; *e.g.,* " It will make you *strong.*"

Figure of speech. Certain devices of expression that may be used for making discourse interesting, effective, or beautiful are called figures of speech; others are not included under this term.

Which of them are included cannot be stated briefly, for the application of the term is arbitrary, being based simply on custom and not on any common peculiarity of the devices included. Of the devices mentioned in this book, the following are figures of speech: simile, metaphor, climax, irony (see these words in this vocabulary), and the use of the historical present (technically called vision).

Finite. See **Mode.**

Future tense. See **Tense.**

Future perfect tense. See **Tense.**

Gerund. A verb-form ending in *ing* is called a gerund when it is used as a noun. When such a form is used as an adjective, it is called a **participle.** In the sentence, " Coming close, he whispered," " coming " is used as an adjective modifying " he " and is therefore a participle. In the sentence " His coming was expected," " coming " is used as a noun, the subject of " was expected," and is therefore a gerund. A gerund may fulfill the principal offices of a noun. It may be the subject of a verb (*e.g.*, " Fishing is tiresome "); the object of a verb (*e.g.*, " I hate fishing "); the object of a preposition (*e.g.*, " I have an aversion to fishing "); a predicate noun (*e.g.*, " What I most detest is fishing "); an appositive (*e.g.*, " That detestable amusement, fishing, I cannot endure "); or an absolute noun (*e.g.*, " Fishing being my aversion, let us not fish ").

Gerund phrase. See **Phrase.**

Govern. The relation between a verb and its object may be stated either by saying that the substantive is the object of the verb, or by saying that the verb governs the substantive. Likewise the relation between a preposition and its object may be stated by saying that the preposition governs the substantive. A clause, whether principal or subordinate, on which another clause depends, is said to govern the latter clause. In the sentence " She wept when she saw the injury that had been done," the clause " she wept " governs the clause " when she saw the injury," and the latter clause governs the clause " that had been done."

Grammar. The science that deals with (1) the classification of words with reference to the functions they perform in discourse (see **Parts of speech**); (2) the inflection of words (see **Inflection**); and (3) the relations that words bear to one another in discourse (see **Syntax**). Grammar is distinguished from **rhetoric** by the following fact: The statements comprising the science of grammar tell us how words *may* be inflected, used singly and combined. The statements comprising the science of rhetoric tell us how words *should* be used and combined in order to make discourse clear and effective.

Indefinite pronoun. The words *each, either, neither, some, any, many, few, all, both, one, none, aught, naught, somebody, something, somewhat, anybody, anything, everybody, everything, nobody,* and *nothing,* when they are used as substantives, are called indefinite pronouns.

Indicative. The set of inflectional forms and of combinations with auxiliary verbs that a speaker uses when he conceives the action of a verb as a fact, is not the same as the set he uses when he conceives the action as doubtful. Compare, for example, the sentences " He *is* a coward " and " If he *be* a coward, he should be dismissed." The former set is called the **indicative mode** of a verb; the latter the **subjunctive mode.** The indicative and subjunctive forms of a typical verb are shown on pages 314 ff.

Indirect question. See **Direct quotation.**

Indirect quotation. See **Direct quotation.**

Infinitive. That inflectional form of a verb which may be combined with *to* (as in the sentences " To err is human," " I wish to go," " He refused to move," " It is impossible to see ") is called an infinitive when it is used in one of the following ways: (1) in combination with *to,* as illustrated above; (2) in combination with an auxiliary verb (*e.g.,* " I will go," " I can see "); (3) as the predicate of another substantive, the whole predication being the object of another verb (*e.g.,* " It made me gasp," " I saw him smile "); (4) in one of the constructions of a substantive (*e.g.,* " Do you dare go in? " in which " go " is the object of " dare "). The word *to,* when it is combined with an infinitive, is not a preposition; it is merely a sort of prefix, serving no grammatical purpose except to show that the verb-form following is an infinitive. For this reason it is called the **sign of the infinitive** or the **infinitive-sign.** The infinitive-sign is not a necessary part of the infinitive. In the sentences " I cannot see," " I dare go," " Will you come? " " I heard the clock strike," " You had better speak," the words " see," " go," " come," " strike," and " speak " are infinitives, though the infinitive-sign does not accompany them. In mentioning an infinitive, the infinitive sign may with equal correctness be put before the infinitive or be omitted; thus we may say either " The verbs *to stand* and *to sit* are intransitive," or " The verbs *stand* and *sit* are intransitive." — The use of infinitives in various substantive constructions is an important matter for the student to understand. An infinitive may be used (1) as the subject of a verb (*e.g.*, " To read history is instructive "); (2) as the object of a verb (*e.g.*, " I like to read history "); (3) as a predicate noun (*e.g.*, " An instructive occupation is to read history "); (4) as an appositive (*e.g.*, " It is instructive to read history "); (5) as an absolute noun (*e.g.*, " To read history being so instructive, let us read it "); (6) as an adverbial noun (*e.g.*, " History is instructive to read ").

Infinitive-sign.   See **Infinitive.**

Inflection.   Change in the form of a word to show variation of meaning (as with inflections of number, comparison, and tense), or to show the relation of a word to another word (as with the inflections of case and person).   The inflection of substantives is called **declension,** that of adjectives and adverbs **comparison** (*q.v.*), and that of verbs **conjugation.**   The various forms that a word receives in inflection are its **inflectional forms**; *e.g.*, *love, lovest, loveth, loved, lovedst,* and *loving* are the inflectional forms of the verb *to love; man, man's, men, men's,* are the inflectional forms of the noun *man;* see also the tables under **Substantive** and opposite **Verb.**

Intensive.   The pronouns *myself, thyself, himself, herself, itself, ourselves, yourself, yourselves, themselves,* and *oneself,* when they are used in apposition, are called intensives (*e.g.*, " I myself will do it," " He saw the bishop himself ").   When they are used as the object of a verb and designate the same person or thing as the subject of that verb, they are called **reflexives** (*e.g.*, " I hurt myself," " They benefit themselves ").

Interjection.   A word that expresses emotion and that has no syntactic relations with other words; *e.g.*, *oh, alas, ha, ah, hello, hurrah, huzza.*

Interrogative pronoun.   The words *who, what, which,* and *whether* (archaic), when they are used as substantives and in an interrogative sense (*e.g.*, " Who are you? " " What do you want? " " Which do you choose? " " Whether of the twain is justified? "), are called interrogative pronouns.   *What* and *which,* when they are used as adjectives and in an interrogative sense (*e.g.*, " What song did you sing? " " Which book do you choose? "), are called **interrogative adjectives.**

Intransitive.   See **Transitive.**

Irony.   The suggestion of a thought or fact by an expression which, if taken literally, would convey the opposite of what is meant.

" You are very kind," spoken in a certain tone to a bully who has been abusing the speaker, is irony. In the expression " arsenic, corrosive sublimate, prussic acid, and other *mild* and *harmless* drugs " the italicized words are ironical. — **Sarcasm,** as applied to discourse, is contemptuous, taunting, or intentionally irritating discourse. Sarcasm may or may not be ironical, and irony may or may not be sarcastic.

Metaphor. The denoting of a person or thing or the stating of a thought or fact by the use of an expression which, if taken literally, would designate not what is meant but something resembling it, is called metaphor, or is said to be metaphorical; *e.g.,* (*a*) " These words cut me to the heart." A single word or expression used metaphorically is said to be a metaphor; *e.g.,* the word *cut* in example *a* and the italicized words in the following sentences are metaphors: (*b*) " He *poured* out a *flood* of eloquence." (*c*) " That is a *knotty* problem." — An explicit statement that a person or thing or fact is like another is a **simile;** *e.g.,* (*d*) " The enemy are fleeing like frightened rabbits." — Metaphor and simile both show resemblance — metaphor by suggestion or implication, simile by explicit statement (usually by the use of *like, as, seem,* or some other such word). For this reason any metaphor may be changed to a simile, and *vice versa.* The metaphors in *a, b,* and *c,* above may be changed to similes thus: (*a*) " On hearing these words, I felt as if I had been cut to the heart." (*b*) " Eloquence seemed to pour like a flood from his lips." (*c*) " It is as difficult to deal with that problem as it is to saw a knotty log." And the simile in example *d* may be changed to a metaphor thus: (*d*) " The enemy are fleeing — the frightened rabbits! "

Mode. A mode of a verb is that set of inflectional forms and verb phrases which a speaker uses to represent the action of the verb in a certain mode (*i.e.,* manner). The set which he uses to represent the action as a fact is the **indicative mode;** that which he uses to represent the action as doubtful, the **subjunctive mode;** that which he uses to represent the action as permitted or possible, the **potential mode;** that which he uses in giving a command, the **imperative mode;** that which he uses when he employs the verb as a substantive, the **infinitive mode** (of the forms constituting this mode some are called **infinitives** and others **gerunds**); that which he uses when he employs the verb as an adjective, the **participial mode** (the forms constituting this mode are called **participles**). The indicative, subjunctive, conditional, potential, obligative, and imperative modes are called **finite (predicative) modes;** the others, **non-finite (non-predicative)**

modes. (See also **Indicative, Infinitive, Gerund,** and **Participle.**)
The different modes of a typical verb are shown on pages 314 ff.[1]

Modifier. See **Modify.**

Modify. A word which, by being combined in discourse with another
word or expression, is made to mean something different from
what it would mean if it stood alone, is said to be modified by
that other word or expression. Thus, the meaning of the sentence " I dislike oranges " is changed if we insert *sour*, so that the
sentence reads " I dislike sour oranges "; it is changed because
" sour oranges " means something different from " oranges ";
" sour " is therefore said to modify (*i.e.*, change) " oranges."
Likewise " many men " and " few men " mean something
different from " men "; " many " and " few " modify " men."
" Call softly " means something different from " call "; " softly "
modifies " call." " I hate women who use slang " means something different from " I hate women "; " who use slang "
modifies " women." A word or expression which thus changes
the meaning of another word is called a **modifier.** — The modifiers of substantives are adjectives (including participles),
adjective-phrases, adjective clauses, appositives, and substantives in the possessive case. The modifiers of adjectives, verbs
and adverbs are adverbs, adverb-phrases, adverbial clauses, and
adverbial objectives. Vocatives (nominatives of address) and
absolute phrases may be considered modifiers of predications.

Passive. See **Voice.**

Past tense. See **Tense.**

Past perfect. See **Tense.**

Perfect. See **Tense.**

Person. The words *I* (with its inflectional forms, — *me, we,* etc.; see
the tables under **Substantive**), *myself, ourselves,* and the relative
who, when its antecedent is one of the foregoing words, are called
pronouns of the first person. The words *thou* (with its inflectional
forms, — *thee, you,* etc.; see **Substantive**), *thyself, yourself, your-*

---

[1] The classification of certain verb-phrases as the conditional mode and
the obligative mode has been omitted here and in the paradigm on pp. 314 ff.,
on philological grounds. The considerations on which these modes are still
retained in some grammatical treatises are stated in Whitney's *Essentials of
English Grammar*, pp. 120 ff., particularly 126; and MacEwan's *The Essentials of the English Sentence*, p. 53. The *Report of the Joint Committee on
Grammatical Nomenclature* recognizes only three modes (moods), the indicative, imperative, and subjunctive.

selves, and the relative *who,* when its antecedent is one of the foregoing words, are called **pronouns of the second person.** The relative *who,* when used otherwise than as above mentioned, all other pronouns than those above mentioned, and all nouns, are said to belong to the **third person.** — A verb-form or verb-phrase that may correctly be used with a subject in the first person is said to belong to the **first person of the verb** (*e.g., am, are bound*); one that may correctly be used with a subject in the second person is said to belong to the **second person of the verb** (*e.g., art, hast gone*); one that may correctly be used with a subject in the third person is said to belong to the **third person of the verb** (*e.g., is, does, has gone*). (See pages 314 ff.) — Discourse is said to be **in the first person** when the speaker designates himself by pronouns of the first person (*e.g.,* the Twenty-third Psalm); **in the second person** when the speaker addresses some person or thing, using pronouns of the second person (*e.g.,* the Lord's Prayer); **in the third person** when neither pronouns of the first person nor pronouns of the second person are used (*e.g.,* the first three letters on page 250).

Personal pronouns. The words *I, thou, he, she,* and *it,* together with their inflectional forms (see the tables under **Substantive**), are called personal pronouns.

Phrase. The term *phrase* is often used to mean any short group of words; as " the slang phrase ' That's hard lines.' " But as the term is used in grammar, a phrase is a group of words not constituting or containing a predication. A **verb-phrase** is a combination of a principal verb and one or more auxiliaries that is analogous to a single inflectional form (*e.g., has gone, shall have done*). A **preposition-phrase** is a combination of words analogous to a single preposition (*e.g., in regard to, as for*). An **adjective-phrase** is a phrase used to modify a substantive (*e.g.,* " A machine *of great value* "). An **adverb-phrase** is a phrase used analogously to an adverb (*e.g.,* " He fell *into the water* "). Any phrase consisting of a preposition and its object is a **prepositional phrase** (a term not to be confused with *preposition-phrase*); *e.g.,* the adjective- and adverb-phrases above quoted are prepositional phrases. A **participial phrase** is a phrase consisting of a participle and its adjuncts (*e.g.,* " *Looking to the north,* I saw the lake "). A **gerund-phrase** is a prepositional phrase in which the preposition governs a gerund (*e.g., in talking, instead of shooting*). Concerning **absolute phrases,** see **Absolute.**

Plural. See **Number.**

Possessive adjective. The words *my, mine, our, ours, thy, thine, your, yours, his, her, hers, its, their, theirs,* and *whose* are called possessive adjectives, or possessives, as well as inflectional forms of the personal pronouns.

Possessive (genitive) case. See **Case.**

Predicate. See **Subject.**

Predicate adjective. See **Predicate substantive.**

Predicate complement. See **Predicate substantive.**

Predicate substantive. A substantive designating what a verb asserts a person or thing to be is a predicate substantive (*e.g.*, " He is a *carpenter*," " These are *strawberries* "). An adjective designating a quality which a verb asserts belongs to a person or thing is a **predicate adjective** (*e.g.*, " He is *skillful*," " These berries are *sweet* "). A predicate substantive, or a predicate adjective, or a phrase or clause used as the one or the other, is said to be the **predicate complement** of the verb it completes.

Predication. Any group of words consisting of a single subject and predicate, whether a simple sentence or a clause.

Preposition. A word used to show the relation of a substantive to another word; *e.g.*, *in, on, into, toward, from, for, against, of, between, with, without, within, before, behind, under, over, above, among, at, by, around, about, through, throughout, beyond, across, along, beside.* A preposition always requires to complete its meaning a substantive, with which it combines into what is felt to be a unit of expression; *e.g.*, " in the water," " into the house," " among the leaves," " behind the house." This fact distinguishes prepositions from adverbs, which do not require a substantive to complete them; *e.g.*, " Go out," " Come in," " Please walk before." (*In, before, on, for, but, across,* and many other English words belong each one to several parts of *speech;* there is a preposition *across* and an adverb *across,* a preposition *for* and a conjunction *for,* etc.) For the distinction between prepositions and conjunctions, see **Conjunction.** The substantive combined with a preposition in the manner illustrated above is called the **object of the preposition.**

Preposition-phrase. See **Phrase.**

Present. See **Tense.**

Principal clause. See **Clause.**

Principal parts. The principal parts of any verb are (1) the present infinitive, (2) the past first singular, and (3) the past participle (see **Verb**); *e.g.*, *flee, fled, fled; choose, chose, chosen; love, loved, loved; set, set, set.*

Principal verb. A verb not used as an auxiliary, including the auxiliaries themselves when they are used independently (*e.g.*, " I *have* a boat," " he *did* wonders").

Pronoun. See **Substantive.**

Proper name. See **Common noun.**

Proper noun. See **Common noun.**

Relative adjectives. See **Relative pronoun.**

Relative clause. See **Adjective clause.**

Relative pronoun. The words *that, who, what, which, whoever, whatever,* and *whichever,* when they are used as substantives and in such a way that the clauses in which they stand are made adjective clauses (*q.v.*), are called **relative pronouns.** The words *what, which, whatever,* and *whichever,* when they are used as adjectives and in such a way that the clauses in which they stand are made adjective clauses, are called **relative adjectives.**

Rhetoric. See **Grammar.**

Sentence. The word *sentence* means (1) a group of words composed of a subject (with or without adjuncts) and a predicate (with or without adjuncts) and not grammatically dependent on any words outside itself (*e.g.*, " I will go," " I, being the person best acquainted with the situation, will go as soon as the carriage which I ordered has come "); or (2) two or more such groups joined by coördinating conjunctions or presented in such a way as to show that they are to be taken as a unit. A sentence of type 2 is called a **compound sentence.** Sentences of type 1 are divided into two classes, — **simple sentences** and **complex sentences.** All sentences are therefore usually said to fall into three classes, simple, complex, and compound. These are described in this vocabulary under their several names.

Sentence-element. A subject, a predicate, a predicate substantive or adjective, an absolute phrase, a modifier, a clause, or any other unit of sentence-structure. Any sentence-element other than a principal clause falls under the term **subordinate sentence-element,** as used in this book.

Sign of the infinitive. See **Infinitive.**

Simile. See **Metaphor.**

Simple conjunction. See **Conjunction.**

Simple sentence. A simple sentence has one subject and one predicate, either or both of which may be compound.

Singular. See **Number.**

Subject. A substantive combined in discourse with a verb (except a gerund or a participle) and representing the person or thing regarding which the verb asserts something is called the **subject** of the verb; and the verb, in turn, is called the **predicate** of the substantive, or is said to be **predicated** of the substantive. Thus, in the expression " He goes," " he " is the subject of " goes," and " goes " is the predicate of " he." The words *subject* and *predicate* are often (in this book and elsewhere) used to designate respectively a subject and a predicate, as above defined, together with any adjuncts they may have. Thus in the sentence " The ploughman homeward plods his weary way," the phrase " the ploughman " may be said to be the subject and the phrase " homeward plods his weary way " the predicate; or the noun " ploughman " alone may be said to be the subject and the verb " plods " the predicate.

Subjunctive. See **Mode** and also **Indicative.**

Subordinate clause. See **Clause.**

Subordinate sentence-element. See **Sentence-element.**

Substantive. A substantive is a word by which, as by a name, some person or thing is called; *e.g., man, house, happiness, beauty, song, speech, Jupiter, Charlemagne, he, she.* A few substantives are called **pronouns**; these are as follows: *I, thou, he, she, it,* and their compounds ending in *self* or *selves; this, that, who, what, which, whether,* and their compounds ending in *ever,* or *soever; each, either, neither, some, any, many, few, all, both, aught, naught, such, other, one, none,* and a few others. The pronouns are divided into five classes: personal, demonstrative, interrogative, relative, and indefinite pronouns (see these headings in the Vocabulary). All substantives other than pronouns are called **nouns.** — The declension of typical nouns and of the principal pronouns that are inflected is shown in the following tables:

DECLENSION OF NOUNS

	Singular	*Plural*
Nom.	boy	boys
Poss. (Gen.)	boy's	boys'
Obj. (Acc.)	boy	boys
Nom.	man	men
Poss. (Gen.)	man's	men's
Obj. (Acc.)	man	men

DECLENSION OF PRONOUNS

	Singular	Plural
Nom.	I	we
Poss. (Gen.)	my, mine	our, ours
Obj. (Acc.)	me	us
Nom.	you	you
Poss. (Gen.)	your	your, yours
Obj. (Acc.)	you	you
Nom.	he	they
Poss. (Gen.)	his	their, theirs
Obj. (Acc.)	him	them
Nom.	she	they
Poss. (Gen.)	her, hers	their, theirs
Obj. (Acc.)	her	them
Nom.	it	they
Poss. (Gen.)	its	their, theirs
Obj. (Acc.)	it	them
Nom.	who	who
Poss. (Gen.)	whose	whose
Obj. (Acc.)	whom	whom

A substantive may be used syntactically in the following ways (which are explained in this Vocabulary under the appropriate headings): (1) as a subject, (2) as a predicate substantive, (3) as an appositive, (4) as a possessive (genitive) substantive, (5) as the object of a verb, (6) as the object of a preposition, (7) as an adverbial substantive, and (8) as an absolute substantive.

Substantive clause. A clause may be used as the subject of a verb (*e.g.*, " *That he is a scholar* is certain "); as the object of a verb (*e.g.*, " I know *that he is a scholar* "); as the object of a preposition (*e.g.*, " There is no doubt as to *whether he is a scholar* "); as a predicate substantive (*e.g.*, " Truth is *that he is a scholar* "); as an appositive (*e.g.*, " This is certain — *that he is a scholar* "); as an adverbial substantive (*e.g.*, " I am sure *that he is a scholar* "); and as an absolute substantive (*e.g.*, " Granted *that he is a scholar*, he may yet be mistaken "). A clause used in one of these ways is a substantive clause.

Superlative. See **Comparison.**

Syntactic. See **Syntax.**

Syntax. The relations that words, when they are combined in discourse, bear to one another (*e.g.*, the relation of " he " to " goes "

in the sentence " He goes," or of " carpenter " to " Nelson,"
in the sentence " Nelson, the carpenter, is here ") are called
syntactic relations, or collectively syntax. Syntactic relations
comprise (1) the relations a single word may bear to another
word or to a group of words (*e.g.*, the relation of a subject to
a verb, of an adjective to a substantive, of a noun to an adjective-phrase, of a vocative substantive to a sentence); and
(2) the relations a predication may bear to another predication
(*viz.*, the relation between a principal and a dependent clause
and the relation between coördinate clauses).

Tense. The several sets of forms and combinations that a verb has
when it represents action as occurring at different points of time
are called its tenses. Of these sets there are six, called respectively the **present tense,** the **past tense,** the **future tense,** the
perfect (present perfect) tense, the **past perfect tense,** and the
future perfect tense. The tenses of a typical verb are shown
on pages 314 ff.

Transitive. A verb representing an action that necessarily affects
some person or thing in such a way that the name of that person
or thing may be made the direct object of the verb, is called a
transitive verb; *e.g., love, hate, have, carry, build.* A verb representing an action of such a kind that a direct object cannot
logically be used with the verb is called an **intransitive verb;**
e.g., stand, arise, become, whimper, bark, quarrel. Many verbs
may be used either transitively or intransitively; *e.g.,* " The
fire burns brightly " (" burns " is intransitive); " He burns the
paper " (" burns " is transitive); " The corn has grown " (" has
grown " is intransitive); " He has grown a beard " (" has
grown " is transitive).

Verb. A word used to assert an action, a condition, or the undergoing
of an action; *e.g., stand, strike, choose, be, become, remain, suffer,
undergo.*
  The various inflections and combinations (see **Voice, Mode,
Tense, Person,** and **Number**) of a typical verb are shown in the
table on pages 314–318. The words *I, you, he, we, they,* and
it are inserted merely to show the way in which the forms they
precede are used; they should not be regarded as necessary parts
of those forms, for they are not parts at all. Words inclosed in
parentheses are variants of the words they follow.

Vocative substantive (nominative of address). A substantive used in
direct address. See **Direct address.**

Voice. A verb is said to be in the **active voice** when it asserts that the
person or thing represented by the subject is, does, or undergoes

something; *e.g.*, " He strikes," " He heard," " I see." A verb is said to be in the **passive voice** when it asserts that something is done to the person or thing represented by the subject; *e.g.*, " He is struck," " He was heard," " I am seen." With one exception all the passive forms of any verb are composed of the several forms of the auxiliary *to be*, and the past participle of the principal verb; the one exception is the past participle itself. See the table on page 314.

Vowel. The letters *a, e, i, o,* and *u* are vowels. The letters *b, c, d, f, g, h, j, k, l, m, n, p, q, r, s, t, v, x,* and *z* are consonants. *W* when used as in *weak*, and *y* when used as in *young* are consonants; *w* when used as in *how*, and *y* when used as in *try* **are vowels.**

CONJUGATION OF THE VERB **TO TAKE** [1]

PRINCIPAL PARTS: **take, took, taken**

	ACTIVE VOICE		PASSIVE VOICE	
	Indicative mode			
	SINGULAR	PLURAL	SINGULAR	PLURAL
PRESENT TENSE	SIMPLE 1. I take 2. you take 3. he takes	we take you take they take	SIMPLE 1. I am taken 2. you are taken 3. he is taken	we are taken you are taken they are taken
	EMPHATIC 1. I do take 2. you take 3. he takes	we do take you do take they do take		
	PROGRESSIVE 1. I am taking 2. you are taking 3. he is taking	we are taking you are taking they are taking		
PAST TENSE	SIMPLE 1. I took 2. you took 3. he took	we took you took they took	SIMPLE 1. I was taken 2. you were taken 3. he was taken	we were taken you were taken they were taken
	EMPHATIC 1. I did take 2. you did take 3. he did take	we did take you did take they did take		
	PROGRESSIVE 1. I was taking 2. you were tak- ing 3. he was taking	we were taking you were taking they were taking		
FUTURE TENSE	SIMPLE 1. I shall (will) take 2. you will (shall) take 3. he will (shall) take	we shall (will) take you will (shall) take they will (shall) take	I shall (will) be taken, etc.	
	PROGRESSIVE I shall (will) be taking, etc.			

[1] See the explanatory remarks under **Verb**.

	ACTIVE VOICE		PASSIVE VOICE

Indicative mode — continued

	SINGULAR	PLURAL	
PERFECT TENSE	SIMPLE 1. I have taken 2. you have taken 3. he has taken	we have taken you have taken they have taken	I have been taken, etc.
	PROGRESSIVE I have been taking, etc.		
PAST PERFECT TENSE	SIMPLE 1. I had taken 2. you had taken 3. he had taken	we had taken you had taken they had taken	I had been taken, etc.
	PROGRESSIVE I had been taking, etc.		
FUTURE PERFECT TENSE	SIMPLE I shall (will) have taken, etc.		I shall (will) have been taken, etc.
	PROGRESSIVE I shall (will) have been taking, etc.		

Subjunctive mode

	SINGULAR	PLURAL	SINGULAR	PLURAL
PRESENT TENSE	SIMPLE 1. if I take 2. if you take 3. if he take	if we take if you take if they take	1. if I be taken 2. if you be taken 3. if he be taken	if we be taken if you be taken if they be taken
	EMPHATIC 1. if I do take 2. if you do take 3. if he do take	if we do take if you do take if they do take		
	PROGRESSIVE 1. if I be taking 2. if you be taking 3. if he be taking	if we be taking if you be taking if they be taking		

	ACTIVE VOICE		PASSIVE VOICE	

Subjunctive mode — continued

	SINGULAR	PLURAL	SINGULAR	PLURAL
PAST TENSE	**SIMPLE**		1. if I were taken	if we were taken
	1. if I took	if we took	2. if you were taken	if you were taken
	2. if you took	if you took	3. if he were taken	if they were taken
	3. if he took	if they took		
	EMPHATIC			
	1. if I did take	if we did take		
	2. if you did take	if you did take		
	3. if he did take	if they did take		
	PROGRESSIVE			
	1. if I were taking	if we were taking		
	2. if you were taking	if you were taking		
	3. if he were taking	if they were taking		
FUTURE TENSE	[The future subjunctive is exactly like the future indicative.]			
PERFECT TENSE	[The perfect subjunctive is exactly like the perfect indicative.]			
PAST PERFECT TENSE	[The past perfect subjunctive is exactly like the past perfect indicative.]			
FUTURE PERFECT TENSE	[The future perfect subjunctive is exactly like the future perfect indicative.]			

	ACTIVE VOICE		PASSIVE VOICE
	Potential mode [1]		
	SINGULAR	PLURAL	
PRESENT TENSE	SIMPLE 1. I may *or* can take 2. you may *or* can take 3. he may *or* can take PROGRESSIVE I may *or* can be taking, etc.	we may *or* can take you may *or* can take they may *or* can take	I may *or* can be taken, etc.
PAST TENSE	SIMPLE 1. I might *or* could take 2. you might *or* could take 3. he might *or* could take PROGRESSIVE I might *or* could be taking, etc.	we might *or* could take you might *or* could take they might *or* could take	I might *or* could be taken, etc.
PERFECT TENSE	SIMPLE I may *or* can have taken, etc. PROGRESSIVE I may *or* can have been taking, etc.		I may *or* can have been taken, etc.
PAST PERFECT TENSE	SIMPLE I might *or* could have taken, etc. PROGRESSIVE I might *or* could have been taking, etc.		I might *or* could have been taken, etc.
	Imperative mode		
	SIMPLE: take EMPHATIC: do take PROGRESSIVE: be taking		be taken

[1] See the footnote on page 306.

	ACTIVE VOICE	PASSIVE VOICE
	Infinitive mode	
PRESENT TENSE	SIMPLE INFINITIVE: to take PROGRESSIVE INFINITIVE: to be taking GERUND: taking	INFINITIVE: to be taken GERUND: being taken
PERFECT TENSE	SIMPLE INFINITIVE: to have taken PROGRESSIVE INFINITIVE: to have been taking GERUND: having taken	INFINITIVE: to have been taken GERUND: having been taken
	Participial mode, or *participles*	
PRESENT TENSE	taking	being taken
PAST TENSE	[There is no past participle in the active voice.]	taken
PERFECT TENSE	SIMPLE: having taken PROGRESSIVE: having been taking	having been taken

APPENDIX B

A List of Words that are often Mispronounced

In the case of a few words in the following list, pronunciations different from those indicated in the right-hand column are admitted by some authorities; these words are marked with an asterisk (*). The pronunciations given opposite such words are those favored by the great majority of lexicographers. In the case of all the words not marked with an asterisk, the pronunciations indicated are the only correct ones.

The accentual and diacritical marks are not intended to give an exhaustive description of the pronunciation of each word, but only to point out common errors. Of the signs that are not self-explanatory the meanings are shown in the following table:

ă is pronounced like *a* in *at.*
ā is pronounced like *a* in *mate.*
ȧ is pronounced like *a* in *climate.*
ä is pronounced like *a* in *arm.*
à is pronounced like *a* in *ask.*
ĕ is pronounced like *e* in *men.*
ē is pronounced like *ee* in *see.*
ĕ is pronounced like *e* in the first syllable of *event.*
ē is pronounced like *e* in *fern.*
ĭ is pronounced like *i* in *tin.*
ī is pronounced like *i* in *wine.*
ŏ is pronounced like *o* in *lot.*
ō is pronounced like *o* in *host.*
ŭ is pronounced like *u* in *bun.*
ū is pronounced like *u* in *use.*
ů is pronounced like *u* in *unite.*
ṵ is pronounced like *u* in *bull.*
o͞o is pronounced like *oo* in *tool.*
o͝o is pronounced like *oo* in *foot.*
ou is pronounced as in *thou.*
zh is pronounced like *z* in *azure*

Correct pronunciation

Words often accented on the wrong syllable		
	abdomen*	ab dō′men
	accent (verb)	ac cent′
	acclimate*	ac clī′mate
	acumen	a cū′men
	address	ad dress′
	admirable	ad′mirable
	adult	a dult′
	adverse	ad′verse
	adversary	ad′ver sa ry
	albumen	al bu′men
	alias	ā′lias
	alloy	al loy′
	ally*	al ly′
	alternate* (adjective and noun)	al tĕr′nate
	ancestral	an ses′tral
	applicable	ap′plicable
	apropos	ăp′rō pō′
	brigand	brĭg′and
	choleric	kŏl′eric
	comparable	com′par a ble
	condolence	con dō′lence
	construe*	con′strue
	contour*	con tour′
	contrary	con′tra ry
	conversant	con′ver sant
	cuckoo	kŏŏk′ōō
	defects	de fects′
	deficit	def′i cit
	despicable	des′picable
	detail	de tail′
	detour	de tour′
	dirigible	dir′i ji ble
	discharge	dis charge′
	discourse	dis course′
	divan	di van′
	elevated	el′e vat ed
	encore	en core′
	entire	en tire′
	exquisite	ex′quisite

Correct pronunciation

extant*	ex'tant
formidable	for'midable
gondola	gon'dola
grimace	gri māce'
guardian	guard'i an
harass	hăr'ass
Herculean	Her cū'le an
hospitable	hos'pitable
illustrate*	il lus'trate
impious	im'pĭ ous
incognito	in cog'nito
incomparable	in com'parable
inevitable	in ev'itable
inquiry	in quĭ'ry
lamentable	lam'entable
mediocre	mē'di o cre
mischievous	mis'chie vous
misconstrue*	mis con'strue
municipal	mu nis'i pal
obligatory*	ob'ligatory
orchestra	or'chestra
orchestral	or kes' tral
pariah*	pä'riah
peremptory*	pĕr'emptory
pianist*	pĭ an'ist
piquant	pēk'ant *or* pĭk'ant
positively	pos'i tive ly
precedence	prĕ cēd'ence
precedent (adjective)	prĕ cēd'ent
precedent (noun)	prĕs'e dent
presage (noun)	prē'sage *or* prĕs'age
presage (verb)	pre sāge'
primarily	pri'ma ri ly
recall	re call'
recourse	re course'
research	re search'
robust	ro bust'
romance	ro mance'
sepulture	sĕp'ulture
theater	the'a ter
vagary	và gā'ry

Correct pronunciation

Words in
which cer-
tain vowels
are often
mispro-
nounced

Adonis	A dō'nis
alma mater	alma mā ter
altercation*	ăltercation
amenable	a mē'nable
apparatus	apparātus
apricot*	āpricot
aviator	a'vi a tor
Basil	Băz'il
biographical	bīographical
biography	bīography
bouquet	bōō kā' *or* bōō'kā (not "bō-")
brooch*	brōch
brougham	brōō'am *or* brōōm
brusque*	brōōsk
cantaloupe*	can'ta lōōp
chock-full	Pronounced as spelled; not "chuck-full."
choler	kŏl'er
Cleopatra	Cleopātra
clique	klēk
constable	kŭn stable
coupon	kōō'pon
courtesan*	kŭr te zan
creek	krēk
crotch	Pronounced as spelled; not "crutch."
culinary	kū'linary
defalcate	dē făl'cate (not "-fawl-")
defalcation	dē făl cation *or* dĕf ăl ca-tion (not "-fawl-")
data	dā'ta (not dat ta)
demise	dē mīz'
describe	dē scribe'
destruction	dē struc'tion
directly	di rect'ly
extol*	ex tŏl'
faucet	faw'set
gape*	gāp
garrulous	găr rụ lous (not "găr yu-lous")

Correct pronunciation

genealogy	jĕn e ălogy *or* jē ne ălogy (not "-ology")
genuine	jen u ĭn (not "-īn")
ghoul	go͞ol
gratis	grā tis
hearth	härth
heinous	hā nous
historian	his to′ ri an
hoof	ho͞of
hypocrisy	hĭ poc′ri sy
ignoramus	ig no rā′mus
implacable	im plā′cable
Italian	Ĭ tal yan (not "Ī-")
joust	jŭst *or* jo͞ost
jugular	jū gŭ lar (not "jŭg-")
literature	lit er a tŭre (not "-toor")
mineralogy	min er ăl ogy (not "-ology")
nape	nāp
Pall Mall	Pĕl Mĕl
panegyric	pan e jĭr ic *or* pan e jĕr ic
pathos	pā thos
penalize	pē′nal ize
premise (noun)	prĕm′iss
premise (verb)	prĕ mīz′
presentation	prĕz entation
pretty	prĭt y
programme	prō′grăm (not "-grum")
quay	kē
radiator	ra′di a tor
regular	reg yu lar
rinse	Pronounced as spelled; not "rense."
roily	Pronounced as spelled; not "rī ly."
roof	ro͞of
root	ro͞ot
route*	ro͞ot
sacrilegious	sac ri lē′jus (not "-religious")
salve*	säv

Correct pronunciation

simultaneous*	sīmultaneous
sinecure	sī ne cure
sleek	slēk
slough (noun, *mire*)	slōō
slough (noun, *cast skin*)	slŭf
slough (verb)	slŭf
status	stā tus
trow	trō
ultimatum	ul ti mā tum
verbatim	ver bā′tim
virulent	vĭr′ụ lent (not "-yulent")
xylophone	zī lophone
zoölogy	zō ŏl ogy (not "zōō-")

Words in which certain certain consonants are often mispronounced

archipelago	ar ki pel′ a go
aversion	a ver shun (not "-zhun")
banquet	bang′quet
bequeath	be queath′ (to rhyme with "breathe.")
cello	chel′o
chaise	shāz
English	ing′glish
flaccid	flak′sid (See Rule 153, note.)
handkerchief	hang′ker chief
has (in expressions like *He has to go*)	hăz (not "hăss")
have (in expressions like *I have to go*)	hăv (not "hăf")
oleo-margarine	The *g* is hard, as in *get*. (See Rule 153, note.)
partner	Pronounced as spelled; not "pard ner."
schism	sizm
turgid	tur jid (See Rule 153, note.)
used (when followed by *to*)	ūzd (not "ūst")
version	ver shun (not "-zhun")
with	The *th* is pronounced as in *thus*.

Correct pronunciation

accidentally	ac ci dent′ al ly	Words from
arctic	arc′tic	which
artistically	ar tis′ti cal ly	certain
authoritatively	au thor′i ta tive ly	sounds are
auxiliary*	aux il i ary	often in-
cemetery	cem′e ter y	correctly
considerable	con sid′er a ble	omitted
cruel	cru′el	
factory	fac′tory	
facts	fakts	
February	Feb ru ary	
geometry	ge om′et ry	
government	gov′ern ment	
laboratory	lab′o ra to ry	
library	li′bra ry	
Messrs.*	mĕsh yĕrz *or* mĕs′yĕrz	
	("Messerz" is wholly	
	unauthorized.)	
piano-forte	piano-for′te	
pumpkin	pump kin	
recognize	rec′og nize	
almond*	ä′mond	Words to
athlete	ath′lete	which an
athletic	ath let′ic	additional
buoy	bwoi *or* boi	sound is
casualty	caz′u al ty (not "-al′i ty")	often in-
cerement	sēr ment	correctly
chasm	kasm	added
column	kol um (not "-yum")	
conduit	kŏn′dit *or* kŭn′dit	
daguerreotype	da ger′ o type	
elm	One syllable	
enthusiasm	en thū zi asm	
falcon*	faw con	
film	One syllable	
grievous	grēv′ous	
helm	One syllable	
mischievous	mis′chĕv ous	
often	of en	

Correct pronunciation

poignant* poi′nănt *or* poin′yănt

salmon să mon

Words often mispro- nounced in various ways

ad infinitum ad in fi nī′tum

charivari sha rē′va rē′ (not "shiv- eree")

debut dă′bu̧

dishabille* dis′a bĭl′ *or* dĭs á bēl′

dishevel di shev′el

dramatis personæ dram′a tis per sō′nē

finis fī′nis

foyer* (*e.g.*, the *foyer* of a theater) fwà′yā′ *or* foy′er

gaol jāl

irrelevant Pronounced as spelled; not "irrevelant."

larynx lăr′inx *or* lā′rinx (not "lar nix")

posthumous pŏst′humous *or* pŏs′tu- mous

rendezvous rĕn de voo *or* rŏn de voo

sarsaparilla sär sa pa ril la (not "săss- parilla")

sough* sŭf

vaudeville vōd′vĭl

viz. An arbitrary sign for the Latin word *videlicet* (pro- nounced vi dĕl′ i set). In reading *viz.* aloud, say either "videl- icet" or "namely" (the English equivalent of *videlicet*); do not say "vizz."

INDEX

Explanations of grammatical and other technical terms are in general not cited below, since they can easily be found in the alphabetical vocabulary on pp. 297 ff.

Comments on the spelling, writing "solid" or not "solid," hyphening, and pronunciation of particular words, are in general not cited under the words; such comments can easily be found through the citations under *Spelling, Solid, Hyphen,* and *Pronunciation.*

Bold-face figures refer to paragraph numbers, other figures to pages.